MEZZATERRA

MEZZATERRA

Fragments from the Common Ground

AHDAF SOUEIF

BLOOMSBURY

First published in Great Britain 2004

Copyright © 2004 by Ahdaf Soueif

The moral right of the author has been asserted

Some of these essays and reviews originally appeared in the *Guardian*, *al-Hayat*, *al-Ahram Weekly*, *Granta*, *New Statesman*, *Index on Censorship*, *Observer*, *London Review of Books*, *New Society*, *Washington Post*, *Sunday Telegraph*, *Times Literary Supplement*, *Journal of Palestine Studies*, *New York Review of Books*, *Nation*, *Bogliasco Foundation* as acknowledged in the text. The acknowledgement page constitutes an extension of this page. The names of private living individuals in some essays have been changed

Bloomsbury Publishing Plc, 38 Soho Square, London W1D 3HB

A CIP catalogue record for this book is available from the British Library

ISBN 0 7475 7725 0

10 9 8 7 6 5 4 3 2 1

All paper used by Bloomsbury Publishing is a natural, recyclable product made from wood grown in well-managed forests. The manufacturing processes conform to the environmental regulations of the country of origin

Typeset by Hewer Text Limited, Edinburgh
Printed in Great Britain by Clays Ltd, St Ives plc

www.bloomsbury.com/ahdafsoueif

For my sons, Omar Robert and Ismail
Richard, and all other inhabitants of
the common ground.

'O Mankind, We have created you from male and female, and made you into Nations and Tribes that you may get to know one another. The one that God honours most among you is the one that fears Him most. And God is knowing of all things.'

Qur'ān, al-Hujurat, 13

Contents

Preface

Holland Park. He came towards me through the crowd in the drawing room of the grand house that I'd never been in before and have never been in since. 'Come,' he said, 'I'll show you the menagerie.' That was twenty-five years ago. I have, in some sense, been examining the menagerie ever since.

I had thought it made no difference where one lived: Cairo, London, what was a four-and-a-half-hour flight? We were citizens of the world and the world was fast becoming more connected. I saw the difficulty only in terms of the personal life: on the one hand, how much would I miss my family, my friends, the sun, the food, the – life? On the other, what was life worth without this miraculous new love?

We married in 1981. But I did not move to London permanently until 1984 when our first child was born. The pieces collected in this book span the years from then to now.

I think of myself as a writer of fiction. But fiction follows its own rhythms; it cannot be forced. In my experience, fiction – except of a certain raw kind – will not be born today out of today's events. The impressions, insights and feelings of today need to be laid into the rag-bag a writer takes along everywhere. Later, much later perhaps, you will draw them out and examine them: which have held their colour and which have faded? You'll position them this way, that way: what patterns might they offer?

Journalism, on the other hand, responds to the day's most pressing concerns, tries, even, to nudge them on to a different track. These non-fiction pieces, then, are the direct product of the interaction between my self and the condition of living in the UK.

That I was not aware of the nature of the situation I had stepped into is, with hindsight, clear in the earliest two pieces in the book. Looking at them now they seem to me to be written in a space free of pressing political concerns, confident of the goodwill of the reader, easy with just having some fun. More than twenty years later, the difference between the mood of 'Many Flights into Egypt' and 'Genoa: City of Light and Shadow' reflects more, I think, than the passage of years.

There were specific lessons to be learned: the article about the family-planning campaign, 'The Circus Comes to Town' was, under an *Observer* syndication agreement, published in Israel without my knowledge. It looked as though I, an Egyptian, was making fun of an Egyptian project in an Israeli newspaper. I learned to retain my copyright.

I shared, of course, in the general life of the country that had become my other home. I supported Spurs, kept an eye on house prices, formed political opinions and found that whatever view I might hold about Thatcher or Europe or the NHS, I was bound to find it expressed somewhere in the common discourse of the mainstream media. Where I felt myself out of step was when this discourse had anything to do with Egypt, the Arabs or Islam. I had become used to what was at the time an unequivocal support for Israel in the British media, but it troubled me that in almost every book, article, film, TV or radio programme that claimed to be about the part of the world that I came from I could never recognise myself or anyone I knew. I was constantly coming face to face with distortions of my reality.

I reasoned that this must be the experience of every 'alien' everywhere and that it shouldn't be taken personally. But it was a constant irritant – and world geo-politics meant that interest in where I came from was growing. Lebanon was suffering the tail end of both the Israeli invasion and its own civil war (which was the direct result of the troubles in

2

Palestine). Afghanistan became the crucible in which thousands of disaffected, young – mainly Arab – Muslim men were being transformed into a fighting force pitted against the USSR. Then the Soviet Union imploded. The Gulf War came and with it the imposition of sanctions on Iraq, the basing of US troops in the Arabian peninsula and talk of a New World Order. In the run up to the Gulf War, Israelis and Palestinians were summoned to negotiations in Spain and Norway and the world applauded while a perceptive few foresaw the mess for which the Oslo accords laid the ground plan.

It was impossible – apart from a few notable exceptions – to find in the media of the West coherent interpretations of all this that did justice to the people of the region and their history. If the New World Order was a mechanism to control the Arab and the Muslim worlds then I felt that the media of the West was complicit in it; for they always represented those worlds in terms that excused or even invited the imposition of control.

Was this misrepresentation reciprocal? If I were an American or British person living in Egypt, and if I knew Arabic well enough to read the mainstream Arabic press, would I constantly be brought up short by skewed accounts of my history and culture? Would I switch on the television to find a doom-laden voice intoning about how the Celts worshipped the massive stones placed on Salisbury Plain by astral beings? Would I switch on my car radio and hear an account of yet another outbreak of 'Christian paedophilia', with a background theme of church bells and Christmas carols? Would I wander into the movies and come face to face with an evil American character bent on destroying the 'third' world so the cinema audience cheers when the Arab hero kills him? I have to say the answer is a resounding no. Where the Arab media is interested in the West it tends to focus on what the West is producing today: policies, technology and art, for example – particularly as those connect to the

Arab world. The Arab media has complete access to English and other European languages and to the world's news agencies. Interpretative or analytic essays are mostly by writers who read the European and American press and have experience of the West. The informed Arab public does not view the West as one monolithic unit; it is aware of dissent, of the fact that people often do not agree with policy, of the role of the judiciary. Above all, an Arab assumes that a Westerner is, at heart, very much like her – or him. Many times I have heard Palestinian village women, speaking of the Israeli soldiers who torment them, ask 'Does his mother know he's doing this?'

Living in London, I know that I am not alone in the experience of alienation; there are hundreds of thousands of us: people with an Arab or a Muslim background living in the West and doing daily double-takes when faced with their reflection in a Western mirror.

Looking at my essays now I find that they are mainly concerned with the problem of representation, and that this theme was established with the 1985 review of William Golding's *Egyptian Journal*. This was not a policy; it simply happened. I felt upset and angered by the misrepresentations I encountered constantly and I felt grateful when a clear-eyed truth was spoken about us.

And then again, who was 'us'?

I went to school in London briefly when I was thirteen. Mayfield Comprehensive in Putney. There, the white girls thought I was white (or thought I was close enough to white to want to be thought of as white) and the black girls thought I was black (or close enough to black to make identifying with the whites suspect). But that did not mean I could associate freely where I chose; it meant that I had to make a choice and stick with it. And whichever group I opted for I would be despised by the other. After three months I refused to go to school. Thinking about it now, I see this as my first serious exposure to the 'with us or against us' mentality; the mentality that forces you to self-identify as

4

one thing despite your certain knowledge that you are a bit of this and a bit of that.

Growing up Egyptian in the Sixties meant growing up Muslim / Christian / Egyptian / Arab / African / Mediterranean / Non-aligned / Socialist but happy with small-scale capitalism. On top of that, if you were urban / professional the chances were that you spoke English and / or French and danced to the Stones as readily as to Abd el-Haleem.

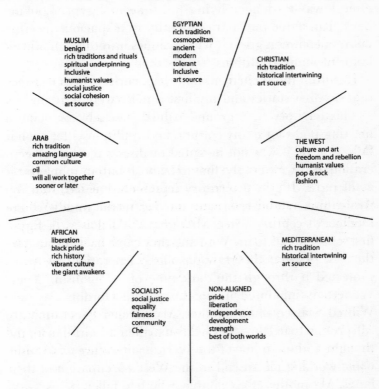

In Cairo on any one night you could go see an Arabic, English, French, Italian or Russian film. One week the Russian *Hamlet* was playing at Cinema Odeon, Christopher Plummer's *Hamlet* at Cinema Qasr el-Nil and Karam Mutawi's *Hamlet* at the Egyptian National Theatre. We were modern and experimental. We believed in Art and Science. We cared passionately for Freedom and Social

Justice. We saw ourselves as occupying a ground common to both Arab and Western culture, Russian culture was in there too, and Indian, and a lot of South America. The question of identity as something that needed to be defined and defended did not occupy us. We were not looking inward at ourselves but outward at the world. We knew who we were. Or thought we did. In fact I never came across the Arabic word for identity, *huwiyyah*, until long after I was no longer living full-time in Egypt. Looking back, I imagine our Sixties identity as a spacious meeting point, a common ground with avenues into the rich hinterlands of many traditions.

It is from the excitement and the security of this territory that my first stories and my first articles were written.

This territory, this ground valued precisely for being a meeting-point for many cultures and traditions – let's call it 'Mezzaterra' – was not invented or discovered by my generation. But we were the first to be born into it, to inhabit it as of right. It was a territory imagined, created even, by Arab thinkers and reformers starting in the middle of the nineteenth century when Muhammad Ali Pasha of Egypt first sent students to the West and they came back inspired by the best of what they saw on offer. Generations of Arabs protected it through the dark time of colonialism. A few Westerners inhabited it too: Lucy Duff Gordon was one, Wilfred Scawen Blunt another. My parents' generation are still around to tell how they held on to their admiration for the thought and discipline of the West, its literature and music, while working for an end to the West's occupation of their lands. My mother, for example, who had fallen in love with the literature of Britain at school, and who could not be appointed English lecturer at Cairo University until the British had left, did not consider that rejecting British imperialism involved rejecting English literature. She might say that true appreciation and enjoyment of English literature is not possible unless you are free of British colonialism and can engage with the culture on an equal footing. This is the stance that Edward Said describes: 'what distinguished the great liberationist cultural movements that stood against Western imperialism was that they wanted liberation within the same universe of discourse inhabited by Western culture'.

They believed this was possible because they recognised an affinity between the best of Western and the best of Arab culture. Ideals of social justice, public service and equality, identified in modern times as Western, are to be found in the Qur'ān and the traditions of the Prophet. If science flourishes in the West now, it had flourished in the Arab and Muslim lands from the tenth to the fourteenth centuries. The principles of objective scientific enquiry described by Roger Bacon in 1286 are the same as those expressed by al-Hasan ibn al-Haytham in 1020. Taxation and philanthropy produced free health care in Baghdad in the tenth century as they did in London in the twentieth. In both cultures a system of patronage had been the midwife to great architecture, literature and music. And as the European Renaissance had blossomed in the sixteenth century out of the mix of Europe's availing itself of Arab science while discovering its own classical heritage and enjoying an economic boom, so the Arabs looked to build their twentieth-century renaissance on their adoption of Western science and the rediscovery of their own classical heritage. This was precisely the creative fusion behind, for example, the extraordinarily innovative revival in Arabic poetry in the second half of the twentieth century.

Generations of Arab Mezzaterrans had, I guess, believed what Western culture said of itself: that its values were universalist, democratic and humane. They believed that once you peeled off military and political dominance, the world so liberated would be one where everyone could engage freely in the exchange of ideas, art forms, technologies. This was the world that my generation believed we had inherited: a fertile land; an area of overlap, where one culture shaded into the other, where echoes and reflections added depth and perspective, where differences were interesting rather than threatening, because they were foregrounded against a backdrop of affinities.

The rewards of inhabiting the Mezzaterra are enormous. At its best it endows each thing, at the same moment, with the shine of the new, the patina of the old; the language, the people, the landscape, the food of one culture constantly reflected off the other. This is not a process of comparison, not a 'which is better than which' project but rather at once a distillation and an enrichment of each thing, each idea. It means, for example, that you are both on the inside and the outside of language, that within each culture your stance cannot help but be both critical and empathetic.

But as the Eighties rolled into the Nineties the political direction the world was taking seemed to undermine every aspect of this identity. Our open and hospitable Mezzaterra was under attack from all sides:

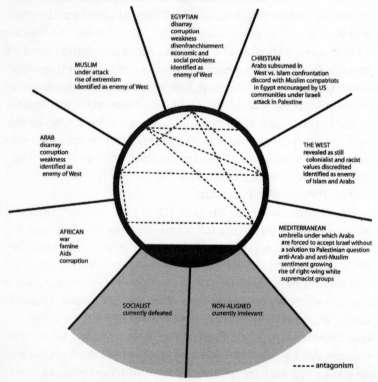

EGYPTIAN
disarray
corruption
weakness
disenfranchisement
economic and
social problems
identified as
enemy of West

CHRISTIAN
Arabs subsumed in
West vs. Islam confrontation
discord with Muslim compatriots
in Egypt encouraged by US
communities under Israeli
attack in Palestine

MUSLIM
under attack
rise of extremism
identified as enemy of West

ARAB
disarray
corruption
weakness
identified as
enemy of West

THE WEST
revealed as still
colonialist and racist
values discredited
identified as enemy
of Islam and Arabs

AFRICAN
war
famine
Aids
corruption

MEDITERRANEAN
umbrella under which Arabs
are forced to accept Israel without
a solution to Palestinian question
anti-Arab and anti-Muslim
sentiment growing
rise of right-wing white
supremacist groups

SOCIALIST
currently defeated

NON-ALIGNED
currently irrelevant

----- antagonism

Personally, I find the situation so grave that in the last four years I have written hardly anything which does not have direct bearing on it. The common ground, after all, is the only home that I and those whom I love can inhabit.

As components of my Mezzaterra have hardened, as some have sought to invade and grab territory and others have thrown up barricades, I have seen my space shrink and felt the ground beneath my feet tremble. Tectonic plates shift into new positions and what was once an open and level plain twists into a jagged, treacherous land. But in today's world a separatist option does not exist; a version of this common ground is where we all, finally, must live if we are to live at all. And yet the loudest voices are the ones that deny its very existence; that trumpet a 'clash of civilisations'. My non-fiction, then, from the second half of the Eighties, through the Nineties, rather than celebrating Mezzaterra, became a defence of it, an attempt to demonstrate its existence.

Throughout the Nineties the world was treated to the spectacle of the Iraqi people suffering under sanctions because their dictator had invaded Kuwait, while next door the democratically elected Labour government of Israel speeded up its theft of Palestinian lands and resources under cover of the Oslo peace accords. Neither process could have taken place without the backing of the United States, the world's one remaining superpower.

The effect was to radicalise Arab opinion and expose the weakness and complicity of Arab rulers. In the West, public opinion was slowly starting to shift towards a more balanced view of the Palestinian–Israeli issue. For a brief moment at the end of the Clinton administration it seemed that a solution with which both sides could live was within reach. It is said that Arafat was willing to accept the offer Clinton put to him at Taba but was advised to wait until after the American elections. The reasoning ran: Clinton is on the way out. He can't do any more good. George W. Bush is our man; his Arab oil connections go back a generation. Let *him* be the one to sign the peace between the Palestinians and the Israelis. But before this could happen Sharon had gone for his promenade through the Noble Sanctuary, the Intifada had erupted, Barak was out and a Likud government was in and all deals were off. True to form, most of the UK and the American media presented the Intifada as essentially a religious protest to Sharon entering the Haram. Hardly any mention was made of the fact central to the preceding seven years of collective Palestinian life: that the Oslo accords had been a new screen behind which Israel could continue to dispossess the Palestinians. It was as though a simple-mindedness descended on the media when it reported on matters to do with Arabs, Islam and, particularly, Palestine. No, it's a bit deeper than that: it is that the media attributes simple and immediate motivation to Arabs and Muslims as though they were all one-celled creatures. Watching the news on the BBC or CNN on the one hand and al-Jazeera on the other was like seeing reports from two different planets.

When the *Guardian* offered me the opportunity to go to Palestine in November 2000, I grabbed it. The articles in the Political Essays section of this collection start here. What I have tried to do throughout is to establish a direct and authentic channel between the reader of English and the perceptions, feelings and ideas of the people whose countries – whose lives, in fact – are the main theatre in which the dramas of the last four years have been played out. In doing this I have hoped to help in demythologising the representation of the Muslim and the Arab and to place the current conflicts in the arena where they belong: politics and economics. I have hoped to add my voice to those of Edward Said and other obstinate inhabitants of the common ground.

As we now know, the New World Order announced at the beginning of the Nineties was, by the beginning of the new millennium, mutating into the Project for the New American Century. An extreme strand of American ideology deemed the omens propitious for America's 'manifest destiny' to be actualised: it was time for the US to dominate the world. The key to this would be strategic control of geography and of the main energy resource of the planet: oil. Dominance in central Asia and the Arab world would both control the oil and prevent those parts of the world from forming alliances with China or Russia.

But the US could not underwrite Israeli policies and ambitions in the region and at the same time be regarded by the Arab people as a friend. The Palestinian issue was largely at the heart of this, but so also was the Arab reading of Israel's desire to become the local superpower. In addition to the questions over the Syrian Golan Heights, the Lebanese Shab'a farms and the never quite renounced expansionist 'Eretz Israel' idea, Israel's footprint was to be found in many issues critical to the well-being of its neighbours, such as the debate over Egypt's share of Nile water, the surreptitious introduction of GM crops into the region's agriculture, or the growing drug trade. America, therefore (and this is before September 11, 2001), could not seek to secure its interests in the region through a positive or mutually beneficial relationship with the Arabs.

This is never spelt out by the American media for the American public: that the discord between the Arab world and the US is entirely to do with Israel. The International Court of Justice, environmental policies, globalisation problems – these are issues between America and the entire world. Between America and the Arabs specifically there is only Israel – or was, until the US-led invasion of Iraq in 2003.

In the early months of 2001 the Intifada had unmasked the bankruptcy of the Oslo agreements, Israel was using increasingly violent measures against Palestinians and against Israeli Arabs, the people in Arab countries were agitating, collecting donations and demanding action from their unwilling governments. In the face of the Palestinians' refusal to back down and accept their dispossession, and with world public opinion shifting to support them, the US was essentially left with four choices. It could:

1. Dissociate itself from Israel, or
2. Pressure Israel into a true peace deal with the Palestinians, or
3. Pressure Israel into disguising or deferring its ambitions and pressure the Palestinian leadership into conceding more ground to Israel, or
4. Accept the hostility of the Arab world and a growing part of the rest of the world and decide how to deal with it.

The first option was unrealistic. US domestic dynamics precluded it. Every American President, presidential candidate and Secretary of State has felt obliged to swear an oath of allegiance to Israel in front of the powerful American Israeli Public Affairs Committee (AIPAC). The recruitment, in the late Nineties, of the Bible-belt right (now estimated to form 18 per cent of voters and 33 per cent of Republican voters) to Israel's cause made it even more unlikely.

The second option was not possible for the same reasons as the first.

Options three and four have formed the basis of US strategy for almost forty years. Every American administration from 1967 to 2001 has tried to conclude interim peace deals which buy Israel time to create more facts on the ground. Since Richard Nixon's visit to Egypt in the early Seventies, American tactics for dealing with Arab hostility to US policies were to increase the region's (particularly Egypt's) dependency on the US through USAID projects, to support corrupt Arab rulers and corrupt them further, to advise and cooperate with regimes in silencing opposition and to attempt to co-opt local elites. Regimes that have balked at the American line have been branded 'rogue' and sanctioned.

Yet this unquestioning pro-Israeli stance was becoming

problematic. Awareness of the plight of the Palestinian people had begun to increase in the US through the alternative media, the Internet and the efforts of second-generation Arab Americans. The day might have come when American taxpayers realised that the billions of dollars they were paying to subsidise Israel were simply buying them the anger of the Arabs and the Muslims and nudging them out of step with the rest of the world. They might have asked why this support continued to be necessary when Israel was the only nuclear power in the region and had the fourth strongest army in the world and was refusing to abide by international law even though it was no longer under an existential threat.

It is conceivable that had the events of September 11 not taken place, George W. Bush would have continued along the lines of options three and four: being a declared non-interventionist and having big oil interests, he might have pushed Israel harder and got something like the Taba proposals back on the table. After September 11 the total identification that has taken place between the US administration and the Likud government seems to preclude even that.

The events of September 11, 2001, played straight into what would appear to be the Neo-conservative dream scenario. The theoretical groundwork for dealing with the Arab world in terms of pure power had been laid by Neo-cons, who were now in crucial positions in government. The ideological framework for a confrontation with 'Islam' had been fashioned by Samuel Huntington and his followers out of the anti-Islamic discourse prevalent in the US since Khomeini's revolution in Iran. With the collapse of the Soviet Union the US no longer needed the Islamist fighters it had helped to create in Afghanistan. In fact they had become a nuisance since the US refused to cede to the demand of its one-time ally, Osama bin Laden, that American troops be pulled out of Saudi Arabia. Now the 'War on Terror' was declared. Israeli politicians leapt to claim common cause with America – or rather to declare that their cause had always been the War on Terror and now, at last, America had joined it.

It was now possible to move the conflict from the political into the metaphysical sphere: a conflict with an enemy so nebulous as to be found anywhere where resistance to American or Israeli policies might lurk.

It was within this rubric that the 2003 war on Iraq was started and it blazes on as I write. The old language of colonialism surfaces once again. Politicians and pundits insist on describing Iraqis in ethnic and religious terms although Iraqis describe themselves (in the Arabic media) in political and economic terms. The US insists on ramming a vicious form of global capitalism down Iraq's throat. In the Western media Arabic is consistently mistranslated and mistranscribed and so leaves an archaic and inchoate impression. British and American heads are constantly to be seen on screen discussing what 'we' should do about Iraq, while coalition troops have until now killed more than 11,000 Iraqi civilians and 80 per cent of the population of Iraq want them to leave their country. Expert Western voices are raised every day against this adventure but leave no trace on events.

To date, the effect of American policies on the Arab world has been the complete opposite of their stated aims. In Palestine America defined itself as the 'honest broker' between the Palestinians and Israelis and proceeded to place matters in the hands of US Special Envoys, almost every one of whom was a graduate of AIPAC. Today, after more than thirty years of an American-sponsored 'peace process', thousands of Palestinians and hundreds of Israelis have been murdered, Jerusalem is encircled by illegal settlements, the West Bank is decimated, an apartheid barrier is being constructed and the President of the US has taken it upon himself to absolve Israel of any obligation to conform to past agreements, to international law or to the declared will of the world. Gaza and Rafah are seeing killings and demolitions of homes on a scale unparalleled since 1948.

In Egypt, the late Anwar Sadat invited the US to set up its stall promising peace, democracy and prosperity and the regime has toed the American line faithfully since then. The country now has unprecedented levels of poverty, huge disparities between rich and poor, and a shattered middle class. What small intimations of representative government there were have been strangled; Egyptians have been ruled by emergency law for the past twenty-three years and the abuse of citizens' human rights has become endemic. So bad is the situation that Egyptians have reversed the trend dominant for some 6,000 years and now seek to emigrate from their land.

Similar effects can be seen in every 'Third World' country that bought into American promises or had them forced upon it. And still the media burble on about the 'peace process' and bringing 'democracy' to the Arabs. Almost 300 years ago Giambattista Vico pointed out that the first symptom of the barbarisation of thought is the corruption of language. The media has a clear duty here: the US administration and the British government should be made to define very precisely what they mean by 'sovereignty', 'democracy', 'freedom', 'stability', 'peace' and 'terrorism'. These people are not vague idealists; they are lawyers and businessmen, they know all about fine print. They run democratically elected governments answerable to the re- presentative houses and to the people. The media should demand that they spell out the fine print in their pronounce- ments to their electorates. We could even limit the question and ask what do the British and the American governments mean by these terms in the context of their dealings with the Arab world? Then, depending on how the definitions agree with those in the *OED*, say, we could find different terms for the commodities Bush and Blair are so keen to export to the region.

And since the Western media is now blithely using Arabic words, it would be useful if they could demonstrate their understanding of those too. They can start with 'jihad', 'fatwa' and 'shaheed', all of which are far more layered and subtle than you would guess if you just came across them in English.

The whole question of Islam and the West needs to be examined honestly. The current pieties that say 'we know so little of each other' or, in the words of Lord Carey, the ex-Archbishop of Canterbury, 'we must get rid of the deep hatred we have for each other', may be well intentioned but they rest on untrue premises and are not helpful. The huge populations of Arab Christians and the Christians who live in Muslim countries know a great deal about Muslims and there is no evidence that they 'hate' them. In fact Arab Christians have fought side by side with their Muslim compatriots against the Crusaders and against the Western colonialists of more recent times. And Muslims are very well informed about Christians. Eastern Christians have been their compatriots, neighbours and friends for fourteen centuries. And Muslims have had to learn about Western Christians if only because the West has been the dominant power in Muslim lives for the last 200 years. As for hatred, a 'secular' Muslim cannot, by definition, hate a Christian on the grounds of religion. A 'believing' Muslim cannot hate a Christian or a Jew because of who they are since Islam is clear that Muslims must live in fellowship with people of the Book. There is, though, an important difference between Christians and Muslims in terms of belief. Since Islam came after Christianity and Judaism and saw itself as a continuation of their traditions, it is part of the faith of a Muslim to believe in Christ, Moses and the prophets of the Old and New Testaments. This is stated in the Qur'ān and it is not open to choice. A believing Christian or Jew, on the other hand, can choose whether or not to believe that Muhammad was a prophet and, therefore, whether Islam too came from the God of Christianity and Judaism. This difference is well demonstrated in the language used by extremists on both sides which – while equally foul – differs in one respect: Christian extremists call Muslims idolators and regularly describe Islam and the Prophet in abusive terms. The most recent high-level example is the Chief of US Military Intelligence, Lt.-Gen. William Boykin, who, while under investigation for boasting that 'my God is bigger than his [a Muslim fighter's] god. My God is a real God, his god is an idol', is also being linked to the torture of detainees in Guantanamo and Iraq. Islamist extremists at their most virulent never attack Christianity, Christ, or 'the Christian God'. They never speak against 'Christians'; the term they use is always 'Crusader'.

A linked and recurrent theme is to claim that Arabs use Israel and the West as an alibi, an excuse for their passivity, that they should get on with fixing their lives, with developing. Here it is essential to differentiate between the Arabs and their rulers. The rulers will do nothing because their only interest is to remain in power. They have failed in their primary task of protecting their nations' sovereignty and steering their countries' resources towards providing the people with a decent life. Their positions are now so precarious that they dare not move one way for fear that their people's anger will finally unseat them, and they dare not move the other way for fear of offending America. As for the people, they are doing plenty. First they are surviving – by the skin of their teeth. The poor are poorer then they have ever been. The middle classes are often running two jobs just to make a living: civil servants are driving taxis, lawyers are working as car park attendants, graduates are working on food stalls. Even so, local NGOs challenge governments on human rights, on trade union laws, on constitutional reforms. Citizens challenge government officers on corruption. They take cases to court and they win. Artists paint and musicians sing. Newspapers are full of analysis and debate. And this against a background of arbitrary detention, of torture, not just in prisons, but in police stations. Protests are organised despite the thousands of armed security forces the state puts on the streets. And despite the sullying of these terms, people still campaign for democracy and freedom.

What does the Western media report of all this? When British and American newspapers took up the case of Sa'd el-Din Ibrahim, the Egyptian academic with strong American ties who had fallen out with the government, you would have thought that all of Egypt was baying for his blood. No mention was made of the fact that Egyptian human rights lawyers across the political spectrum – including leftists unenthusiastic about certain of his American connections – volunteered to defend him. Similarly in the ongoing case of the three young British Muslims accused (with twenty Egyptians) of belonging to the outlawed Hizb al-Tahrir, reports in British newspapers make no mention of the panel of Egyptian lawyers – again from right, left and centre – who are defending them. When the United Nations Development Program report on the Arab countries came out with its abysmal findings, where was the logical concern about the measly percentage of state budgets devoted to research and development and the trillions spent on importing Western arms? Instead the headlines screamed about how 50 per cent of Arab women were still illiterate. But another finding was that in the last two decades Arab women outstripped every other group of women in the world in the advances they had made. Why was that not a headline?

It should be said that representation in the Western media is not high among the priorities of my friends in Egypt and other Arab countries. Nor should it be. But for those of us who live in the West this fashioning of an image that is so at variance with the truth is very troubling. As Jean Genet observed in *Un captif amoureux*, the mask of the image can be used to manipulate reality to sinister ends. And while it would not be correct to attribute malign motives to the media in general, it is not unreasonable to feel that by promoting a picture of the Arab world that is essentially passive, primitive and hopeless, a picture that hardly ever depicts Arabs as agents of action (except for terrorists and suicide bombers), the media validates the politicians' dreams of domination.

This, also, is where a certain breed of Arab intellectual plays a crucial role. Decrying the political oppression rampant in their countries of birth and exposing the atrocities that take place there, these intellectuals (the majority of whom are to be found in Washington, DC) will implicitly widen their critique to discredit the very culture and people of these countries. They therefore provide the ideological justification to 'save these people from themselves'. This has been seen in action recently in the writings of Arab intellectuals embedded with the US administration encouraging it into its disastrous Iraqi adventure.

The long Editors' Note published by the *New York Times* in the 26 May 2004 issue, regarding its coverage of the Iraq affair, admits that 'editors at several levels who should have been challenging reporters and pressing for more scepticism were perhaps too intent on rushing scoops into the paper . . . Articles based on dire claims about Iraq tended to get prominent display, while follow-up articles that called the original ones into question were sometimes buried.' But the Note itself is published at the bottom of page A10 and, as Michael Massing points out in the 24 June *New York Review of Books*, does not address the underlying causes of this failure. It is interesting that the bravest and most objective analyses of the events of the past four years have tended to come from the cultural rather than the news media.

It has become commonplace to say that the world has never known such dangerous times. It's possibly true. The givens we live with at the moment are well rehearsed: the absence of a world-power alternative to that of the United States, the US's umbilical links with the global ambitions of capital and corporatism, and the reach and power of contemporary weapons.

I would add to these that the identification (despite the efforts at blurring) of Islam as 'the enemy' is particularly dangerous. When the West identified the USSR as the enemy, it had to construct 'the Evil Empire' from scratch. But with Islam, the idealogues and propagandists of the

West need only revive old colonialist and orientalist ideas of Islam as an inherently fanatical, violent ideological system that rejects modernity. They can play to deep-seated fears and prejudices with roots stretching back into the Middle Ages. When, at the height of the Troubles, the IRA launched a bombing campaign on the mainland, the suggestion that this was a manifestation of 'Catholic fanaticism' was a marginal one. However repellent their bombing of civilians, it had to be regarded and dealt with as a politically motivated act. A similar reaction was afforded the African National Congress's bombing campaign – no reasonable person suggested that this was 'black fanaticism'. From 1970 to 2000 the United States has been directly implicated in creating and nurturing Islamist groups to counter secular national liberation movements in Palestine and other Arab countries. It, and the Arab regimes, have succeeded in pushing most political opposition into the cloak of Islamism. Now that the most militant of the Islamist extremists, whose lands are the 'objects' of Western policies, are no longer content for the battles to be fought exclusively on their home ground and have brought a sample of the carnage into the territory of the West, we hear a ready-made discourse on 'nihilistic Islamic fanatics' who are on the rampage because they hate the democracy, freedom and prosperity of the West. One does not have to condone the killing of civilians to admit the political demands behind it. In fact denying the existence of those political demands guarantees the continuation and escalation of the conflict and the deaths of yet more innocents.

The role of Israel here needs to be clearly acknowledged, for Israel has always predicated its value to the West on the premise that there is an unresolvable conflict between the West and the Muslim hordes. Today, allied to the American Christian right, its role is to exaggerate and escalate the conflict.

Imagine George W. Bush elected for a second term. The Neo-cons will have four more years in which to implement their vision for the New American Century in such a way as to make it stick. They will go all out for world domination.

Imagine a new atrocity taking place in the US. General Tommy Franks has said that if that happens he can envisage the US being put under military law. All American dissidence will be suppressed; the administration will not even need to talk about democracy and freedom and beacons of light. And in response to America's deadly activities across the world will come a continuous asymmetrical terror.

Now imagine that this scenario is actually desired by the Christian Zionists who have allied themselves to Israel and who believe literally in Armageddon and cannot wait for 'the Rapture', the moment when they, as good pious Christians, will be – in George Monbiot's phrase – 'wafted out of their pyjamas' and seated at the right hand of God to watch what befalls us sinners. Among those people are some powerful officers of the American state, and they are interested in fomenting conflict, not resolving it.

A bleak, bleak picture. And yet there *is* still hope. Hope lies in a unity of conscience between the people of the world for whom this phrase itself carries any meaning. We have seen this conscience in action in the demonstrations that swept the planet before the invasion of Iraq, in the anger of Americans and Europeans at the pictures coming out of Abu Ghraib prison in Iraq, in the courageous stand of the Israelis refusing to serve the occupation and the private citizens from every part of the world who have tried – and some have paid with their lives – to stand between the Palestinians and their destruction. We see it every day in the writings of the brave and dogged few in the mainstream media and in the tireless work of the alternative and fringe media. It expresses itself in the myriad grass-roots movements that have coalesced into a worldwide effort to influence and modify the course of global capitalism.

For all these voices, these consciences, to be effective, however, Western democracies have to live up to their own values. It is shameful that on questions of international politics there is so little to choose between the governing parties and the opposition in the US and Britain. Democracy presupposes vigorous opposition on matters of national importance; it also presupposes a free and informed media which sees its task as making the facts available to the electorate. The current attacks on civil rights on both sides of the Atlantic, the drive to place security concerns before every other concern, the attempts to tamper with education and the law to serve a political agenda remind me of nothing so much as the activities of the ruling regimes in the Arab world for the last several decades; activities that have now brought the Arab world to what Arab intellectuals argue is the lowest point in its history.

The question of Palestine is of paramount importance not just because of humanitarian concerns about the plight of the Palestinians. It matters that now, in full view of the world and in utter defiance of the mechanisms the international community has put into place to regulate disputes between nations, a favoured state can commit vast illegal acts of brutality and be allowed to gain by them. If the world allows Israel to steal the West Bank and Jerusalem and to deny the history of the people it dispossessed in 1948 and 1967 then the world will have admitted it is a lawless place, and the world will suffer the consequences of this admission. The question of Palestine is also where the influence of the USA on world affairs is most sharply in focus. If there is no just solution to the Palestinian problem, if the ordinary citizens of Palestine and Israel are not permitted the conditions which would allow them to live their daily lives in a human way, then the influence of the world's only superpower will be proved to be irredeemably malign.

Globalisation is happening. It is driven by economics, economic ideology and communications. But does this have to entail the economic, political, cultural annexation of chunks of the world by whoever is the most powerful at any given moment? Surely that is the path to constant conflict, to grief and misery.

There is another way and that is to inhabit and broaden the common ground. This is the ground where everybody is welcome, the ground we need to defend and to expand. It is to Mezzaterra that every responsible person on this planet now needs to migrate. And it is there that we need to make our stand.

London, June 2004

POLITICAL ESSAYS

Mystery surrounds rules of engagement

The rules of engagement used by the Israeli Defense Force and the border police have always been something of a mystery …

Since the intifada, Israeli security forces have frequently used live ammunition against demonstrators despite the absence of firearms on the Palestinian side, producing a steady stream of deaths.
Guardian, Tuesday October 3, 2000

Intifada 2000 dwarfs the original

The slings and stones may be familiar, but the past weeks of Palestinian-Israeli violence bear little resemblance to the intifada of 1987-93. They make it look almost gentlemanly …

Mr Najjar recalls the mass arrests and bones broken deliberately by Israeli security forces.

'This time,' he says, 'they aim to kill.'
Guardian, Friday October 27, 2000

Under the Gun: A Palestinian Journey[1]

I have never, to my knowledge, seen an Israeli except on television. I have never spoken to one. I cannot say I have wanted to. My life, like the life of every Egyptian of my generation, has been overcast by the shadow of Israel. I have longed to go to Palestine, but have not wished to go to Israel. And now I am going there.

I have not felt such anticipation or such fear since I was a child. For the past two months I have been following the news of the Intifada.[2] I have compared the images on the BBC and CNN with those on al-Jazeera and other Arab channels. I have unspun stories, fumed at the American newspapers and been grateful for some of the reporting in some of the British press. I have started and ended my days reading appeals for help on the Internet. And again and again I have asked myself: 'What is it that I can do?' Now at last I can do something; I can go see for myself, and write. But going means going *there*.

Sunday 26 November 2000
My suitcase is open, almost packed, on the bed. I bought it yesterday – with wheels in case I have to drag it through barricades. The minicab is due in half an hour.

Monday 27 November 2000
It is the first day of Ramadan and we are on the road from Amman to the bridge and I am staring out at the desert and

[1] The *Guardian*, 18 and 19 December 2000 published this in a shorter form. The full article appears here.
[2] The word *Intifada* derives from the root *nfd*, to make a sudden, violent movement. It carries connotations of 'involuntary', as when in shock or when hit by a sudden realisation. It also carries connotations of shaking something off: dust, lethargy.

thinking – as I always do – how much I miss it when I'm in England: ten minutes of rolling dunes, then rock formations rising like huge chocolate gateaux followed by dunes again; but this time rippling as though having a joke, then a bend in the road and a green valley opens up and suddenly a row of bedouin women walking elegantly along a ridge, then sand again and we are at the Jordanian terminal which seems almost empty. We unload and our driver makes enquiries. The West Bank, al-Daffa, is closed. He points to a large, low building and through the windows we see that it is crammed with people. 'But Jerusalem?' the woman with whom I've shared the taxi asks. Jerusalem, apparently, is open.

I know nothing of this woman except that the small daughter on the seat next to her is called 'Malak', Angel. An orthodox priest in black robes and his hair in a long grey braid comes out of the building and takes a taxi back to Amman. We go to another part of the terminal. Buses are waiting, loaded with people. Angel's mother decides to go VIP for the sake of the child. I walk along behind her. We hand over our passports and are ushered into a large room with sofas and Arabic newspapers. An official says that because I have a British passport I must go with the 'foreigners' on the bus.

'But she'll sit there for hours,' Angel's mother says.

The man shrugs.

'She's Egyptian', she says, 'and it's her first time here. Let her stay with us.'

He asks me in Arabic if I'm Egyptian. I am. Am I willing to pay the eighteen dinar VIP fee? I am. He disappears. An exhausted woman comes in. She says she sat in this room yesterday from two till eight then was told Jerusalem was closed and had to go back to Amman. But the man comes back and waves us out.

A van this time and when we get off, there it is – 'Al-Jisr,' Umm Angel[3] says – the bridge. A wooden construction, just

---

[3] *Umm* is mother. A traditional form of referring to someone is through the name of their child, so Umm Angel is Angel's mother. Angel's father would be Abu Angel.

like in the pictures, with wooden walls so you can't jump off and into the Jordan river. The Jordan river is a mere trickle of water. We walk across, two women and a flame-haired child and there, above our heads, are Israeli soldiers just as I've seen them on television for four decades: their eyes behind shades, their faces behind machine guns and above them two crossed Israeli flags; one fluttering in the breeze, the other caught in a spike of machinery and lying limp.

We stop at a kiosk and hand our passports in through a window to a young woman in army uniform. She waves us on. Another van and on to another terminal building. Had there been Jordanian soldiers and guns on the other side? I didn't see any, but maybe I just didn't notice.

We are sitting in a smallish, brightly lit room with vivid blue armchairs. Serious attempts at decor have been made: a cactus growing out of a half coconut shell tilts on an Arab-style carved wooden table, rubber plants and plastic flowers droop from dusty glass shelves, an empty drinks dispenser glows coldly in the corner. On the walls are three reproductions: two are Kandinsky-like, but the third is a large close-up of the two forefingers of God and Adam just failing to meet.

A polite young Israeli comes in and asks me in broken Arabic to fill out some forms. Then he comes back to escort us to the passport window.

I say: 'I don't want my passport stamped.'

He says: 'I know.'

Al-Quds, Jerusalem, 2.30 p.m.

I head out of the hotel and start walking. Every car I pass I imagine exploding into flames. How far away does one have to be not to be killed by an exploding car? But the sun is shining as I head down Salah el-Din Street – and I am at home. The street is lined with bakeries, haberdasheries, shoe shops, small grocers, hairdressers. Girls in school uniform and headscarves walk in groups, chatting, laughing. Boys loiter and watch them. The names on the shops and the doctors' signs are the familiar mix of Christian and Muslim Arab, French and Armenian. The French cultural centre has wide-open doors and an inviting garden; there is a smell of roasting coffee. It's like a smaller, cleaner, uncrowded Cairo. But two buildings look different from the others: they are modern, precise, their angles are sharp, they fly the Israeli flag, and they are the only ones where the gates are made of steel bars – and are closed.

But then appearing in front of me are the walls of the old city. Closer in I see the ancient gateway and beside it an Israeli army car and five soldiers armed with machine guns. I tie a scarf under my chin and walk past them, through Bab al-Zahra,[4] and I am in a medieval Arab city: Orshalim al-Quds, Jerusalem the Sacred, a city made of rose-hued stone. The streets are paved with it; like cobbles, only larger, the stones are worn smooth and shine in the light. Down steps, round bends and another rosy alley stretches ahead. The houses seem to grow out of the street. Around many of their green iron doors are the decorations which mean that the resident has made the pilgrimage to Makkah. You see these in any Egyptian village, but here, instead of the representations of the pilgrim and his or her transport, you get delicate drawings of flowers and birds.

A small handwritten sign on the wall points to al-Aqsa. I walk down Mujahedin Street. A small boy, maybe four years old, skips along chanting, 'Ya Saddam, ya habeeb, come and blow up Tel Abeeb.' A few steps behind him his mother smiles at me. And now I am in front of the gateway to al-Haram al-Sharif (the Noble Sanctuary). Inside the gateway, sitting at a wooden table are three armed soldiers. One stands up and blocks my path: 'Papers.' I don't like the look of the soldiers. I am one and they are three. My passport is British but it says born in Cairo. Egypt has just recalled its ambassador from Tel Aviv. But a couple of local

[4] *Bab* is door or gate. Bab el-Zahra is al-Zahra Gate. Interestingly the Arabic and English names of the gates of Jerusalem are different. So what in Arabic is Bab al-Khalil in English is the New Gate.

men from the administration of the mosque are standing just inside the gateway. I hand over my passport. The soldier flicks through it.

'In England, you live?' He has a heavy, East European accent.

'Yes.'

I've been told don't explain, don't justify, don't be defensive. Minimal response.

'What town?'

'London.'

'Why you are going in?'

I decide: 'To pray.'

'You are Muslim?'

'Yes.'

The Israelis have closed the Haram to all Palestinians except residents of Jerusalem. And Jerusalemite men under the age of forty-five are also not allowed to go in. The soldier goes through my handbag which I have emptied of everything except purse, tissues and comb. The other soldiers look into the bag, too. He motions me on with his head.

A few steps and I am in the vast enclosure of the Haram. Brown earth with shrubs, patches of grass, trees. The Haram wall to my left forms part of the wall of the old city itself, to my right it forms the backs of houses and churches. Stretching in front of me the path rises to meet a wide set of pale steps leading to a great stone terrace and out of that rises the golden Dome of the Rock. I sit on a low stone wall under the open sky surrounded by small Mameluke structures and sense utter peace.

Later the women come out of prayers. They look at me with open curiosity: 'Salamu aleikum!'

I return the greeting.

'From where is the sister?'

'From Egypt.'

They want to know if I have somewhere to stay, otherwise any one of them will take me home. They all live in the old city, the Dome of the Rock is their local mosque; they nip down every day to pray.

Two minutes takes me round a corner, up some stairs and into Umm Yasir's home. Her two young daughters-in-law are both students. They whisper and laugh together over their books.

'She got married three days ago,' Umm Yasir says, pointing to one of the girls. 'Just over a cup of coffee. Who can have a proper wedding now when people are being killed every day?'

'Does the situation affect you here, in the old city?'

'Look!' Umm Yasir says, taking me to her door, pointing at the shuttered house across the lane: 'The settlers took it over. They put chairs out here in the lane and pick quarrels with the young people coming and going.'

But how did they take it over?

'Since Ariel Sharon bought two houses here he's made it easy for them.'

But how? Who would sell to Sharon?

'Awwad Abu Sneina. Everybody knew he was a spy. He vanished from the neighbourhood and next thing we knew the Israeli flag went up on the house and Sharon had bought it. But when Abu Sneina died there wasn't a burial ground that would take him. One day my son was playing football and the ball hit one of them [the settlers], they grabbed him and said they'd call the police. We said go ahead, call the police. But they called some other settlers instead. Two hundred of them came from Atarot Cohunim and beat us with everything they had – even their walkie-talkies. The people praying in the mosque heard the noise and came to our help and it was a battle. The police said we were the aggressors. At the Hadasa hospital they would not treat us under the insurance. They made us pay 450 shekels. Affect us? They do what they like to us.'

She talks of tear gas pumped into houses, of rubber bullets which the Palestinian children peel to extract the steel marble within, which they brace into their slingshots and aim back at the soldiers. She talks of the threat to her mosque, of an ambulance bringing a seventy-eight-year-old neighbour back from hospital, how soldiers searched it and stripped it down to the radiator: 'They've grown afraid of the air itself.' I feel dizzy with the detail piling up in my head. It is getting close to sunset and I leave before I can be made to stay and eat.

Through Bab el-Silsila I see several young Jewish men in black clothes hurrying along and into the tunnel which – I assume – leads to the Wailing Wall. Further along a mild-looking man wearing a yarmulke and leading two children steps out of a building. From within I hear the sound of children chanting in Hebrew.

The sun has set and it is time to break my fast. In Bab el-Amoud a man at a stall fills me a pitta bread with falafel, salad and tahina. He finds a chair for me and places a glass of water on the ground at my side. I sit inside the ancient gateway and eat – within sight of the army car and the soldiers and beyond them a beautiful, Indian-looking building standing alone. Two young men lean against a wall discussing what the Arab states can reasonably be expected to do. If only Egypt and Jordan would open the borders, they say, so we're not mice in a trap like this.

Back at the hotel I phone a journalist contact. I ask a few questions then my enthusiasm for this city bursts forth – and is met with silence.

'What? You don't agree?'

'Well, yes,' she says. 'It's just that I think everything would be so much easier if it wasn't there.'

I go out to the grocery next door. I want to buy some yoghurt and dates for my pre-dawn meal. The TV set on the wall is tuned into a Palestinian channel showing the news. Every pot of yoghurt I pick up is labelled in Hebrew only. 'Don't you have any Palestinian yoghurt?' I ask and the owner points me to another refrigerator.

The news comes through of five workers killed by settlers. A sixth man had managed to get away. The ambulances had raced to the scene but been stopped by the army. Everybody in the shop has stopped in mid-motion and is watching the set. The tears roll down my face as someone's wife wails on the screen, but everybody else is impassive. When the item is over they go back to what they were doing.

The door to my hotel room will not lock from the inside. From the outside I can lock it, but not from the inside. I try and try. I feel uneasy about alerting people to the fact that my door does not lock. I decide that I'm safe enough here. I sit down to write today's notes.

Soon I will have to try to meet some Israelis.

Al-Khalil, Tuesday 28 November 2000

Abraham, Ibrahim al-Khalil, the Friend of God, father of the Arabs through Ismael son of Hager, and of the Jews through Isaac son of Sarah. At midday I am in the city that bears his name and houses his magnificent mosque. We have circuited two roadblocks to get here, turning a journey of half an hour into one of an hour and a half. Our car has Israeli licence plates and so – as we pass the Uruba refugee camp – my driver puts a large sign saying 'Press' in Arabic against the windscreen to prevent us being pelted with stones. But behind the wire-mesh fences the Palestinian youths are quiet.

When we pass the giant settlement of Kiryat Araba, my driver turns the Arabic sign over to display the English 'Press'.

'They came in 1969,' he says. 'They pretended they were a group of Swedish tourists and stayed in a hotel. Their leader was Moshe Levinger. Then they started clashing with the people and they were backed by the military governor, they stole the land and built the settlement.'

Think of al-Khalil (or Hebron) as two parts: the old city surrounding the mosque, and the new suburbs that have grown out of it. The main square of the modern part is teeming with people. Vegetable and fruit stalls teeter on the edges of pavements and on traffic islands. The Israelis have expropriated the old marketplace and bulldozed it. Raise your eyes from the bustle and you see the evidence of shells and mortars on the buildings surrounding the square. A gaping hole where the offices of *al-Ayyam*[5] newspaper used to be. Doctors' clinics, toy shops, a hairdresser: rubble, soot, shattered glass and pockmarks. Raise your eyes further and you see Israeli soldiers sandbagged on people's rooftops, their guns trained on the throng below. 'Twelve tonnes of equipment on my roof,' a man tells me, 'and they urinate in our water tanks.'

Al-Shuhada Street leads into the old city. It is empty and the shops are shuttered. At its far end I can see concrete roadblocks and, as I watch, a soldier emerges from behind a building beyond the blocks. He surveys us, his machine gun aimed, then steps back again behind the building. I start walking down the road towards him.

My guide pulls me back: 'No. There's already been shooting today.'

The soldier reappears, followed by another. There are maybe twenty metres between us.

A young man says: 'You don't need to be scared of them. Look!' He runs a few paces towards the soldiers, jumps up and down stamps his feet flaps his arms and yells out the Arabic equivalent of 'Boo!' The soldiers duck behind the wall. 'See! They're cowards!' he laughs and saunters off.

As we stand talking a tall man appears carrying a camera and wearing a white helmet and a white bullet-proof vest with 'Press' written in black across it. Awad Awad works for Agence France Presse. He stops to talk and my guide tells him I'm writing an article for the *Guardian*.

'You want to go in?' he asks.

'Yes. But I don't want to be shot.'

'You won't be shot if you're behind them.'

'She's my responsibility. I can't let anything happen to her—'

---

[5] *The Days*, the main Palestinian daily newspaper.

'Nothing will happen,' the photographer says easily. 'Come.'

I follow him through the roadblock and round a corner. Now I can see the soldiers grouped behind the wall at the end of al-Shuhada Street. Behind a building at the other side of the street are a journalist and three more photographers. We walk past the soldiers then Awad says 'Run!' and we run across the street and join the posse of cameras on the other side. We introduce ourselves and shake hands.

'What are they doing?' a man asks, nodding towards the seven soldiers huddled behind the wall.

'Making a plan,' another laughs.

The soldiers break up and three of them run across the road towards us. They crouch behind the concrete blocks, their guns aimed at the empty street. If I stretched out my hand I could touch their backpacks. After a moment a stone crashes into one of the concrete blocks and splinters off. A boy dances across the street. A shot is fired. It is alarmingly loud. The same event is repeated six times in the next half-hour. Twice, in the silence following a shot a woman walks quickly across the street. Three people in blue dungarees and helmets with IPIF written in red across their bullet-proof vests stand across the road.[6] I cannot make out if they are men or women. They carry clipboards and timers and seem to be recording the times of the shots. The photographers tell me that when there is going to be any real action the soldiers simply shoo away the observers. A mobile rings and it is my guide begging me to come back.

I want to go into the old city but my guide and driver are fearful and reluctant. As we argue in the street a woman stops and asks where I'm from. I'm an Egyptian from London writing a piece for a British paper. 'Then you should take her in,' she says, and starts to describe a route. They will not listen to her. An imposing man in a grey cashmere

---

[6] International observers.

overcoat appears. They seem awed by him. I later learn that he is a Palestinian journalist who's been shot in five separate incidents.[7] The woman tells him what's happening and he says, 'Come on, chaps. It's your duty to take her in. You've got Israeli licence plates. She's got a British passport. Take her in.'

Reluctantly they make a detour and try to drive into the old city. Forty thousand people live here under curfew. Twelve thousand children cannot go to school. Fifteen mosques are closed. In the centre, armed, live what Israel says are 400 settlers and the Palestinians say are 100. All this is for their benefit.

'If the army were to go away', I ask, 'and the settlers were content to live here among you, would you let them?'

'They wouldn't. They would go away.'

'But if they wanted to stay, could they?'

'They've taken people's homes. If you could go into the centre you would see families camped by their homes, refusing to leave, and the settlers throw rubbish on them and beat them up. They're not even proper settlers; they are religious students, mostly from the United States, volunteering to come for one or two years to do their religious duty by being here—'

The city is beautiful. Like old Jerusalem it is made of pink stone. The narrow streets wind up and down like the streets of an Etruscan town. The houses lean against each other, one house's roof forming the other's patio. Ornate stone balconies look out on to the empty street. The sun shines, the air is clean and fresh, the light is so perfect we could be on a film set. A dark green patrol car passes and does not stop us. The microphone blares out in accented Arabic: 'O people of al-Khalil. Beware breaking the curfew.' Round the next bend a yellow taxi is at a stop in the middle of the road, leaning to one side. A group of children has gathered round

---

[7] This was Mazin Da'na, who worked for Reuters. He was killed by the Americans in 2003 while filming in Baghdad.

it watching, hushed and still. We pull in by a wall and park. A woman leans against the taxi with a baby in her arms. 'I know it's a curfew,' the driver says, 'but she has just come out of hospital, and she had the baby, so I drove her. Look what they've done.' A soldier had taken out a knife, he tells us, and slashed the two tyres on the driver's side. Naturally he has only one spare tyre. With the curfew, how is he going to get another one? Two boys are helping him change one wheel. The other children look on in silence. The woman starts walking off slowly.

We carry on, on foot. Up some steps leading down to the centre an old man is climbing.

'Can we get to the centre?'

'No. They've blocked it off.'

'Is there somewhere from where I can at least see the centre and the mosque?'

'Yes, from my house,' and he turns back to lead the way.

Through a green iron door I step into paradise. Terrace after terrace of pink stone, plants overflowing their pots and flowers growing out of tin cans, trellises with vines, doorways into the hill itself that the old man, Hajj al-Ja'bari, opens with big keys so that we step into vaulted chambers where ancient Sufis meditated and prayed to be vouchsafed a vision. Some of the chambers have Mameluk niches where I imagine the Sufis kept their jars of water and bundles of dates. In one chamber photographs of three young men trimmed with black are propped up against the wall. 'My wife's nephews,' he says.

I emerge from a chamber to find myself looking at a wall with wire-mesh windows and above them the Israeli flag. 'Yes. They are here,' he says. The soldiers are looking at us and we keep our eyes averted. 'They occupied the building next door and they tried to get me out of this. I said I would bring out my sword and kill the first man to step over my threshold.'

'What happened?'

'They put iron doors on the street openings between my

house and the mosque – and they set up this surveillance camera up there.'

'And now they leave you alone?' as I take a photo of the camera.

'I have no children now or young men to make trouble. There is just me and my wife. The [Palestinian] Authority came and said give us the biggest vault we'll make it into a museum.'

'And?'

'I threatened them too with my sword. They would have turned it over to the Israelis sooner or later.'

An elderly woman appears on a balcony and calls to him to bring the guests into the house. On the patio outside, two very old Singer sewing machines sit side by side.

'I just oiled them yesterday.' He spins the wheel to prove that they work beautifully. In the living room there is another sewing machine, 'But this one can do embroidery,' he says, and pulls out a length of cloth to show us the different stitches.

'I don't know what he wants with all these old machines,' his wife says. On the wall there are the three young men. On each photograph there is written a name prefaced by 'The Martyr'. 'My nephews,' the woman says. 'Come, you can see the mosque from the kitchen window.'

I see the rose-pink walls of Ibrahim's Sanctuary and beyond them, in the central town square, the army camp with the sandbags, the guns, the soldiers and the white flag with the blue star. My guide tells me that Saturday is the worst day here because the settlers have more time to walk around upturning vegetable stalls and kicking people. The army protects them, he says, because the army has to behave within its orders but the settlers are accountable to the religious courts and cannot be punished for harming a non-Jew.

My driver loses patience: 'We've gone down the road of "peace" as we were asked to. Meetings and summits without end. And what's the result? Is this right? That a wronged

41

population should be punished? In '94 Baruch Goldstein murders the worshippers and this is what we get? The mosque is divided and now with the curfew this old man who has prayed in it every day of his life cannot set foot in it?'

'The unjust will be visited with retribution,' our host says gently, 'and I pray on my terrace within sight of the Sanctuary walls.'

I think of the decisive battle, in 1517, when Mameluk Egypt fell to the Ottoman Turks. When the dashing Mameluk knights, till then the finest fighting force in the world, rode out to do battle against the invaders, they found themselves with the modern technology of Ottoman guns in front of them and treachery at their backs.

Back on the road the taxi is still there. We drive out of al-Khalil, negotiate roadblocks, get on to the motorway. Ahead of us is an army truck. The soldier at the wheel drives slowly and we are not allowed to overtake him. In the back three young soldiers watch us. It is getting near to sunset and time to break the fast. A roadblock near Bethlehem and we are pulled over. My driver opens his window and hands over his papers. I stare ahead but suddenly my door is flung open.

A rather plump young soldier bends down, smiling: 'What did they thay today? The Tanthim? That they would thtop the shooting?'

Somehow the lisp reassures me.

'Who?' I ask.

'The Tanthim.'

When I look blank he says: 'Fatah: What did they thay today?'

'I'm frightfully sorry,' I say, speaking posh, 'I don't know. I've been out all day and haven't seen the news.'

'But you have a radio in the car?'

My driver leans over and speaks in Hebrew: 'What would she know? Can't you see she's foreign?'

They wave us on.

'Son of a bitch,' my driver laughs. 'They don't miss a trick.'

Maybe there are cafés in West Jerusalem or Tel Aviv where intellectuals, artists, people, sit around and debate the condition of the country and the 'Palestinian problem'. Maybe they debate the ethics of an army of occupation holding a population hostage, or the civil rights of an Arab population in a Zionist state; but these places – the places that are lit up at night – how do I find them? In the entertainment guide I look at the listings: films, recitals, cabarets. I consider taking a taxi and simply buying a ticket. But the thought makes me uneasy.

Last night I walked back to my hotel up Salah el-Din Street. I was still wearing the headscarf I wore at al-Aqsa and my dress reached to just above my ankles. I passed the barred building which I now know is the Israeli Court. In front of it was the armoured car and four soldiers with the obligatory machine guns. They were laughing together and I also thought that in the space of two days my fear had disappeared, my heart did not lurch. I must have taken thirty paces or so and was about to turn the corner when I felt something hit my left shoulder hard and heard the crack as whatever it was ricocheted off me and hit – I suppose – the ground. What did I feel? I felt shock as I turned ice cold then hot. I felt my throat block up and the tears rise to my eyes, and then I felt pure anger and I turned. As I looked at the ground to try to identify what had hit me one of the transits that carry people between towns screeched to a stop by my side. The door was pulled open and inside I saw women who looked like me, and children.

The driver leaned over: 'Are you all right?'

'Yes,' I said. I found that I was feeling ashamed, ashamed of having been hit. 'Did you see who hit me?' I looked around the street. It was deserted except for the soldiers.

'No, we just heard the sound. Do you need help? We're going to Ramallah.'

'My hotel's just round the corner.'

'Don't wait here. Get in. I'll take you to the hotel.'

'I'm all right,' I said.

'God will punish them,' a woman said. They did not drive off until I was round the corner and out of sight.

When I got to my room I pushed the heavy table with my suitcase on it against the door. I took off my coat and dress. In the mirror I could see the purple bruise on my left shoulder. It did not hurt, but in my mind I kept walking back to the soldiers, challenging: 'Did you see who hit me?'

Wednesday 29 November 2000

We start early for Ramallah and a couple of minutes from my hotel I see two Israeli flags fixed to the flat roof of a house. Next to them four boys in civilian clothes nurse machine guns. My driver, Abu Karim, says these are four houses that have recently been taken from their Arab residents.

Out of Jerusalem, major roads are being built to connect up with the settlements. The roadworks are guarded by Israeli army trucks.

The road north to Ramallah – the road that the Palestinians may use – will lead us through the town of Bireh and the news is that Bireh was shelled last night. Soon we see the concrete blocks, the waiting cars, the soldiers. We swerve off to the right and drive through dirt roads. Abu Karim points to a rectangular crater in the middle of the road the size of a grave. The army, he says, do this just to make life more difficult. A bone-jolting twenty minutes later we rejoin the main road about one kilometre up from where we had left it.

An hour and a half later (and a distance equivalent to, say, Chelsea to Kingston) we are sitting in Rima Tarazi's living room talking to her and her friend Fatima Jibril.[8] The women, one Christian, the other Muslim, are founders of

[8] Fatima Jibril died in 2003.

44

the National Union of Palestinian Women (NUPW) and worked hard to establish the Centre for the Support of the Family in Ramallah, a day centre where children were taught music and encouraged to draw: 'The children are not allowed to see maps of Palestine or learn their own history,' they tell me. Eighteen months ago the Israelis closed the centre down for 'inspiring sedition'.

'Sedition!' snorts Mrs Jibril. 'We were trying to help the mothers give their children a "normal" childhood. You know what the children sing? They sing: *Papa bought me a trifle/A machine gun and a rifle*. We were struggling to get them to sing normal children's songs. But normal children's songs have nothing to with the reality of their lives.'

'When the children said "The Jews came and took my cousin, threw our rice into the flour and the sugar—" we would say don't say the Jews, it's the Israelis, the Zionists. We were battling with the ethics of language—'

'The media in Britain', I say, 'ask why mothers allow their children to go out and throw stones at the army.'

'Allow?' says Rima Tarazi. 'You should see the quantities of valium we've dispensed to women in the camps simply to enable them to cope with their lives: when their children go out to play they're playing under the guns of the army observation post above them – these people have been living under "temporary" emergency conditions for thirty-three years – and some since '48. They don't go looking for the army, the army is right on their doorstep—'

'There isn't a child', says Fatima Jibril 'who doesn't have a father or a brother banished or jailed or killed. When the soldiers come in and beat up a father, the kids see it – all they've got is one room. They see their father being beaten. What do you think it does to them? They ask us if people in the whole world live like this. What can we tell them? A three-year-old comes in and tells me, "The Jews came and beat my father and his tummy fell out on to the floor but we got him to hospital and they're going to mend him." '

'When they arrested me—' Fatima Jibril says. I sit up. It's

very hard to think of this stately lady being arrested. 'When they arrested me, they took my mother. She was seventy. They blindfolded her and took her for interrogation. And you know what she did? She pretended she was senile, told them she was twenty-five and engaged and started describing her fiancé. They had to let her go.' The two women crack up, repeating 'engaged!'

'We've compromised,' Rima Tarazi says. 'They have West Jerusalem, the Carmel, Yafa and Haifa and so on. They have Israel. But they want everything, it's their nature. They attack us – physically – in three ways: through the army, the settlers, and the Mustaribs.'

The Mustaribs (Israeli agents who pretend to be Arab) apparently mingle with the people during demonstrations: 'They choose a child, grab him, throw their kuffiyas over their faces [so they can mingle again without being identified], whip out their yarmulkes and a gun and rush with the child over to an army car.' The two Israelis lynched in Ramallah were, the women say, Mustaribs.

'The settlers,' they say, 'God protect us from them. They are an army of barbarians; they don't even have the pretence of discipline like the army – and they believe they're acting with a dispensation from God.'

'You know the worst of it', they say, 'is that they keep you guessing. You never know if a road is to be open or closed. When they're going to shut off your water or turn off your electricity. Whether they're going to permit a burial. Whether they're going to give you a permit to travel. You can never ever plan. They create conditions to keep you spinning . . .'

At Oslo, Israel agreed to hand over some major Arab towns to the Palestinian Authority. Israel however retained all the areas surrounding the towns, so to get from one to another the Palestinians had to carry permits which were checked at Israeli checkpoints. With the Intifada the Israeli army simply encircled the towns, preventing the residents from leaving or entering. Critics of Oslo at the time said this was a blueprint for disaster. No one understands why the Palestinian Authority agreed to it. Some say they simply didn't have maps. It is at the soldiers encircling their towns that the youth and children of the Intifada throw stones.

Are there any good Israelis? People of conscience? 'Yes, a few. Look at what Amira Hass writes in *Ha'aretz*. And Uri Avnery. Michael Warschawski[9] is a good man. But they're marginalised.'

What about Peace Now?

'They've fallen silent.'

Why?

'Azmi Beshara[10] says it's because they don't want to oppose Barak. He came in on the "man of peace" ticket. How can a man who's built his career on assassinating Palestinians be a man of peace? Still, if Sharon were Prime Minister they might have spoken up against what's happening.'

Are you in touch with them?

'Not any more. We realised they would go so far and no further. The best of them balks at the Right of Return for the refugees. Even Leah Rabin wanted East Jerusalem. At the beginning of the Intifada they got in touch. We said, "You've been talking to us for years, now it's time for you to talk to your government."'

Back in Jerusalem I break my fast at a small café outside Bab al-Zahra. On the street outside is the army car and the soldiers. At the table behind me three elderly men are

[9] As I work on this book on 6 July 2004, Michael Warschawski, together with Arab Knesset Member, Azmi Beshara, the Chief Judge of the Islamic Court, Sheikh Tayseer Tamimi, the Archmandrite of the Greek Orthodox Church, Father Attallah Hanna, Hatem Abd el-Qader, local member of the Palestinian Legislative Council, Ahmad Ghneim, local leader of Fatah, Abd al-Latif Ghaith of the Popular Front for the Liberation of Palestine, Hani al-Issawi of the Democratic Front for the Liberation of Palestine and seven others are on the fourth day of their hunger strike in East Jerusalem. Their protest is against the Israeli barrier.

[10] Arab-Israeli member of the Knesset.

extolling the days of Gamal Abd el-Nasser and the idea of pan-Arabism. They end up singing popular Egyptian songs of the Sixties: 'Ya Gamal/Beloved of millions' and 'We said we'd build and now we've built/The Hi-i-gh Dam'.

The owner asks me what I'm doing in Jerusalem. I'm an odd sight breaking my fast alone – no family, no friends. He treats me to tamarind juice and pudding on the house and asks if I'm OK at my hotel. His family would have been glad to take me in but they're in al-Khalil. He used to commute, it's only half an hour, but now with the closures he can only manage to sneak in to see them once a week.

A silent candlelit demonstration outside Bab al-Khalil. Sixty candles flicker in the hands of sixty Palestinian women just outside the Gate. Opposite them, on the other side of the road, fifteen Israeli women dressed in black hold fifteen candles.

This is the third night now that I have stayed up writing past 2 a.m. and yet I have not recorded everything I have heard and everything I have seen. I have not even really thought about all I have heard and seen – that will come later. For now the present facts are all I can manage.

Al-Quds, Jerusalem, Thursday 30 November 2000

Albert Agazerian teaches History at Bir Zeit University. He meets me just inside Bab al-Khalil and we walk towards the house where he lives with his family inside the Armenian convent grounds. He points out the first British Consulate and the first British church: 'Layers of history,' he says. 'Dig here and you come up with at least seventeen layers of history – and the stories are all woven together. Here in Jerusalem we have what the whole world today is headed for: plurality. But the Israelis want to cancel everybody's story except their own.'

Madeleine, his wife, insists on giving me a jar of their olives. Her family has always got their olives from a farm near Nablus. Now the farmers are fighting not only the closures but the settlers who set fire to the olive groves or take chainsaws to the trees. 'The farmers', she tells me, 'slip out on Friday night and steal their own harvest while the settlers have their Sabbath.'

My attempts to examine the other side of all this have so far not been successful. Shlomo Ben Ami, sometime Israeli ambassador to Egypt, cannot see me because he is investigating the killings of thirteen[11] Arab-Israelis in Israel.

Could we not talk about broader issues?

'No. They are all related.'

I am still trying to speak to someone from the Yesha Council to arrange a meeting with a settler. It's not simple. From the first word it's not simple: I have often been asked whether I have a problem with English as the 'language of my oppressor'. I understand the question but I do not feel it; the British occupation was out of Egypt before I was born. English was the language of my first reading and I love it. When the voice at the other end of the phone said 'Shalom' I said 'Shalom' back out of courtesy but I was left with a nasty feeling; a feeling that I had been compromised. For the remaining seven calls I would respond with 'Good morning/evening'. When the Israeli army of occupation has been removed from the streets of the West Bank and East Jerusalem I will say 'Shalom' to Jewish visitors to the Holy Land.

And if a meeting should be arranged, how would I get there? My Palestinian driver won't go near a settlement. And who will I get to go in with me – for there's no way I'm going alone.

4.30 p.m.

I am sitting in the lobby of the hotel when Judy Blanc walks in. Stylish and small with her grey hair worn short and close-fitting, she is unmistakably a New Yorker. Her husband got

[11] During peaceful protest demonstrations within Israel in October 2000, thirteen Palestinian citizens of Israel were killed by the Israeli police and security forces, and hundreds more were injured. For more information on this and related issues see www.alternativenews.org.

a job as Professor of Arabic at the Hebrew University in '54 and she came with him. I have been told by my Palestinian friends that she is 'one in a million'. I ask her if this is true and she laughs: 'Not quite.' She says that the recent events – terrible as they are – have been useful in clarifying the Palestinians' priorities. That the Israeli government can no longer manipulate the confusion between principles and negotiating positions.

I ask her – this place seems to make it necessary to ask basic questions – where the 'good' Israelis are? How can people, aware that their government is subduing an entire population, cutting off their water and electricity, beating them up – I feel embarrassed at listing the misdeeds of the Israeli government to her – how can people, people with souls, tolerate this?

'But they're not aware,' she says. 'It's so easy not to see it. You live in West Jerusalem or in Tel Aviv. You don't need to notice the Palestinians. If they're there they're in the background. And there is a fundamental racism in this society that makes it possible for people to delude themselves, to not see what's happening. If you want to know what's happening you have to go looking for it, to East Jerusalem or the West Bank. Not many Israelis will do that.'

Are there any Israelis working with Palestinians now?

'No. The Palestinians saw that the liberal position of making contact one on one was corrupting the political process. Now they do what the University of Bir Zeit has always done: any joint activity between Palestinians and Israelis has to be based upon the Israelis' articulated commitment to the minimum demands of the Palestinians: Resolution 242 and the Right of Return.'

What about Peace Now and similar organisations?

'They have a problem. They supported Barak and now they say he's gone as far as he can and the violence has to stop. The TV liberals are really hampered by the fact that they supported him. Do you know, one of my friends, a good liberal, said to me last week, "I finally understood that Oslo was not the same for the Palestinians as it was for us." It took her seven years.'

What about Israeli Arabs? What's the liberal position there?

'That's also a problem. In fact it is *the* problem: the inherent contradiction between a "Jewish" state and a fully democratic state. Two years ago Azmi Beshara coined a slogan: "Israel: A State for All Its Citizens." The liberals were really unhappy with that. They refuse to use it and talk instead about "full equality for all".'

Judy works with Women in Black, Four Mothers and other organisations (mostly of women) who support Palestinian rights.

'Judy,' I ask, 'How much of a price have you paid for your stand?'

'A price? My dear, if you are a Jew in Israel you never have to pay a price.'

Al-Quds, Jerusalem, Friday 1 December 2000

This is the first Friday of Ramadan and Barak, in a move designed to 'achieve quiet during the month of Ramadan', has repealed the ban on Jerusalemite men under forty-five praying at the al-Aqsa mosque.

Israeli mounted police, armed and dressed in riot gear, guard the gates of the old city as though we were armed and dangerous hooligans. We pass through Bab al-Zahra in single file between two rows of soldiers with machine guns. Each man has to stop and show his identity papers. The women, if they keep their heads bowed and their eyes on the ground, are left alone. At Bab Hutta, the actual gate to al-Haram al-Sharif, there are more soldiers with guns. Inside, the men head for al-Aqsa, the women for that choice jewel, the Dome of the Rock. Because the Israeli amnesty does not extend to the people of the West Bank, there are maybe 20,000–25,000 people here today instead of the half a million you would normally expect.

At the Dome I squeeze in through Bab al-Janna (the Gate

51

of Paradise). In straight lines, shoulder to shoulder, we pray then sit to listen to the sermon. The imam preaches patience, steadfastness and resistance. He reminds us of the Prophet's saying that there are those who fast and gain nothing except hunger; to fast is to renounce falsehood, hypocrisy and all bad deeds. He lists the crimes of the Israeli military occupation against the people. He lists the demands of the people: an end to the occupation, the implementation of UN Resolution 242 and the return to the borders of 4 June 1967, an independent and sovereign Palestinian state in the West Bank, Gaza and East Jerusalem, the release of Palestinian prisoners from Israeli jails, the Right of Return to the homeland of all Palestinian refugees. He repeats God's promise that the righteous shall prevail, then he prays for al-Aqsa itself. Again and again he implores God to protect it from the plots being woven against it, again and again the women's voices from the Dome and the men's voices from al-Aqsa rise: Amen.

The al-Aqsa, where the men pray, is close to Bab el-Magharba[12] which is close to the Wailing Wall. As prayers end, groups of young men and boys start gathering there. But the army and police are solidly waiting and everyone knows that if one stone hits the Wall someone will be shot. But the shabab[13] are in the grip of fervour and a man who some say is a 'Fatah element' starts yelling Hamas slogans and, playing Pied Piper, leads them away from the certain danger of Bab el-Magharba and through the terraces of al-Haram to the relative safety of Bab el-Sabbat. There they stop.

Outside the gateway is a police station that they set fire to a couple of weeks ago. The administrators of the mosque rush to place wooden barriers between the shabab and the

[12] The Gate of the Moroccans, named after the Moroccan quarter which stood just outside it. When Israel took East Jerusalem in 1967 it bulldozed the whole quarter to create the piazza now in front of the Wailing Wall.
[13] The word means 'young people'. It is now used in Palestine specifically for young men confronting the Israeli army.

small army of soldiers and police taking up positions outside with guns aimed. The shabab chant of the Prophet's victory against the Jews at Khaybar in the seventh century, some of them rush back into the Haram and try to break down the iron door leading to the stairs of a minaret. It will not break. One young man climbs a wall and tries to open a higher door into the minaret.

On the walls of the terraces hundreds of women and older men stand and watch. The atmosphere is almost one of carnival. Maybe a thousand shabab are facing the soldiers, but the gate is narrow so it's not too hard for the elders to hold them back. On the steps just opposite the gate, the steps leading up to the top of the city wall, the photographers stand with their cameras, helmets and bullet-proof vests. Something happens outside and the shabab scatter for a moment then regroup. A woman in an embroidered bedouin dress pushes forward into their midst, yelling along with them and a man tries to hold her back: 'They might shoot you!'

'Let them shoot me. Am I worth more than any of these youngsters?'

Another woman, in horn-rimmed spectacles, waves her arms at the soldiers from the wall where she's standing: 'Get out!' she shouts, 'Get out! You've strangled us, may God strangle you.'

One young man is ordering his little brother to go home. 'Let me stay,' the kid begs, 'just for a few minutes. Let me stay.' It takes a cuff on the side of the head to send him home.

A couple of smallish stones are pitched across the wall. 'Bet that landed on our car,' a stylishly dressed, slim young man says to his companion.

A well-built youth picks up a large rock and throws it to the ground to smash it. It doesn't smash and he picks it up again. As he raises it a mosque caretaker runs up and takes it from him, quietly, without a word. He places it carefully under a tree and the young man walks away.

An argument is breaking out on the side: 'They shouldn't

make trouble,' a tall, fair man shouts. 'The Israelis will close it down. Let people pray.'

A bystander laughs: 'You've been praying for fifty years. What good has it done you?'

A diminutive sheikh in a very trim costume and brand-new red cleric's hat is marching measuredly up and down beside the yelling demonstrators with a megaphone: 'Your presence here incites them. Disperse. Disperse.' No one pays any attention to him except one man who says to his neighbour: 'This is all he ever has to say. He does this every Friday.'

There are women and girls sitting chatting under the trees. Eventually the shabab start to drift away. It has taken two hours but this time, here, the Palestinians have no martyrs.

Ramallah, Saturday 2 December 2000, 12 p.m.

The great hall of Our Lady of the Gospels Independent School in Ramallah is filling up with students. Hundreds of girls and boys crowd into the seats talking and laughing. On stage the principal, Mrs Samira, and the guest speaker, Dr Mustafa Barghouti are setting up the overhead projector. Dr Barghouti is one of the triumvirate heading the People's Party of Palestine, and he has been organising all the medical aid work for the Intifada. At his office, earlier, he had shown me samples of the bullets the Israeli army uses against the stone-throwing kids.

This talk is part of the independent schools of Ramallah's joint initiative to 'document the truth and demand our legitimate rights before the world'. This group of children is in economic band A, their parents can afford to educate them privately, can stop them going to the barricades. Their hair is glossy, their teeth are good. As Mrs Samira lists the names of the participating schools they cheer and stamp and she outlaws whistling.

They all want to know how they can contribute. They ask why the Authority has not declared Oslo dead. Why it arrests members of Hamas. What is the Authority doing to protect civilians from the attacks of the settlers? Why does the Authority continue to try to coordinate security with the Israelis? They want a programme to support the thousands of workers who've lost their jobs inside Israel. They want the leadership to pull together and an end to the factions. They want to talk to the world. They want independence and they want to know what they can do.

Dr Barghouti tells them they can join his NGO across the road. They can be trained in first aid and primary care, in crisis management. They can do media work, monitor the net, respond to articles . . .

They crowd around to put their names down before they rush off to be picked up by parents at 2.30 p.m. sharp.

Ramallah, 3 p.m.

Another Barghouti (it's a massive family), Marwan Barghouti,[14] is mostly on the move. He is forty-one, the Chief Executive Officer of Fatah. Since the Intifada he's been on the streets with the shabab and he has formed the People's Watch, groups in each village that try to defend the villagers against the settlers. Everybody says he is targeted by the Israelis (*Ma'ariv* called him one of the 'triangle of terror: Arafat, Barghouti and Rajjoub, head of Palestinian intelligence'). Some say he's targeted by the Palestinian Authority – for being too popular.

In his office, against a huge poster of al-Aqsa, he repeats that the Intifada and negotiations do not preclude each other; that the Intifada is the only way the people have of projecting their own voice, their own will into the negotiations. He points at a poster of Muhammad al-Durra and says: 'We need to get away from the image of the Palestinian as a victim. This is a better poster,' pointing at a poster of a child confronting a tank.

---

[14] Marwan Barghouti was arrested one year later. In June 2004 an Israeli court sentenced him to five life terms.

I say: 'That kid was killed two days later.'

He says: 'Yes, I know.'

I wonder whether there is space to get out of the 'victim' frying-pan without falling into the 'fanatical Islamic terrorist' fire. The margin is terribly narrow. Then a man sitting with us – clearly an old friend – says: 'But I hear Qassam is down at the barricades. Why don't you stop him?' Qassam is Barghouti's sixteen-year-old son. Barghouti waves the question away. His friend insists: 'You have to stop him.'

And for a moment the militia leader looks helpless: 'I can't,' he says. 'How can I?'

Ramallah, 3.45 p.m.

Abu Karim is getting restless. He wants to be home in Jerusalem before sunset, but I have asked to see the barricades and now we examine them. An area of desolation at the edge of the town – which means ten minutes from the centre. After sunset this will turn into a battleground. Concrete blocks, stones, burn marks, some shattered glass. Two Israeli army cars on the other side of the concrete.

A woman appears from nowhere. Fortyish, poor, dressed in black, she is an Egyptian who has married a Palestinian and lived here for twenty-five years. Umm Basim: I have heard of her, heard that she lost her eldest son in the previous Intifada and that she is in the thick of the action at the barricades every night.

Is it because of your son, I ask, that you come here?

'No. I have four more, and they are with me here. I come because this situation has to end. We can't live like this.'

I ask if I may take her photo. She hesitates: 'It won't appear in any Egyptian newspapers? I wouldn't want my mother to know what I'm doing. She'd worry.'

As I take the photo she turns to the man who brought us here: 'I've seen Qassam here. Tell his father to keep him away.'

Psagot. ('Bascot,' the students at Bir Zeit University had said, 'biscuits. Think American cookies.')

Psagot is a settlement built ten years ago on a hilltop just outside Ramallah and Bireh. The Palestinians say it was built by the government on land expropriated from Bireh. They say it was positioned strategically to halt the natural expansion of the town and to control the Arab population. They say the settlers are armed and the army itself can move into the settlement at very short notice. For the past two months Bireh and Ramallah have been shelled every night from Psagot.

My calls to the Yesha Council have paid off and they have sent me here to meet Chaim Bloch.

A Western journalist connects me to a taxi driver who will go to a settlement (but charges triple), and from the start the journey is unlike any other I've made here. Smooth, wide roads, speeding cars, no roadblocks. And Psagot, like almost every settlement, on the top of a hill like a lookout, like the spooky small town of *Edward Scissorhands*. Barak's proposed budget for the coming year would spend $300 million on settlements.

Chaim Bloch is courteously waiting for us outside his house. He is dressed in a suit with a buttoned-up shirt and no tie. He has a longish light-brown beard and speaks softly and carefully. His father, a textile engineer, was offered a job in Israel thirty-one years ago and within two weeks the family had moved over from Baltimore. I work out that Mr Bloch is thirty-nine. He looks older.

In Israel, if you choose to do religious studies you are exempt from military service. For the young men who want to do both, special yeshivas exist. There are thirty of them round the country. Bloch is a graduate of one and, until recently, he had always taught at another. Now he teaches Jewish law as it relates to monetary management as a kind of 'continuing education' course. He has been in Psagot nine years.

Why Psagot?

'Because this is the land of Judea and Samaria. It is here that the Israeli destiny is to be decided.'

The people across the valley, in Ramallah and Bireh, say this land was expropriated from them. How do you feel about that?

'The government of Israel never takes land without paying for it. The Arabs tried to bring a court case against us and in the end they begged us to allow them to drop it because they were going to be ruined.'

There are UN resolutions stating that the West Bank and Gaza are illegally occupied.

'Israel is a law-abiding nation but there can be differences in the interpretation of the law. What we are doing here is not against international law.' Then, without pause: 'Even if I was one hundred per cent sure that international law was against me it would not change my views. Just because international law says something does not make it so.'

But if not the law, what is your reference?

'God promised us this land. The state of Israel was here two thousand years ago and God promised this land to our forefathers thirty-seven thousand years ago. There was never a state of Palestine here.'

The one thought that I have is that I am not afraid any more, not even uneasy. I feel nothing. I am conducting an interview.

Well, I say, there was never Syria or Lebanon or Jordan or Iraq. As states. It was all part of the Ottoman empire and was carved up by the British and the French.

'This is the land promised to us by God.'

OK. You say this land is yours because you were here two thousand years ago. Across the valley there is a man who says this land is his because he has been here for two thousand years. If – just for a moment – you put yourself in his position . . .

'I do not put myself in his position. You do that for a

friend, on a personal matter. This is a question of nations. And my business is to look after the interests of the Jewish nation.'

So you have no individual moral responsibility in this matter?

'No.'

Well, from your point of view, what should the Palestinians do?

'They can go on living here. No one will throw them out. But they have to understand that they are living in a Jewish state. If they do not like that there are many places where they can go.'

But if they live here, in a Jewish state, they don't have the same rights as the Jews.

'Yes. It is a Jewish state and they live as a minority. Believe me, ninety per cent of Palestinians admire us and want to live in the state of Israel.'

I know that a poll among young Palestinians found that they admired Israeli democracy as it was applied to the Jews. But it is not applied to the Arabs.

'Ninety per cent of Palestinians would be happy to live in the state of Israel. I know this.'

You know that ninety per cent of Palestinians would be happy to live as second-class citizens for ever?

'This is what my Palestinian friends tell me.'

You have Palestinian friends?

'Yes.'

Forgive me but – who are they?

Silence.

I don't want to know their names, just – where did you meet them, for example?

'One is a mechanic. He had to fix something for my car. And the other – he knows him.'

Could I just ask how life on the settlement works – economically?

'How do you mean?'

Well, I've heard that settlements get government help.

'Barak's government has cut back on most of what we got from Netanyahu. We get hardly anything.'

(Judy, who has very kindly accompanied me, ascertains that the house Mr Bloch lives in was bought for one-fifth of the market value. For a settler to travel to and from his or her settlement the government provides an armoured bus and two army car escorts. Water, the main resource under government control, is divided between the Arab population and the Israeli settlers: each settler is allocated 1,450 cubic meters of water per year. Each Palestinian is allowed to use 83 cubic meters. Electricity is regularly shut down in the Palestinian towns while the settlements are lit up.)

Mr Bloch, you have Israel. If you do not allow the Palestinians their own state in the West Bank this conflict will never end.

'Not everything has to be solved now.'

You are happy that your children should inherit this conflict?

'Happy?' His voice rises, but only slightly. 'My sister was on the bus that they blew up. The woman sitting next to her was killed. Children had to have their limbs amputated. I am not happy.'

But you believe your children should inherit this situation?

'Those children on the bus – I pray that God will never ask me to pay such a terrible price. But if He does, I shall pay it.'

As we drive away from Psagot I feel empty. I look at my notes and realise that I have no impression of what the living room we had been in looked like, except that it was bare and functional and sunny – and looked out on Ramallah. The taxi driver (even with $100 in his pocket) is speeding and angry and has an argument with a speeding young Israeli. Through the window I hear: *'Kess ikhtak!'* (Your sister's cunt.)

Is that the same in Hebrew? I ask.

No, that was Arabic, Judy says.

'I see a terrible fire,' Madame Tarazi had said to me, 'a terrible fire coming to swallow us all, Israelis and Palestinians – unless the Palestinian people are freed from their bondage.'

The West Bank, 1.30 p.m.
On the way back to the bridge I see that the army has dug a brand-new trench between the road and the town of Ariha (Jericho).

Exhaustion hits me the minute I get to London. This conflict has been part of my life all my life. But seeing it there, on the ground, is different.

What can I do except bear witness?

I am angrier than before I went. And more incredulous that what is happening in Palestine – every day – to men, women and children, should be allowed by the world to continue.

The choices are in the hands of Israel. They can hand over the West Bank, Gaza and East Jerusalem and live within their borders as a nation among nations. There are no choices for the people of Palestine.

Ilan Halevi, a Jew who fought with the PLO, says it's a question of macho image: 'Israel does not want to be seen as the fat boy of the Middle East.'

Others say Israel does not want to be a 'nation among nations'. It wants the beleaguered, plucky image – and the moral indulgence and trillions of dollars' worth of aid that goes with it. If that is so then the Israeli government has joined others of the region who are not working in the interests of their own people.

Awad Awad says the Israelis have declared they will not renew the licences of any Palestinian photographers working with the international media.

What will you do? I asked him.

'Just carry on taking photographs. I'm a photographer.'

I have seen women pushing their sons behind them, shoving them to run away, screaming at the soldiers: 'Get out of our faces. Stop baiting the kids.'

I have heard a man say: 'I have four sons and no work. I cannot feed them. Let them go out and die if it will help our country; if it will end this state of things.'

I have seen children calmly watch yet another shooting, another funeral. And when I have wept they've said: 'She's new to this.'

I have listened to everybody predict that the leadership would do a deal. 'But if they don't bring us independence and the Right of Return the streets will catch fire.'

Palestinian weddings are celebrated over coffee, but when a young man is killed his mother is held up over his grave. 'Trill out your zaghrouda [ululation], mother,' his friends say, the shabab who might die tomorrow. A mother says to me: 'Our joy-cries now only ring out in the face of death. Our world is upside down.'

Hijackers rammed jetliners into each of New York's World Trade Center towers yesterday, toppling both in a hellish storm of ash, glass, smoke and leaping victims, while a third jetliner crashed into the Pentagon in Virginia. There was no official count, but Pres. Bush said thousands had perished, and in the immediate aftermath the calamity was already being ranked the worst and most audacious terror attack in American history. The attacks seemed carefully co-ordinated. The hijacked planes were all en route to California, and therefore gorged with fuel, and their departures were spaced within an hour and 40 minutes. The first, American Airlines Flight 11, a Boeing 767 out of Boston for Los Angeles, crashed into the north tower at 8:48 a.m. Eighteen minutes later, United Airlines Flight 175, also headed from Boston to Los Angeles, plowed into the south tower. Then an American Airlines Boeing 757, Flight 77, left Washington's Dulles International Airport bound for Los Angeles, but instead hit the western part of the Pentagon, the military headquarters where 24,000 people work, at 9:40 a.m. Finally, United Airlines Flight 93, a Boeing 757 flying from Newark to San Francisco, crashed near Pittsburgh, raising the possibility that its hijackers had failed in whatever their mission was. There were indications that the hijackers on at least two of the planes were armed with knives.

New York Times, 12 September, 2001

In this together

A deluge of hate seems poised to rain down on Arabs and Muslims living in the West, even before those responsible for Tuesday's abominable acts are identified.
Al-Ahram Weekly, 13-19 September, 2001

Our Poor, Our Weak, Our Hungry[1]

Thousands of people have been murdered in New York and Washington; America mourns and the world mourns with it.

The American government is readying itself – and the world – for action. This action would seem to derive from the concept of a 'clash of civilisations', a school of thought that Islamist extremists subscribe to, since they, we are told, view America or even the whole of Western civilisation, as a hegemonous monolith; an enemy to be feared and, if possible, destroyed.

This is exactly the kind of thinking that thinking people must avoid. And yet it is reciprocated (if indeed it was not initiated) by the West. In the past decade there has been a growing tendency to see the terms 'Arab', 'Muslim', 'fanatic', even 'terrorist' as practically interchangeable. When EgyptAir flight 990 fell into the Atlantic in 1999 killing 217 people on board, the US explained within minutes that the Egyptian pilot was an Islamist fanatic who had decided to commit suicide. Even after Egyptian newspapers published a photo of him with his little daughter holding an inflatable Father Christmas, the US insisted he was an Islamist fanatic.

You could almost say that US officialdom, the US media and Hollywood dreamed this nightmare into reality. And ordinary Americans have paid the price. But looking back, it is as though somebody had been working on a series of drafts. A 'fanatic' in an Egyptian aircraft, a mystery boat crashing into the side of the USS *Cole*, and now this horror. Was somebody working out what could be done, what you could get away with? The prime suspect, we are told, is Osama bin

---

[1] The *Guardian*, Saturday 15 September 2001.

Laden. It may have been him. He cannot have expected that this massively criminal act would do him any good, and it has put back – who knows for how long? – the causes he professes to care about.

Why did he do it? Because he hates America and wants to damage her? Because, Iago-like, he revels in his hatred? Then why does he not gloat? Why has he said it was not his doing?[2] The too-easy thing about having a 'fanatic' perpetrator is that you can ignore logical questions to do with purpose and motivation.

What if it wasn't him? What if the men who did it thought they were working for an Arab or Muslim cause – but were not? We saw images of Palestinians dancing in the streets after the news broke. It needs to be said that they were shameful images. It also needs to be said that the same three pictures were shown again and again, that correspondents on Arab news channels said they were isolated incidents and that they occurred when the scale of the disaster had not yet become clear.

Next day nobody was dancing; the US Consul-General in Jerusalem received a twelve-inch stack of faxes and condolences from Palestinians and Palestinian organisations. Later, a correspondent in Jerusalem for the [BBC's] *Today* radio programme reported with surprise that people seemed able to make a distinction between the American people in their bereavement and the American state that had suffered a 'deserved' blow. People in the Middle East have learned to make an automatic distinction between the state and the people. It is a faultline in the region that could become more

---

[2] Immediately after the attacks bin Laden issued a statement denying responsibility. Later, in an interview published in Pakistan's *Daily Ummat* on 28 September 2001, bin Laden says, 'I have already said that I am not involved in the 11 September attacks in the United States. As a Muslim I try my best to avoid telling a lie. I had no knowledge of these attacks, nor do I consider the killing of innocent women, children and other humans as an appreciable act.' Weeks later, at the start of the bombing of Afghanistan, he praised the act and appropriated it within the wider context of the conflict with the US.

dangerous if regimes are pushed further from their people by the need to placate America in the near future.

America needs to look at its foreign policy, its stance on the International Court of Justice and the Kyoto agreement, its contribution to the suffering of the Iraqi people, its bombing of Libya and Sudan, its long-standing position on the Arab–Israeli conflict, and ask itself why sixteen men[3] were prepared to kill and die to bring down the symbols of American commercial and military might.

No price can be put on the pain that has hit so many people in one instant. How can it be prevented from ever happening again? A letter from a Canadian says: 'Nothing justifies what was done on Tuesday. But we must ask ourselves how we have contributed to conditions that cause people to hate us this much. Then we must set about eradicating those conditions and injustices.'

The world has had repeated proof that terrorist actions cannot be combated by security measures alone. The underlying cause, the why, has to be addressed. And listening to official responses I am filled with fear. Experts have opined that the US has to hit 'someone' within ten days, that cruise missiles targeted somewhere in the Middle East are the only appropriate action. The Deputy Secretary of State, Paul Wolfowitz, said that 'the whole civilised world has been shocked . . . and even portions of the uncivilised world have started to wonder whether they're on the wrong side'. How's that for the official American view of the planet? There is talk of a $20 billion war chest, of the full resources of the American government, of combat patrols over Washington.

It will not be enough. The US will be safe only when the puppetmasters can no longer find people willing to lay down their lives to harm it. The nation that once said 'give me your poor, your weak, your hungry' needs to look at itself through the eyes of the world's dispossessed. During the last year, and before the catastrophe, it was starting to do so. It

---

[3] The official figure arrived at later was nineteen.

seemed that the people of the most powerful country in the world were starting to let themselves see more clearly what was happening in the world around them. More articles were appearing, more people were asking questions. Sections of the US administration were even demurring slightly at the unconditional, eternal support they were supposed to extend to the state of Israel.

Those people have now joined the ranks of the grieving. It should not have happened. It should not happen again. Maybe it won't, if in their grief Americans make common cause with other sorrowing humans. There is evidence that many are doing just that. And their leaders should listen to their voices.

Wanted: Dead or Alive

Mr Bush said that he wanted bin Laden's head, evoking dramatic images of the Wild West to make his point. He said: 'I want justice. There's an old poster out West that said "wanted, dead or alive".'
The Times, Tuesday 18 September, 2001

Secret plans for 10-year war

America and Britain are producing secret plans to launch a ten-year 'war on terrorism' – Operation Noble Eagle – involving a completely new military and diplomatic strategy to eliminate terrorist networks and cells around the world.
The Times, Thursday 20 September, 2001

Opening the Doors[1]

In the two weeks or so since the events of September 11, reports of harassment of Muslims across the UK have started coming in. Politicians and commentators have elbowed their way on to television to warn that there should be no reprisals against Britain's Arab or Muslim community. Members of said community (which numbers around two million) have been filmed against 'Islamic' backgrounds and encouraged to denounce 'terror'. They did, but many of them spoke also of the terror of the US's foreign policy and pointed particularly at that policy in Palestine. Notable among them were a group of young people on BBC TV's *Question Time*, who spoke of how much America was 'despised' across the 'developing' (or even stunted) world. The ex-American ambassador to the UK (who was on the panel and seemed a perfectly nice man) felt impelled to share with the viewers his feelings of deep hurt at being so attacked at a time when he felt so vulnerable. This prompted the head of the BBC next day to issue a public apology for the programme, while this apology in turn led to a row in the newspapers about democracy and free speech. Two of the most impassioned and articulate speakers on *Question Time* were young women: one in a hijab which accentuated her round south-Asian face, the other an Anglo-Arab with a great mane of curly, golden hair.

The attacks on the World Trade Center and the Pentagon and the US's reaction to date have highlighted the faultlines in British and no doubt other Western societies including that of America. But increasingly, at least in the UK, voices

[1] *Al-Ahram Weekly*, 27 September–3 October 2001.

are heard rejecting all forms of extremism, arguing for understanding and attempting to bridge the terrifying gaps that threaten our world. They condemn the act which killed six thousand[2] in New York and Washington and they condemn the Western and Israeli policies which have killed tens, even hundreds of thousands all over the world and which led to it. Nowhere has this been more touching than in the statements of the families who lost a brother, a sister or a child in the attacks on the Trade Towers.

But of course neither the US nor the British government (apart from some lone voices such as that of Clare Short, Minister for Overseas Development) accept the linkage between their policies and the events of September 11. As far as officialdom is concerned 'Islamic terrorists' have one simple motive: hatred of the US because it is 'free', it practises 'democracy' and its women are 'full and active citizens'.

'We could be next', cry the British tabloids, shivering deliciously in anticipation. The *Daily Star* has a dream front page, equitably shared between Sex and Violence, Beauty and the Beast: the top half of the page announces the return of the Page 3 girls (topless lovelies who had been screened off for a few days to show respect) and celebrates with a photo of 'Nicola' whom readers are invited to 'phone today'. Underneath Nicola there is the now familiar photograph of Osama bin Laden, looking like butter wouldn't melt in his mouth and the heading 'Bin's Murder Manual', which apparently teaches would-be terrorists how to slit throats with box-cutters. The underlying, ongoing joke is 'Bin Laden' = 'bin liner', i.e. rubbish bag. Another paper has a full frontal of a chap in what appears to be a space suit. Everybody will have to rush out and buy these, it seems, to protect themselves against Anthrax, small pox et al. And yet another front page screams 'THEY'RE HERE!' with news of arrests of three

---

[2] The figure was later amended to: Confirmed dead: 2,948, reported dead: 24, reported missing: 24, total: 2,996. See www.september11victims.com.

Arabs in Birmingham. This 'they' of course is what's at the heart of the matter. Sikhs have been beaten up for wearing turbans, adding injury to the insult of being taken for Muslims. My friends on the *Guardian* and the *Independent* newspapers (who have been arguing ceaselessly for America to face up to the responsibility of its actions in Palestine, Iraq, Afghanistan, Colombia, Nicaragua, etc.) shrug off the tabloids and their readership. But even *The Times*, normally sober if disagreeable, employs a graphologist to interpret bin Laden's signature and draws comfort from the expert's pronouncement that he is 'not a happy man' and that he feels he has 'bitten off more than he can chew'.

Meanwhile an array of weaponry to delight every arms dealer's bank manager is being assembled in Asia.

I suppose this is the warming-up phase of the war, the Battle of the Images. In one corner, George W. Bush, flailing for the first few days, then getting it together for his address to the nation on Capitol Hill. Reassuringly surrounded by symbols of the might of the United States of America, he delivered sound bite after sound bite with authority and with appropriate pauses for his audience to be levered to its feet by its own applause. Up and down and up and down they went. I lost count of the times. At the end you expected a curtain call but got the next best thing: a slow triumphal exit full of resolute bonhomie with senators, congressmen, ministers, army commanders pressing forward to shake his hand, pat him on the back, and if they were too far away to touch him, contenting themselves with a cheery thumbs-up.

In the opposite corner, Osama bin Laden, always alone in close-up in the frame. The only thing you see other than the man himself is his machine gun propped up against the wall. The beard, the turban, the unvarying voice and serene expression of a man at peace with himself. From time to time we get a shot of turbaned fighters scrambling along mountain paths.

This is the encouraged reading of the conflict: a backward fanatical oppressive Islam confronting a liberal inclusive democratic West. But when we look at the two champions in their corners they don't seem too dissimilar: both seek to impose their views on others and so to bipolarise the world, both seek solutions in wholesale killing and both firmly believe that God is on their side.

Well, let's hope most of the world knows that this is a con. That the conflict, far from starting on September 11, has been raging for decades. And that it's President Bush and Mr bin Laden in one corner and in the other the billions of us who simply want decent and human lives – for others as well as for ourselves. For us this coming time should not be about winning, but about winning over.

'We are at war with terrorism'

Blair says Britain will play full part in military strikes

The countdown towards America's fightback against terror begins today, with the ruling Taleban regime in Afghanistan being told to hand over Osama bin Laden within days or face a massive military assault ...

The ultimatum was being prepared as Tony Blair yesterday said for the first time that Britain and America were 'at war' with terrorism.
The Times, Monday 17 September, 2001

Bush: the hour is coming

Mr Bush said that America's grief had turned to anger, and anger to resolution. He said: 'Whether we bring our enemies to justice, or justice to our enemies, justice will be done.' ...

Standing alongside the President, Mr Blair said that no one should doubt their joint resolve to bring to account those behind last week's hijacks.
The Times, Friday 21 September, 2001

The battle is joined

America and Britain went to war against the Taleban last night, unleashing waves of cruise missiles against Afghan cities and airbases.
The Times, Monday 8 October, 2001

Battle of Kabul is days away

A ground assault on Kabul appeared imminent last night ...

Donald Rumsfeld said American planes were dropping bombs to assist the Northern Alliance, and working from intelligence from the rebel forces ...
The Times, Friday 12 October, 2001

Nile Blues[1]

Right there, at my feet, the Nile spreads out in a shimmering, flowing mass. The water reflects the lights of small boats, of floating restaurants, of the bridges flung across the river. From the centre rises Gezira island, on it the lit-up dome of the Opera House and the tall, slim lotus of the Cairo Tower. The scene is spectacularly beautiful, and over it all hangs the thick pall that Cairenes call 'the black cloud'. No one seems certain where it comes from. They say it's the farmers burning husks of rice in Sharqiyya province. They say it's Cairo rubbish burning in several places – two of the fires out of control. They say it's a component in the new unleaded petrol. It hangs over everything, but Cairenes live with it, because – so far – they can still breathe.

'I don't know who I feel more alienated from, the Americans or the Taliban,' says Nadra. She hitches her heel to the seat of her chair, hugs her knee to her chest. 'The Americans' language is so sleazily self-laudatory.' Nadra and her American husband are photographers. He has been in San Diego for three months. She was supposed to join him on 15 September and they had planned to come back together in January. But now she can't bring herself to go.

'Do you watch CNN?' she asks. 'Should journalists collude with government? Or do the media have an agenda of their own? They're trying to frighten us all so we each stay in our little hole and don't talk to each other.' She tells me that on 12 September she received international calls from seven agencies, all working for clients in the American media. 'Go

[1] The *Guardian*, 6 November 2001; *Voices for Peace*, 30 November 2001.

out,' they said, 'and photograph the people rejoicing in the streets.' 'But nobody's rejoicing in the streets,' she said. 'In the coffee shops then. Photograph the people laughing and celebrating in the coffee shops.' 'People are glued to their TVs,' she told them. 'Everybody's in shock.' Still they pressed her. Eventually, she said if they wanted her photographs they could send her to Jenin (on the West Bank) and she'd photograph Israeli tanks entering the city.

That was my first night in Cairo. The city is, as usual, humming with energy. The Cairo film festival awards its special jury prize to the Iranian director Tahmina, who is in trouble in Iran for including a shot of two chador-clad women handing out communist leaflets in her film *The Hidden Half*. The Hanager theatre workshop is showing an Egyptian *Phaedre*. The feast of Sayyida Zeinab,[2] grand-daughter of the Prophet and one of the most popular members of his household, is reaching its climax, with thousands of people from all over the country converging on al-Sayyida, the district which contains her mosque and bears her name. The walls of downtown Cairo are chaotic with posters for the trade union elections due to take place in a few days. The demonstrations that have so far been contained within the campuses of Cairo's five universities ebb and flow with news of Afghan civilian casualties and new Israeli incursions into Palestinian towns.

The mood is not explosive but tense, expectant. There is also puzzlement, a deep exhaustion and a cold, amused cynicism. Nobody even bothers to discuss the 'clash of civilisations' theory except to marvel that the West wastes any time on it at all. Can't they see, people ask, how much of their culture we've adopted? Practically every major work of Western literature or thought is translated into Arabic. The Cairo Opera House is home to the Cairo Symphony Orchestra and the Egyptian Ballet as well as the Arab Music Ensemble. English is taught in every school and the British

[2] *Sayyida* is Arabic for 'Lady'.

Council in Cairo is the largest of their operations worldwide because of its English language courses. Yes, there are aspects of Western society that we don't like, they say, but they are the aspects that the West itself regards as problematic: widespread drug abuse, violent crime, the disintegration of the family, teenage pregnancies, lack of a sense of community, rampant consumerism. What's wrong with not wanting those for ourselves?

The 'Islam versus the West' theory is dismissed by both Muslim and Christian clerics. In an interview with al-Jazeera, Sheikh Qaradawi echoes what Nadra has been saying: 'It is unfair to lump people together in one basket,' he says. 'The American people are the prisoners of their media. They're ordinary people, concerned with their daily lives, with earning a living. We must try to reach them through debate, not through hostility.' Sayyid Hasan Nasrallah, the secretary-general of Hezbollah warns: 'We should not deal with this war [in Afghanistan] as if it is a Christian war against Islam.'

A columnist in *al-Ahram Weekly*, the major national newspaper of Egypt, reminds readers that in 1977, when Anwar Sadat made his peace visit to Israel, the Coptic Pope, Shenuda III, insisted that no Arab Christian would visit Jerusalem until they could visit alongside their Muslim brothers and sisters.

We are fourteen people sitting down to dinner at the Arabesque: Egyptian, Palestinian, American and Iraqi. On the table is a choice of wine, water and guava juice:

'It's sheer ignorance, this equation of the East with Islam.'

'Where did Christianity come from in the first place?'

'Bethlehem, Beit Sahour, Beit Jala, all essentially Christian Palestinian towns, bombarded by the Israelis every day.'

'And where do they think *we* are, the twelve million Egyptian Christians, in all this?'

'And the Jews would have still been here if it hadn't been for the creation of Israel.'

One of the gravest fears in Egypt is of the threat that Islamic extremism poses to the fourteen centuries of national unity between Egyptian Copts and Egyptian Muslims. The 'clash of civilisations' rhetoric coming out of the West, the transformation of Osama bin Laden from a fringe figure into a hero, the shoe-horning of what people see as a political and economic conflict into a religious mould, are all appallingly dangerous for the very fabric of Egyptian society, where the two communities are so intertwined that they share all the rituals of both joy and sorrow; where Christian women visit the mosque of Sayyida Zeinab to ask for help and Muslims visit the Church of Santa Teresa, the Rose of Lisieux, to plead for her aid.

Bush and Blair's repeated affirmations of the essential goodness of Islam are seen as so much hot air designed to appease the uneducated masses, who, naturally, will never believe them. People smile as they remind you of the German propaganda asserting that 'Hajji Muhammad Hitler' was a true friend of Islam, or the rumour put about by the French 150 years earlier that Bonaparte had converted to the 'true faith'. Religion, people believe, is being used both as a smoke-screen and a mobilisation device. When, people ask, has bin Laden ever spoken of Iraq or Palestine? Only after the bombings started. His mission, essentially, was to get the Americans out of Saudi Arabia; now he is playing the West at its own game, and millions of aggrieved, desperate young Muslims across the world are likely to listen to him.

'And what does your chap think he's up to? What's his name?' I'm asked.

'Blair?' I venture.

'Yes. Is he outbidding the Americans? He comes over here with a list of names he wants handed over and six of them are in the Sudanese Cabinet.'

There is general incredulity at Tony Blair's gung-ho stance and Britain's seeming eagerness to be part of the conflict. Someone asks me what public opinion in the UK is really like. We talk about the anti-war demonstrations, reminiscent of the Suez crisis.

Returning from the Middle East after his first whirlwind visit last month, the Prime Minister seemed to think that his problem was one of communication. He has suggested that Britain needs to do more PR in the Arab world. His personal efforts seem to have been a resounding failure. Why, people ask, is he rushing around with such zeal? Why does he look so pleased with himself? A cartoon in a newspaper has a flunky saying to a government minister: 'But of course there's nothing wrong with Your Excellency taking a second job to augment your income. Look at the British Prime Minister – he's got an extra job as PR manager for America's campaign in Afghanistan.' Blair might save the Downing Street spin doctors' efforts for internal affairs. Spin will get nowhere with people who have for a long time not trusted their own governments, far less the governments of the West.

Nobody condones what is happening in Afghanistan. The anger is given more edge, yes, by the fact that it is a Muslim country, but more by the perception that the Afghan people have been used and abused for more than twenty years. Everyone is aware of the responsibility of the US in creating the circumstances for the appearance of the Taliban, who are then pointed at as proof of the backwardness of Islam in general. Yet Afghanistan, before the Russian invasion, was finding its own way towards modernity; otherwise, how come there are so many Afghan women professionals in the opposition camped up north?

An article in the Egyptian press maps the relationship between oil, arms and key members of the American administration. Not a conspiracy theory, rather a practical acknowledgment that 'oil, defence and politics . . . are not mutually exclusive interests'.

Nobody is surprised by any of this. After all, a democracy where you need millions of dollars to get into the White House is hardly likely to be free of corporate influence. But a journalist asks why America needs a pretext at all. Why paint itself into a corner with all the 'bin Laden, dead or alive' rhetoric? Maybe we understand why it needs Russia and Europe on board, but why the pressure on the Arab countries? Is it necessary? Several letters in *al-Ahram Weekly* suggest that not everyone thinks so. In the past five weeks the paper has received hundreds of hostile letters from Westerners – many of them taking that classical orientalist image of a penetrative relationship between West and East to contemporary levels of frankness and violence.

Why does America assume conflict and confrontation with the Arab world? My aunt reminds me of the crowds that welcomed Richard Nixon, then the US president, to Egypt in 1974: 'Remember all the talk of USAID and the democratising process and how the co-ops were full of frozen American chickens? America was synonymous then with plenty, with progress and liberalisation. But none of it came through.' My aunt is a doctor, but right now she's lying in bed with a drip attached to her arm. Her left hand is swollen with a bad infection and a powerful antibiotic is blasting its way through her veins. Her son has had to scour Cairo and pay over the odds because the public-sector lab that produces the drug has just burned down. Next the lab will be sold at a rock-bottom price to a well-connected private investor, many of its workforce will be laid off, and the medicine, when production is resumed, will be more expensive than before. This is part of the privatisation process, the economic 'reforms' the country is being pushed into. 'None of it came through.' In fact, I remember wondering, when I first came in touch with USAID in 1980, why – if it was such a benevolent operation – did its officials seem so jittery? Why did they drive around in black-windowed limos? And why had their embassy been turned into a marine-guarded fortress?

Over turkish coffee in the Café Riche, Ahmad Hamad, who works for Legal Aid (a non-governmental organisation funded by a sister NGO in Holland) reminds me of the US-encouraged domestic policies of President Anwar Sadat.

People were ready to give them a try. America was democratic and free and more fun than the dour, totalitarian Russians. But what 'democratisation' amounted to was a clampdown on all left-wing, Nasserist and pan-Arab views and organisations, and eventually on all opposition. 'They nurtured the Islamists as a way of hitting the left. They created and funded Islamist organisations. They manipulated elections so that Islamists took control of the student unions and the professional syndicates. What they didn't understand was that the Islamists took themselves seriously and eventually, of course, they assassinated Sadat himself.' It is the same game that the US played in Afghanistan: to fund and aid an 'Islamist' opposition to the Russians and fail to recognise the consequences.

Since the three attacks by armed Islamist extremists on tourists in Egypt in the mid-Nineties, the tourist industry has become extremely sensitive. Last week some 50 per cent of its employed workers were forced to take indefinite unpaid leave. For the self-employed there is hardly any work. Entire resorts in Sinai are closed down. Around two million Egyptians rely directly on tourism for their livelihoods, and the worry in the country is palpable.

Practically every American or American-influenced intervention in Egypt has been bad for every one of the sixty-five million Egyptians – except the few thousand who have become fabulously wealthy in the new economy. Debt-ridden farmers, disenfranchised workers, the decimated middle class, the silenced intellectuals and students – all of them will tell you that they have America's influence to thank for their problems. Yes, Egyptians have internal problems with their government and inter-Arab problems with their neighbours, but these problems are made ever more intractable by American intervention. And then there's the question of Palestine.

Egyptian official media, on the whole, play down what is happening in the Palestinian territories. Egyptian television, for example, does not show the images of brutality, destruction and grief coming out of the West Bank and Gaza. But half of Cairo is tuned in to the al-Jazeera satellite channel. On top of every building you can see the dishes facing up towards ArabSat. And every taxi driver you talk to says: 'Isn't that terrorism, what they're doing to the Palestinians?'

The Egyptian Committee for Solidarity with the Palestinian Intifada (ECSPI) formed itself in October 2000 to provide humanitarian aid to the people of the West Bank and Gaza. It now has volunteers in every city across Egypt. When I meet four of its members in a coffee shop they are shadowed by a chap from the state security service, who sits down at the next table. Their phones are bugged and their every move is monitored. The people I meet are two men and two women. One of the women, May, is Christian, the other, Nadra, is a Muslim in a complete veil. She tells me she used to be my student, and it turns into a joke since there's no way that I can recognise her. The ECSPI volunteers go into the towns and villages to collect donations for the Palestinians. 'There isn't a house that doesn't give us something,' May tells me, 'and people have so little. We collected three tons of sugar, half-kilo by half-kilo.'

On 10 September a long-planned petition on behalf of the Palestinian people was due to be handed in to the American embassy in Cairo. As the delegation met in Tahrir Square it grew to some 300 people. The police surrounded it and refused to let it proceed. A group of ten was chosen and headed for the embassy, where the ambassador refused to meet them and the embassy refused to take delivery of the petition.

America's support for Israel is a dominant issue in Egyptian–American relations. I have not had a conversation in Cairo where it has not come up. When American officials talk about the lives lost in New York and Washington, about New Yorkers' inalienable right to freedom of movement, about US citizens' right to safety, a voice inside the head of every Arab will echo: 'True. And what about the rights of the Palestinians?' President Bush has spoken for the first time about a 'Palestinian state', but he has not used the word 'viable'. People remember that when the West was drumming up the coalition against Iraq it made noises about Palestine and set up the Madrid conference, resulting in the Oslo agreements, which have been disastrous for peace. They suspect a similar agenda now. Yet the hope is that if one good thing can come out of the current horrors it would be that America recognises that a truly workable formula for a reasonably just peace has to be imposed on the Israeli–Palestinian conflict.

A few days after the failed attempt to deliver the petition, Farid Zahran, the vice-chair of the organisation, was abducted by state security and vanished for three weeks. He was released only after 250 members of ECSPI and Legal Aid insisted on turning themselves in to the public attorney, signing an affidavit against themselves that they were complicit with Zahran in whatever he was accused of. 'The government was giving us a warning,' Nadra says: 'We'll let you carry on collecting medicines and stuff, but any attempt to mobilise the street and we'll come down on you hard.' This is made possible by the emergency laws operating since the assassination of Sadat in 1981 and further strengthened by anti-terrorism laws formulated in the mid-Nineties – essentially the same type of law that is under discussion now both in the US and here in the UK.

People I speak to are alarmed at the prospect of Americans giving up their civil liberties. 'It's one of the organising principles of their society,' someone says. 'How will their society hold without it?'

An article in the Egyptian press reports that Americans, apparently, are 'cocooning'. They're staying at home, hiring videos, talking to each other, visiting family and friends nearby, and buying only what they need. It seems, to the Egyptian reader, like a good way to live. But the report is alarmed: two-thirds of the American economy is consumer spending; if people don't get out there to the malls, the economy will collapse. Egyptian people feel sorry for them. The poor Americans, they say, they're whipped out to work more and earn more, then they're whipped out to spend it; is that the freedom they're so proud of?

I walk down Sheikh Rihan Street with an American graduate student who tells me that he first learned of the attacks by phone from his parents. 'They were so worried they scared me. They kept telling me to come home. I stayed in the apartment for three days then I thought I can't go on like this and I went out. The man at the kiosk on the corner of my street came out to shake my hand. He said he'd been worried about me and asked if my people were OK. Everything was normal; people were friendly and concerned.' He had been approached to be interviewed on NBC. They called him for a pre-interview, he says. He kept his answers neutral, but truthful. In the end they said they'd call him back – they never did.

There is general agreement among people who have access to Western media that Americans are being kept ignorant. 'They're under media siege,' was how one journalist put it.

'Our only hope', Nadra says, 'is to talk to them. Sensible people everywhere should make themselves heard so that we don't personally witness the end of the world.'

A young, slim, professional woman in casual trousers and a loose shirt, the canvas bag slung over her shoulder bulging with lenses, tapes, papers and somewhere, I suppose, a comb and some lip salve. I watch her walk away from me down the avenue of flame trees. Is the road tightening round her? Narrowing down? Or is it just my perspective?

A federal judge's decision to release Muslim lawyer Brandon Mayfield rallied critics of the Justice Department on Friday, who decried his jailing in Oregon on dubious fingerprint evidence as a new example of government disregard for civil liberties ...

Questions about the case linger, compounded by [the judge's] decision to continue a gag order that prevents lawyers and Mayfield from talking publicly ...

Stanley Cohen, a New York criminal defense attorney ... said the Mayfield case had made federal investigators 'put their tails between their legs'. Cohen said it called into question not just the general way the government was pursuing terrorism cases, but also how it collected evidence. The Mayfield case reflects 'incompetence' among FBI forensics experts, and a tendency among federal investigators to reach a conclusion first, and then make the evidence fit the conclusion, Cohen said.

'The FBI is now the political police of this government,' Cohen said.

The Nation, Saturday 22 May, 2004

The Bush regime is using the Treasury Department to hound the Anti-war activists who courageously went to pre-war Iraq to act as human shields in an effort to stop the war.

Faith Fippinger, a sixty-two-year-old school teacher was one of those human shields. She refuses to pay a fine of $10,000 and now faces up to twelve years in prison for her stand against the regime's illegal invasion of Iraq. If she doesn't pay the fine, the regime threatens to increase the amount and to take the money out of her retirement check, her social security benefits and any assets she may have.

Les Blough, www.axisoflogic.com, Wednesday 13 August, 2003

Seisint Inc., a key player in the government's Matrix project, has produced a list of 120,000 people who showed a statistical likelihood of being terrorists. The scoring incorporated such factors as age, gender, ethnicity, credit history, 'investigational data', information about pilot and driver licenses, and connections to 'dirty' addresses known to have been used by other suspects.

Scarier still is news that the Justice Dept. acted on the company's findings – triggering investigations and arrests by the INS and other agencies. Officials say neither this data nor the statistical methods used in creating the list will be used in Matrix – short for Multistate Anti-Terrorism Information Exchange. Though it appears the damage may already have been done.

Oj, www.alternet.org, Friday 21 May, 2004

America[1]

There was something so free, so untethered about them: *The Daring Young Man on the Flying Trapeze*, *A Perfect Day for Banana-fish*. The stories themselves were, perhaps, not so different from the stories of other nations, but their titles were more kooky, more exhilarating. *Tender Is the Night*. I was entranced that a book with a title that could have come off the cover of one of the Mills and Boon novels I was supposed to despise was considered serious – or in bookstore code 'literary' – fiction. *Baby Doll* and *As I Lay Dying* opened up worlds that seemed at once more immediate and more dangerous than those of the European novels I was reading at the same time. *Giovanni's Room* was the first narrative I recognised as 'gay' and broke down more barriers in my mind.

While my mother's library shaped my fictive world, my musical one had already been formed by my father's taste. Louis Armstrong's gentle growl had eased its way between Beethoven's Sonata No. 5 and Abd el-Wahhab's pre-1920 recordings and into my seven-year-old soul. I wondered at the undertow of sadness in even his happiest songs; where did it come from and how was it achieved? If the words and the rhythm were quite jolly, what was that sorrow plucking at my heart? My first intimations of adult ambiguities.

Summer of 1966, the last 'normal' summer of my child-hood, for the following June was to bring the Six Day War – and yet, not quite so normal. My youngest aunt, the doctor, had gone to New York to complete her medical training and the annual family migration to Alexandria had lost one

[1] *Granta*, spring 2002.

member. That was the summer 'Abd el-Haleem sang *'Ala hizb wdad galbi* and I read Orwell's *1984* and rushed off, away from Room 101 and into the cool night air. For ever, now, a bar from that song will plant me back in the sand of Ma'mura beach at night-time, the orange and white paperback tucked under my arm, the music drifting out of the nearby palm-walled disco, the sea black and gently roaring ahead of me and beyond it no longer only the familiar Europe I knew but further, much much further beyond that: America.

The America we watched on television then was the America of *Bonanza* and *The Virginian*, neither of which, as far as I can remember, went much for the 'Cowboy and Injun' stuff that I found troubling. My problem, at that early age, was that the 'Indians' never got to put their side of the story. We were not expected to grieve when several of their yelling, galloping braves were cut down, nor did we ever see them in their 'normal' lives which, presumably, they had. Or had had before the righteous gun-toting (white) heroes came on the scene. But, that problem apart, my America, in the Sixties, was still blues and fiction but also Who Killed JFK? It was Vietnam protests and civil rights marches, campus demos and Sharpeville; all at a distance, 'out there'. At home one seemed to have no need to be aware or beware of political America – except for the CIA. There was a general sense that an American you met in Egypt would most likely be working for the CIA, and the CIA was implicated in the murder of Che Guevara. But then you didn't really meet Americans around Cairo. Not, anyway, in the way that you met British, French, Italian, German, Spanish and Russian people living and working in the city. I think that the first time I was struck by a gross misuse of language was when I was told that the 'Peace Corps' was really a tool of the CIA.

And yet, of course, I knew that we had a problem of some kind with America. I suppose I thought it was because Egypt was a leading player in the Non-Aligned group, together with countries like India, Indonesia, Yugoslavia and so on. And the Soviets were helping us build the High Dam when Europe and America tried to block it. It seemed fair to me that we should get help where we could find it. I didn't understand, for example, why America had it in for Nasser. The bond between the USA and Israel had not yet, I guess, become so starkly clear. When the June '67 war broke out many fingers pointed at America, speaking of its collusion with Israel, both in the setting up and in the execution of the war. Then films like *Z* and *Missing* spelt out the extent of CIA meddling in the affairs of other nations. But it was as though you could somehow disband the CIA and be left with the America of fiction and jazz, the America that seemed such fun, so democratic, so egalitarian and so free.

Still, when it was time to go abroad to study for a Ph.D. I chose not to go to America: it was too far from home. I studied in Lancaster instead. I had no idea how far from home that would turn out to be. And it was in Lancaster that I first saw *Casablanca* and while the aficionados enthused about the film I wondered silently, underneath my liking for it, about the Arabs. Where were the Moroccans? And how come the only non-European character with a dramatic role to play was a sleaze-bag? But maybe the longing for home was making me too thin-skinned.

Perhaps films were the reason why when for Christmas 1978 I went to New York for the first time the city was entirely familiar to me. Which is not to say that it had no impact; it was electrifying. Electrifying and homey. In the doorways of giant skyscrapers men stood idle, chewing gum, watching the Cadillacs go by. Delis handed you your purchases in brown paper bags. The hot pretzels I bought on street corners were identical to our *semeet* and you were even given a twist of salt to dip them into. Paper and harmless bits of rubbish drifted across the roads and run-down general stores nuzzled high-fashion boutiques. Small shops selling women's underwear displayed the same stolid, prosaic busts you saw in Cairo shop windows and everywhere people talked and shouted and argued. The traffic lights said 'DON'T WALK' and a roadside sign said 'Don't even THINK of parking here'. It was at once like being at home and being inside a movie. The accent served as a distancing but endearing factor; I kept thinking everyone I spoke to was being ironic, sending themselves – or something – up.

And it seemed to me, on subsequent visits, that there was plenty to send up. The TV programmes that were interrupted every ten minutes by commercials. The bizarre characters flaunting their far-out personal problems on chat shows. The TV evangelists with their unabashed demands for donations. The fact that 'socialism' was a dirty word.

In the last two decades I've visited America many times and love its vibrancy, its variety, its playfulness. I've made strong and warm and – I hope – enduring friendships with Americans. But in the last two decades America's influence on the world and actions in it have become more and more distasteful. And what is most shameful is that it is all done under the cover of 'freedom', 'democracy' and 'peace'.

Nowhere does the hypocrisy of American foreign policy seem more clear than in its unconditional support for Israel. This is generally explained by citing the power of the Zionist lobby, the misguided identification of 'Jewish' with 'Israeli' or 'Zionist' – an identification which many Jews now openly reject – and the wish to make amends for the Holocaust. But maybe the affinity goes deeper than that. The US too is a (relatively) young nation; a state that came into being at the hands of groups of white Europeans who 'discovered' a land and 'settled' it – never mind that there were (brown) people already there. Maybe America's fondness for Israel is like that of a parent watching a child follow in its footsteps. And now it looks as though the parent will be taught by the child: airborne attacks on civilian populations, illegal detentions, use of torture in interrogation, targeted assassinations worldwide, these have been the stock-in-trade of the Israeli state for fifty years and now America looks to follow suit. But

Israel has a free press and Israel would not dare suggest subjecting its citizens – its Jewish citizens, that is – to the infringements on their civil liberties that America is now proposing for Americans. So maybe the parent can still show the child a trick or two.

At the moment the world dominated by America looks like a nasty place.

I still love my American friends; they're smart and funny and open and warm. Is it really the case that to be good for them America has to be bad for the rest of us?

Hundreds of protesters held a two-hour long rally in the downtown Bar Association. Their repeated attempts to march beyond the syndicate's gates and into the main Rameses thoroughfare were foiled by riot police. Dozens of armoured vehicles surrounded the syndicate's headquarters even before the demonstration began.

Demonstrations are prohibited by the emergency law in force since 1982.

The demonstrators repeated slogans calling for the cutting of diplomatic ties with Israel, the cancelation of the Camp David peace agreement between Egypt and Israel and the waging of jihad. 'Filasteen arabiyya' (Palestine is Arab) roared the demonstrators as they waved the Palestinian flag and pictures of late Egyptian president, Gamal Abdel-Nasser. The slogans criticised Arab regimes and the Saudi peace initiative. 'With our lives, with our blood we will die for you, Palestine,' 'Abdel-Nasser said it a long time ago, the occupation is American,' 'Down with America, down with Israel,' they cried. 'Our first demand is kicking out the Israeli ambassador,' protestors shouted, 'and shutting down the Israeli embassy'.

Thousands in Cairo and Tanta University students also went on similar demonstrations, today. In Cairo University, the students walked out of the campus, headed towards the nearby Israeli Embassy but were repelled by hundreds of anti-riot police. Protesters held small Palestinian flags with 'Palestine is Arab' printed on them. A massive demonstration is expected on Monday in front of Cairo University.

Al-Ahram Weekly, Saturday 30 March, 2002

Defiant Israel ignores UN's demands to pull back forces

In words and deeds Israel yesterday defied a United Nations resolution calling on it to pull out of Ramallah and other Palestinian cities …

An Israeli spokesman said their forces would not withdraw as they continued what they say will be a sustained campaign against Palestinian militants.

Observer, Sunday 31 March, 2002

Dear Mr Blair[1]

Dear Mr Blair,

It is midnight now and I have spent these last three days of Easter here, in London, moving between TV channels, the Internet and the walls of my home as the Israeli army moves into the towns of the West Bank. I feel a tremendous anger and a tremendous frustration. And thousands in Britain, millions in the world, feel the same way. We hate what is happening. We fear what is about to happen.

On Saturday I received an e-mail signed by eight Palestinian and seventeen Israeli academics. They say, among other things: 'We call for the international community not to wait for massacres on the scale of those in Sabra and Shatila in 1982; the time for action is now.'

Now, Mr Blair, now. When you were elected, much was made of your 'ethical' foreign policy. Where are the ethics of your foreign policy now, Mr Blair? Women and children are trapped in their homes. Men are blindfolded and shot in the streets. An entire civilian population is being terrorised in the name of rooting out terror – will you do nothing about it?

Two months ago, in a talk at Westminster, the Israeli anti-occupation activist Jeff Halper told us that Israel will never, ever pull out of the West Bank voluntarily. And why should it? After all, this is how Israel first came into being: bands of settlers taking over land and driving out the original inhabitants. The policy that was adopted in 1905 and which remains unchanged is 'talk peace and create facts on the ground'. This is what every Israeli government has done so

[1] The *Guardian*, 3 April 2002.

far. The Sharons are simply more upfront about their intentions than the Baraks.

But there are differences between then and now. One is that some young Israelis, born in Israel and loyal to their country, are beginning to think differently. Some of them are the soldiers (now numbering 384) who are bravely refusing to serve in the occupied territories. Here is one, Gil Nemesh, staff sergeant, engineering: 'Those terrible things happening in the territories have little to do with the security of Israel and stopping terror. It is all about the settlements. Choking and starving and humiliating millions of people, to provide safety to the settlements.'

Another difference between then and now is the Palestinian people. They have learned the lessons of 1948; have learned what happens to you once you let yourself be terrorised off your land. And so they are staying to the bitter end. And the journey too has been bitter. They have gone the way of negotiations and talks and discussions, and have seen that in thirty-two years it has led them nowhere. In the nine years since the Oslo accord the illegal settlements have doubled while the world is lulled by talk of 'peace processes' and 'stages' and 'negotiations'. Now the Palestinians' backs are to the wall. Bring the occupation to an end and you will have peace in the time it takes to withdraw the Israeli army and the illegal settlers to within the Green Line. The situation is still retrievable – but only just. The vast majority of Palestinians do not condone suicide attacks – or any attacks – upon civilians. Here is another Israeli soldier: Tal Belo, staff sergeant, armoured corps: 'The women of Gaza were the true heroes. While the men were busy tending to the miseries of life and looking for ways to liberate themselves from this or that occupation, the women were busy taking care of the kids, preparing the food and working in the groves . . . All alone there, they cried for their youth and for their dreams; for the sons who were killed or sent to prison, or for the sons who will be killed or will be sent to prison.'

But now young girls – girls who have worked as nurses, pretty girls, teenagers with lives ahead of them – strap explosives to their bodies and blow themselves up. Can you imagine the despair and the anger that would lead a young woman to such an act?

Do you know what happens in the West Bank and Gaza, Mr Blair? What has been happening there for years? Let me tell you – or better still, let another Israeli soldier tell you. You see, Mr Blair, I am quoting heavily from these young men. This is to make up the credibility I may lack as a UK citizen of Egyptian origin and to dispel the prevailing myth that this is a 'religious' conflict rather than a political one. So listen to Assaf Oron, sergeant first class, Infantry: '. . . when, as a sergeant, I found myself in charge, something cracked inside me. Without thinking, I turned into the perfect occupation enforcer. I settled accounts with "upstarts" who didn't show enough respect. I tore up the personal documents of men my father's age. I hit, harassed, served as a bad example . . . I was no aberration. I was exactly the norm . . .'

Have you seen the pictures of the Israeli army stationed on the roofs of people's houses? Do you know what that is like, day by day, hour by hour? Listen to Avner Kohavi, sergeant first class, infantry: 'First, the external walls of the house were black with coffee leftovers spilled by the soldiers from the roof. The yard was full of shit and toilet papers because it served as the soldiers' latrine. On the roof there were piles of trash and empty cans. The military vehicle bringing every new shift in would shatter the pavement and entrance to the house. When a shift changed at 2 a.m., all the tenants would wake up, and since there was a baby in the house he would start wailing. I remember the look on the face of the tenants whenever I bumped into them on the stairway: a look of humiliation.'

And this was in the good old days, before they started making men strip to their underwear to walk through the checkpoints, before they started digging trenches so that people couldn't get to work, before they placed their tanks at hospital gates so women delivered their babies in the streets, before they started the executions. So tell them, Mr Blair, tell them that this life, with no end in sight, is preferable to blowing themselves up and taking a few of their tormentors with them.

The people who get blown up are often not their specific tormentors. A sad and terrible truth. But still, as Tamir Sorek, sergeant first class, army intelligence, writes: 'The deprived [Palestinian] habitants are still desperately demanding their rights. The obvious facts that their uprising includes hideous assaults against innocent privileged [Israeli] people do not subtract from the legitimacy of their claim for freedom from non-elected rule.' How is that for straight, moral thinking?

Do something to stop the occupation, Mr Blair. For days presidents and world leaders have been pleading with Sharon not to harm Chairman Arafat. Arafat's life is not worth more than any other and the man is no picture, but filmed by candlelight he looked like a Rembrandt on the TV screen. That is the image that will fuel the years of anguish that will surely follow if anything happens to him.

The occupation is not negotiable. It is illegal by all accepted international laws. It is immoral, obscene, corrupting. Negotiations about the other issues in question should take place after the occupation is ended. The calls for help are coming not only from the Palestinians but from Israelis too. Listen to them. And tell your friend in the White House that Israel needs to be bound by international law. Tell him that the Arabs' quarrel with America is because of its dishonesty on the Israeli issue; that it cannot pick a fight with Iraq for not heeding international law and at the same time fund the Israeli slaughter of Palestinians with American taxpayers' money. Tell him that if America really played the 'honest broker' in the Holy Land, it would not need to shore up corrupt regimes in Arab countries to protect its legitimate interests.

As Sergeant Oron writes: 'We are the Chinese young man standing in front of the tank [in Tiananmen Square]. And you? If you are nowhere to be seen, you are probably inside the tank, advising the driver.'

Sincerely,

America turns sights on Iraq

As American bombs and missiles struck Taleban targets in four Afghan cities for the second consecutive night, the Bush Administration served formal notice at the United Nations that this could be just the beginning of a worldwide campaign. Some members of the Bush Administration have already identified Iraq as a possible target for reprisals.

The Times, Tuesday 9 October, 2001

Iraq War was about Israel, Bush insider suggests

IPS uncovered the remarks by Philip Zelikow, who is now the executive director of the body set up to investigate the terrorist attacks on the United States in September 2001 – the 9/11 Commission – in which he suggests a prime motive for the invasion just over one year ago was to eliminate a threat to Israel, a staunch US ally in the Middle East …

Zelikow made his statements about 'the unstated threat' during his tenure on a highly knowledgeable and well-connected body known as the President's Foreign Intelligence Advisory Board (PFIAB), which reports directly to the President. He served on the board between 2001 and 2003.

'Why would Iraq attack America or use nuclear weapons against us? I'll tell you what I think the real threat (is) and actually has been since 1990 – it's the threat against Israel,' Zelikow told a crowd at the University of Virginia on Sept. 10, 2002.

www.salon.com, Friday 16 April, 2004

The Worst Story Ever Told[1]

The two musicians seated on the rug on the low platform could have come from an illumination in a Mughal manuscript. A tall window opened on to a mild October night and the passer-by outside would have heard – flowing into the quiet Kensington street – the melody from the sitar, pumped along by the tabla, and carrying with it the longings of all our hearts: English gents in black tie and kids in jeans, a couple of dog collars, white women in saris and Indian women in tailored suits. The book being launched, William Dalrymple's remarkable *White Mughals*, tells a love story; a story of India before the Raj, an India where the newly arrived British mixed with the Indians, where what today would be called 'cultural exchange' took place. Until commercial interests got too big and politics took over and with them came segregation, rigidity and talk of 'superior' cultures. In Leighton House, where the celebration was held, a fountain plays on a mosaic floor, Turkish and Persian tiles line the walls and hanging companionably above them are paintings from the time of Alma Tadema and Burne-Jones. Together they form a unique British house.

Later, at home, we watched President George W. Bush on television and my mother from across the kitchen table said, 'All those cities that one associates with poetry, with art . . .' I let her sentence tail off. She's seventy-five and we're close to midnight. But the names loop through my head: Baghdad and Basra and Kufa, Kabul and Kandahar, Mazar-i Sharif and Jalalabad, Bethlehem, Nazareth, Jerusalem . . .

---

[1] The *New Statesman*, 4 November 2002 published this in a shorter form. The full article appears here.

In the morning a Jordanian friend tells me a joke over the phone: King Abdullah says to George Bush, 'You know I watch *Star Trek* every day and there's white people and black people, Spanish, Chinese, every sort of people. But there are no Arabs. Why are there no Arabs?' And Bush says, 'Because it's set in the future, stupid!'

We have all feared – deep in our hearts – that it might come to this. It affects, infects, your every moment. My children are half-Scots. Should I encourage them to forget their other half? My half? Forget Arabic, forget their family in Cairo and Alexandria. Forget Egypt and the Nile and Fairuz and 'am Ahmad in the grocery on the corner of our street. Should I plug them into MTV and save them?

In the streets of London, as in other cities, hundreds of thousands march, newspapers are full of the anger and fear which President Bush's call to war has engendered across the world. Trade unions have made their positions clear, MPs threaten a revolt, analysts and commentators analyse and comment. What is a novelist to do?

Martin Amis, writing last June, questioned the use or relevance of fiction in the post 9/11 days: 'After a couple of hours at their desks, on September 12, 2001, all the writers on earth were reluctantly considering a change of occupation.' More than two decades ago Philip Roth observed that 'the actuality is continually outdoing our talents'. And Jonathan Franzen has contrasted the slowness of novel-writing and the speed at which everything now moves: 'portents . . . stream uninterruptedly through a cable converter or a modem'.

I open my e-mail to an appeal from the children of al-Khalil to be allowed back to school, a letter from a friend trying to help with the olive harvest near the Ariel settlement on the West Bank describes 'armed settler militias that are seemingly out of control', an appeal from Radio Tariq al-Mahabba (Amity Road) in Nablus to help keep it on the air as it is people's only method of communication after 100 days of curfew, an interview with Archmandrite Dr Theodosios Attallah Hanna describing the designs of the Israeli occupation authorities against the Greek Orthodox Church in Jerusalem . . .

It is impossible to close your eyes to the black spectacle mushrooming before us and concentrate on making things up. Novelists work with patterns, with the logic of an unfolding narrative, with the motivation of characters, with the telling detail. But by the time you've written the novel it's too late. And yet, it's all there: the dramatic curve, the characters, the context. It's being written but we can't afford to wait. So, for what it's worth, here's one novelist's interpretation of the narrative unfolding before us now and where it's likely to end.

Our narrative can begin, if you like, in March this year with US Vice-President Dick Cheney's unsuccessful attempt to drum up Arab support for a war against Iraq, or it can begin with the terrible events of September 11, 2001, and the ensuing 'War on Terror'. It can begin with the Intifada of the Palestinians in September 2000 when they realised that seven years after the Oslo agreements they were further than ever from independence, or with the creation of the state of Israel in 1948. But at whatever point the story begins, its dramatic curve will be seen to originate back in the beginning of the twentieth century: in the Zionists' choice of Arab Palestine as a home for the Jewish people and in the defeat of the Ottoman empire in the First World War and the subsequent division of the Arab lands by Britain and France. A carve-up which, through the mechanism of the British mandate in Palestine, facilitated the implementation of the Zionist dream. The curve will also take in the discovery of oil in the Arabian Peninsula and the West's growing dependence on it during the course of the century.

These, then, are our three plot-shapers: the unnatural divisions of 1916, the continuing interest the great powers of any given moment take in the area because of its oil and its strategic position, and the presence in the heart of the Arab lands of an alien, settler state and, therefore, a dispossessed refugee people. Any one of these, alone, would probably have resolved itself eventually. The three together ensured a rising curve of conflict, held in a kind of balance for the best part of the twentieth century by the cold confrontation between the world's two great powers: the US and the USSR.

That balance vanished with the implosion of the Soviet Union. Shortly afterwards, when, in his invasion of Kuwait, Saddam Hussein overstepped the mark set by the American masters who had till then been perfectly happy to do business with him, Iraq was made an example of. A 'New World Order' was in place. The United States was now in a position to push its interests in the oil and the strategic position of the Arabs on the one hand and to demonstrate more openly its support for the state of Israel on the other. But the two, at the best of times, cannot fit together. And these are not the best of times.

The United States now has the most right-wing, militaristic administration it has ever had. Its political outlook, geared to the metaphysics of the Cold War is about as nuanced as that of a C-grade action movie. And it is isolationist in the sense that it sees only America's interests. Israel has, in Ariel Sharon, a leader who is on the record as saying that Israel's 'dirty work' is not yet done and that he is not afraid of doing it. This is even after what he has accomplished in Qibya, in Beirut, in Sabra and Chatila. The function of Arab governments seems to be mainly to keep their citizens in a stranglehold while tiny elites whose interests are those of global business and the United States run away with their countries' wealth. Arab opposition (to their governments, to the further dispossession of the Palestinians, to the new globalised world order) has been hijacked by practitioners of a brand of puritanical, militant Islam, one of whose weapons is acts of terror. (It is always worth remembering, however, that these 'terrorists' were bred and nurtured in the first place by both their own governments and the United States as a tool with which to destroy liberal, secular opposition to both their economic politics and their politics towards Israel.)

At this point in our story the United States decides to attack Iraq. The arguments against this attack do not need rehearsing here. Neither do we need to rehearse the continual excuses the US administration is putting forward for going to war. But the question remains: Why attack Iraq *now*? And if Iraq has to be attacked, why not minimise the effects on the Arab world by solving the Palestinian problem first? In other words, if you are going to ratchet up the explosive tension of two of your plot-shapers, would it not be wise to neutralise the third one first? Why the insistence on putting the Palestinian question on hold till later? These are questions to do with motivation and therefore with character. Pushing the 'attack now' agenda in the US are Vice-President Cheney and the Department of Defense. It is now understood that they are interested in securing the US position as the only global superpower for the foreseeable future through the strategic positioning of military bases and friendly regimes, securing oil and weakening or fragmenting potential rivals or threats. They also take the view that the road to 'real' security and peace runs through Baghdad. In 1998 Donald Rumsfeld (now Secretary for Defense) and Paul Wolfowitz (now his deputy) wrote to Republican leaders in Congress warning that with weapons of mass destruction Saddam Hussein could become 'the driving force of Middle East politics, including on such important matters as the Middle East peace process'. A year later Wolfowitz said 'the US needs to accelerate Saddam's demise if it truly wants to help the peace process'. In 2000 a report by Cheney, Rumsfeld and Wolfowitz – published by the Project for the New American Century – practically states that the Iraqi President is an excuse for action: 'While the unresolved conflict with Iraq provides the immediate justification, the need for a substantial American force presence in the Gulf transcends the issue of the regime of Saddam Hussein' (*Sunday Herald*). When Rumsfeld came to office in the current administration he appointed Richard Perle (a director of the right-wing Israeli *Jerusalem Post*) as chairman of the United States Defense Policy Board. Douglas Feith, a Perle protégé, was appointed Under Secretary of Defense for Policy. In 1996 Perle and Feith had written an advisory paper for Benyamin Netanyahu (then new Likud Prime Minister of Israel) calling on him to break with Oslo and reassert Israel's claim to the West Bank and Gaza.

The other quarter busily preparing for war is the Israeli government. On 16 August the Associated Press reported Raanan Gissin, an aide to Prime Minister Ariel Sharon, as saying that Israel is urging US officials not to delay a military strike against Iraq's Saddam Hussein: 'any postponement of an attack on Iraq at this stage will serve no purpose'. On 3 October, while Israeli Defense Ministry Director-General, Amos Yaron, held talks in Washington with US Deputy Secretary of State Richard Armitage, Israeli Defense Minister Benjamin Ben-Eliezer estimated that the US would attack Iraq at the end of November so prompting Sharon (who has been invited to Washington by George Bush later this month) to request that 'ministers cease making remarks about Iraq'.

On the last school run of the week before half-term I switched on the car radio and caught Andrew Motion mentioning the 'sliver of ice' in the heart of every artist that makes him/her able to fashion art out of the saddest things. Every night private and public losses mingle; I dream of my husband who died last year and of Nasser who died thirty years ago and wake with a cold fist tight around my heart. The book I'm writing on Cairo is on hold. How can I write about my beloved city when my friends in Ramallah, Nablus and Bethlehem are under curfew in theirs? And are the curfews and the marauding tanks the worst of it, or is there more to fear?

Why does Sharon want war on Iraq? We know that a strong Iraq – particularly a strong, democratic Iraq – could be a real threat to Israeli dominance in the area; it has the demography and the resources. But why war rather than continued containment? War now? Speaking in London three months ago, Azmi Bishara, Arab member of the Knesset, warned against talking of 'transfer' – of the deportation of Palestinians. Once you talk about something you make it closer to happening. I share that caution, but 'transfer' is now openly discussed. And we should remember that as the US started to bomb Afghanistan Sharon moved his army into the West Bank and Gaza.

'Would it not be wise to neutralise the third one first?' Well, no, actually. Not if what both the US and Israel want is the biggest (local) conflagration possible, which eventually is revealed to have burned new facts into the ground. If this were a novel Sharon would be waiting for an extraordinary circumstance under cover of which he would start driving people out of the West Bank, out of Jerusalem. But he needs somewhere to drive them to. And maybe a justification.

Did he hope to do it under cover of the war in Afghanistan? Within hours of the attacks of September 11 he rushed to identify the terror the USA had just suffered with the 'terror' Israel was enduring. Was he paving the way then for his final solution? But the Taliban caved in more quickly than anyone had expected and the war in Afghanistan as a huge and diverting spectacle was over too soon. A war on Iraq now could give him the cover he needs. It could also provide him with the locale of the banishment. He cannot use Sinai – whether because of the peace treaty with Egypt or because he hopes to re-occupy it eventually is open to question. Southern Lebanon is guarded by Hezbollah. Jordan – a friend of the US – already has a huge Palestinian population and would be destabilised by more. It has already closed its borders. How about driving the Palestinians out through Jordan and into a compliant Iraq?

It is likely that the story Israel tells itself about itself, does not allow for it to relinquish – of its own volition – the West Bank. Perhaps it did for a moment during the premiership of Yitzhak Rabin, and he was murdered for it. For if the claim of Israel to the land of Palestine is biblical, then it is a claim not to Tel Aviv and Haifa but to Judea and Samaria.

Indeed, it is a claim to 'Eretz Yisrael', which stretches from the Euphrates to the Nile. Hence Israel has talked peace but built settlements, has talked stopping terror but demolished houses and torn up olive groves. This is why it has to dehumanise the Palestinians, to speak of a society in the grip of fanaticism, of a cult of death. In a recent interview in *Ha'aretz*, chief of staff Moshe Ya'alon described the Palestinians as a 'cancerous manifestation' – although (former Prime Minister) Ehud Barak demurred at this and said they were more like 'a virus'. This is why it is possible for a pro-Israeli Jewish writer to publish a piece in the *LA Times* saying that 'if in 1948, 1956, 1967 or 1973 Israel had acted just a bit like the Third Reich, then today Israelis would shop, eat pizza, marry and celebrate the holy days unmolested. And of course, Jews, not sheikhs, would have that Gulf oil' (7 April 2002). Perhaps Ariel Sharon does not need to articulate a justification for mass transfer – but alarms are being spread that 'in the event of a US attack, Iraq would enlist the aid of the Palestinians in mounting biological attacks' (Radio Israel in Arabic, 3 August 2002). And in the last couple of weeks the reports of settlers attacking Palestinian peasants as they try to harvest their olives have been so harrowing that some of my English friends have dropped everything and gone out to join the International Solidarity Movement and act as human shields.

An interesting plot complication arises from the fact that Israel is indeed a democracy – for its Jewish citizens. And so there are Israeli characters who stand like heroic figures against the current. The wise men of Rabbis for Peace, the soldiers who are refusing to serve in the occupied territories. Scholars like Ilan Pappe or historian and one-time deputy mayor of Jerusalem, Meron Benvenisti, who warned, in *Ha'aretz* on 15 August of 'the possibility of a mass transfer of Palestinians in case of war in Iraq'. Architects who have spoken of the 'vertical' occupation. The members of Gush Shalom who ran an ad last month to tell the world that 'in the imminent chaos created in the Middle East in case of war, Sharon hopes to implement his old scheme to expel the Palestinians from all of Palestine. For this end he is ready to inflict a disaster upon all of us.'

Can these people influence the plot? So far it seems not. And their calls to their countrymen appear to have gone unheeded. A telling phrase in a recent article by David Grossman (*Guardian*, 30 September) says 'the Palestinians begin their timeline for the conflict from, at the latest, 1948, when the state of Israel was founded. Israelis, for the most part, place the starting point of their timeline at September 2000' (the beginning of the Intifada). A crucial difference. But the dissidents add tragic depth to our narrative. And they can provide justification for the United States to refuse to implement Sharon's plans.

In March of this year Crown Prince Abdullah of Saudi Arabia proposed a peace plan that included full normalisation of Arab relations with Israel. President Bush endorsed the plan at first but Cheney and Rumsfeld argued that fighting terror meant supporting Sharon. On 4 April Bush said that 'moral clarity' required an attack on terror in all its forms. So far it seems that the Pentagon is winning the day. And the Pentagon is, by this analysis, not merely 'hawkish' in promotion of US interests but committed to the ambitions – the world-view – of Israel.

And it is Pentagon officials that we find liaising with possible replacements for Saddam Hussein's regime. One possible leader, admired – we are told – by Richard Perle (*New York Times*, 2 October), is Ahmad Chalabi. Chalabi is an interesting character. Some twenty years ago he set up, with the support of (then Crown) Prince Hasan of Jordan, the Petra Bank, which collapsed with debts of some $57 million leaving Chalabi a wealthy man – though unpopular in banking circles. It was said that two warrants were out for his arrest, the standard Interpol warrant and another personally signed by King Hussein. It was also said that he evaded arrest by hiding out in south Lebanon. A few years ago he relaunched himself as the head of the 'Iraq National

Congress'; one of the various groups that have set themselves up as 'Iraqi opposition in exile'. The INC is the group closest to the Pentagon and is funded by the CIA. At an INC meeting with Pentagon officials in Washington last July, Ahmad Chalabi appeared hand in hand with his sometime mentor Prince Hasan who, in a recent interview in the Israeli paper *Yediot Aharanot*, failed to make a single mention of a Palestinian sovereign state.

Flashback here to a deathbed scene: King Hussein of Jordan, days from his end, flies to the US. Then, in a letter to his brother, he removes him from the succession. And the Prince accepts the removal of the kingdom which had been practically guaranteed to him from birth. What was the prize big enough for this to happen? Was it, in fact, oil-rich Iraq – but with a couple of million Palestinians thrown in? Israeli terrorism expert, Ehud Sprinzak, says that the US goal in Iraq is to create a 'united Hashemite kingdom' out of Iraq and Jordan's 'Sunni areas'. Sprinzak states that the authors of this plan are Cheney and Wolfowitz.

It was reported that, in the wake of the September 11 attacks, George Bush consulted with the scriptwriter for the film *Die Hard 2* on how to deal with Arabs and terrorists. Perhaps in the script Bush is shooting now the US, backed by Britain, will blaze into Iraq and come out (at the cost of an 'acceptable' number of American and British dead) having smelted that country into a docile Hashemite kingdom with a Chalabi Karzaid into Prime Minister. This 'beacon', together with a fully Jewish and contented Israel, would then proceed to spread democracy and the principles of the free market in the surrounding Middle East while the rich oilfields of Majnoun and others start to pump their millions of barrels through the pipelines – disused since 1948 – running to Haifa and thence back to the US.

There is another script being written by the Reverend Jerry Falwell and the American Christian fundamentalists so cynically courted by Benyamin Netanyahu. Ed McAteer, a founder of the Moral Majority and known as the godfather of the Christian right says, 'I believe that we are seeing prophecy unfold so rapidly and dramatically and wonderfully, and, without exaggeration, [it] makes me breathless.' For the rest of this narrative and an account of Armageddon see the Book of Revelation.

A realistic novel, however, would acknowledge that this is the fruit-bearing stage of the three plot-shapers planted at the beginning of the century: the world's only superpower, in league with Israel, plots new deployments of the lands and resources of the Arabs, to serve their own, narrowly defined interests. It would also acknowledge the complexities, the heightening in both true knowledge and misunderstanding that the last hundred years have wrought in the relationship of the people of the East to the people of the West. But I fear it would have to portray a massive panorama of war and destruction, men and women carrying their children, their old and their bedclothes and struggling across borders: a new cycle of terror and guilt. The entire Middle East may not erupt immediately but its rulers, supported by the US, will have to use more fire and steel to keep its people down. Across the Third World (and the Second?) Business elites close to the US will leverage themselves closer and closer to government and the people will get hungrier and angrier – even while their old values of patience, acceptance, tolerance and so on are being replaced by the dog-eat-dog, survival-of-the-fittest market-economy values. Desperate anger will express itself in desperate acts; as we have already seen in Bali and Moscow, acts that had once been unthinkable will become commonplace. Governments themselves will perpetrate terror and in so doing make terrorists of their people. The war that Bush has prescribed will indeed last for generations and spread across the world. The people in the dominant countries, in the US and the UK and Israel, that dare to question or talk of causes or write or publish articles like this one will be first sidelined and then criminalised. Fascist measures will eventually be used to control their societies. Think of the occupied territories of Palestine today – then spread that vision across the world. It will take a library of novels to do justice to the American, Arab, British and Israeli – the millions – the fragmented global community of broken hearts.

There is an alternative ending:

The US administration and Mr Blair heed the voice of their people. The UN arms inspectors fly in and Iraq allows them to do their work. Israel (in a spirit of saving it from itself) is pushed to an international negotiating table – in the UK or Europe. The world tells it that it has to pull out of the occupied territories. Not in 2004. Now. UN or international forces are flown to the West Bank and Gaza to protect the Palestinians, oversee the withdrawal and help in securing Israel's borders. The Palestinians have their state. Israel is secure within its pre-1967 borders. The refugee issue is on the table for negotiations towards a workable just solution. The anger of the Arabs and the Muslims is dissipated. Oil flows uninterrupted to America who then sees that it can have oil and world hegemony (of sorts) through genuine aid and cultural ties. With the thorn of the Palestinian–Israeli conflict removed from its heart and the US the friend it once seemed to be, the Arab world can turn its attention to development, to democratisation. Sharon falls and a more thoughtful and humane Prime Minister leads his country. Cheney, Rumsfeld, Wolfowitz, et al. have to save their dreams of world domination for another day. The minor characters and chorus can walk off the page and live ordinary, uneventful, human lives: they can go to celebrations in beautiful houses and listen to sitars or flutes or saxophones and when sadness does come to them may it be only the sadness of the unavoidable – rather than the colossal sorrows I fear we have started to bring upon ourselves.

International Women's Day – 8 March – is marked by a protest against war outside the headquarters of the Arab League in the heart of Cairo.
Al-Ahram Weekly, 13-19 March, 2003

Staying Alive[1]

In Baghdad on any given day you might come across her. I will not tell you her name – but you'll recognise her. She is tall and slim, has silver hair and dresses in black with black trainers and thick black socks. Her husband, now dead, used long ago to be an Iraqi ambassador. Now she sets out from her home every morning and walks. She walks though the streets looking and listening and asking questions. Her project is to memorise what is happening to the people and the daily life of her country. She's eighty-eight and doesn't have much time.

None of us has much time.

Have you ever seen a patched book? Here it is: SJ's slim volume *The Poet*. SJ has a Ph.D. in Arabic literature from Baghdad University. The ancient piece of machinery coaxed into printing her book either dries up or floods. On pages where the damage is too bad SJ writes out the missing words by hand on a piece of paper and glues it in place. 'War gives birth,' she writes, 'and mothers do the bringing up.' She sells *The Poet* at 125 dinars a copy, hoping eventually to pay back the 3,000 dinars it's cost to produce. Three thousand dinars equal one dollar and fifty cents.

I'm asked what Arab women are doing in these critical times. They are doing what they've always done: toughing it out, spreading themselves thin, doing their work, making ends meet, trying to protect their children and support their men, turning to their sisters and their mothers for solidarity and laughs. There was a time, I guess, when women's political action was born of choice, of a desire to change

[1] The *Guardian*, 13 March 2003 published this in a shorter form. The full article appears here.

the world. Now, simply to hold on to our world action is thrust upon us.

F is an Egyptian architect. She has always been active in women's organisations. She did voluntary literacy work with poor urban women and her book on mothers and children was published by the UNDP. Her husband is one of the fourteen anti-war activists detained recently in Cairo. Last Monday she and her two daughters, both engineering students, went to visit him in Tora jail. Her daughters were astounded at the hundreds of women and children waiting to visit political detainees. Children were waiting to visit grandfathers in their seventies. F's husband is from the left but the majority of the detainees are Islamists. The majority are unofficially detained. They have never been to court and there is no document that gives them prisoner status. They are not allowed to give power of attorney to anyone. Without documents wives cannot draw their husband's salaries, cannot travel, cannot marry off a daughter or even bury a child. Because of the conditions in the jail, the detainees' families have to provide them with food, clothes, books, cigarettes. The distance from the centre of Cairo to Tora jail is twenty miles. Because the detainees have no official status there is no agreed system for visits. The women show up and hope that they and their provisions will be allowed in. If they are not they have to come back the next day. F and her colleagues now find themselves campaigning at least for the proper application of the hated emergency laws under which Egyptians have laboured since 1981. In the Arab world today, the human rights of women are indivisible from those of men.

The emergency laws proscribe demonstrations or un-authorised public gatherings. Five of the marches that have taken place in Cairo over the last two weeks have been women's marches called by women's NGOs and timed with the Women in Black demonstrations across the world. Un-like marches involving men they managed to reach both the American and Israeli embassies. Men who demonstrate get shot before they come anywhere near these, but the authorities are still wary of brutalising women in public. It seems, though, that their patience may be wearing thin; the latest demo saw 150 women cornered by some 2,000 riot police so their protest took place in front of Shepheard's Hotel round the corner from the American embassy. Today's demonstration in front of the Arab League headquarters will link Iraq and Palestine, for while the world's attention is on Iraq, Ariel Sharon's army shoots at ambulances and bulldozes houses down on top of pregnant women. Since November 2000, 51 Palestinian women have had to give birth at checkpoints. Twenty-nine of these 51 babies died.

And yet Palestinian women continue to have babies. Is that a political choice? At the centre of most women's lives are the children. Soha, a nursing student, breaks down and cries in her home in Aida Camp when a rocket whizzes through her kitchen window at supper-time and out through the facing wall into the mercifully empty bedroom. Her mother tells her to buck up and not scare the children. It is sobering to note that the first Palestinian woman to make the political decision to become a human bomb was a nurse, caring daily for children injured or maimed by Israeli bullets. In between these two extremes – the giving and the giving up of life – hundreds of thousands of women go about their business as best they can.

A great many of the cultural workers in the West Bank and Gaza are women. Marina Burhan operates a childrens' theatre out of Beit Jala despite her roof having been blown off. Carol Michel keeps the small cultural centre in Bethlehem working – curfews permitting. Suad al-Amiri restores houses in the old city of al-Khalil (Hebron) and takes the Israeli army to court when they try to demolish her work. Vera Tamari makes installations out of cars trashed by said army. Tania Nasir researches traditional embroidery patterns. Adila Laidi stages concerts and painting competitions in Ramallah despite her computers being ripped apart and excrement smeared on her walls again by the army. 'By responding to the occupation, interpreting it through art, we are no longer its victims, we work our own will upon it,' she says. Vera and Tania take advantage of a sudden lifting of curfew to slip out and have highlights put in their hair. They say it makes them feel stronger and able to cope with the soldiers.

Karma, though sixty years younger than our Baghdadi friend, does not walk the streets of Ramallah. She sits at home and compiles the *Hearpalestine* newsletter and website, recording what she can of the daily demolitions, expropriations, arrests and killings. Keeping the children alive. Keeping culture alive. Preserving history and telling the story – these seem to be at the heart of our women's concerns right now.

Peter Hansen, writing in this paper last Wednesday of the terrible hunger in Gaza, says that 'the Palestinian extended family and community network have saved the territories from . . . absolute collapse'. Women are the backbone of these families and networks and they are performing the same function in Iraq. Families who have, share with those who have not, through the agency of the churches and the mosques.

Last night IK told me that her mother, in Baghdad, has sold the Virgin's gold. An icon of the Virgin that has been in the family for more than 300 years. A neighbour in trouble – Christian, Jew or Muslim – would come and whisper a prayer, perhaps make a pledge. When the afflicted was healed, the traveller berthed, the child conceived, the neighbour would fulfil the pledge. Over the decades the Virgin was adorned with the most delicate filaments of gold. To her children's appalled protests that the gold was not hers to sell, their mother replied that the Virgin had no need of gold when there were people in the city who were starving. But what comes next? Where do you go after you've sold the Virgin's gold?

Much to the displeasure of the media covering the first summit of its kind between five Arab leaders and a US president in Sharm El-Sheikh on Tuesday, no questions were permitted after conclusion of the closing statements of President Hosni Mubarak and his American counterpart, President George W. Bush. There was no opportunity to tackle sensitive issues such as the new US 'vision' for the Middle East, the tricky definition of 'terrorism', the precarious status of Palestinian President Yasser Arafat, a guarantee that the roadmap will be implemented, or criticism of Israel's obstructive behaviour during the peace process.

Understandably, perhaps, the less said was deemed the better ...
Al-Ahram Weekly, 5-11 June, 2003

Before the war, Bush connected nonexistent dots between Saddam Hussein and al-Qaida. Now he and his neoconservative brain trust are mapping the Iraq conflict onto the Likud Party agenda in Palestine. This time, however, it's a self-fulfilling prophecy – and one that will have devastating repercussions for US interests in both Iraq and the entire Arab world.

The conflict between the Israelis and Palestinians is so central to US diplomacy in the region that it cannot help affecting every other policy imperative ... Many Arabs, including Iraqis, initially looked upon the US as an honest broker, but its reputation has gradually been sullied ... as of this week, the Bush administration has endorsed the seizure of the land of one party by another in an international dispute.

Neoconservatives, many of them ardent defenders of Israel with strong ties to the Likud, were among the chief intellectual architects of the war on Iraq – they advocated an Iraq war, the destruction of the Oslo peace process, the refusal ever to return territories occupied by Israel in 1967, and using a conquered Iraq as a means of pacifying the Lebanese Hezbollah.

At the time, such positions were regarded as wildly radical: Today they have become US policy – in many minds, there are now two major occupations of Arab land by outside powers, the West Bank and Iraq. This perception is a very dangerous development for Americans seeking legitimacy in Iraq and the Muslim world.
www.salon.com, Friday 16 April, 2004

US forces in Iraq's Sunni triangle have already begun to use tactics that echo Israeli operations in the occupied territories, sealing off centres of resistance with razor wire and razing buildings ...

'This is basically an assassination programme ... This is a hunter-killer team,' said a former senior US intelligence official.
Guardian, Tuesday 9 December, 2003

Contagious Exchanges[1]

Once again it's funny-mirrors time. The world watches the meetings taking place by the Red Sea, and Western media see one process taking place while the Arabs generally see another.

Interpreting these meetings is largely a matter of how you view the relationship between the US and Israel. A few weeks ago I heard a well-known British columnist say he was sick of being told that the Palestinian–Israeli conflict was the 'litmus test' for how people can expect the American Imperium to influence the world. Yet 'Freedom for Palestine' was the demand on millions of the banners in the demonstrations against the war on Iraq that swept the world last February.

America's support for Israel dates to the beginning of the Zionist project in the late nineteenth century and grew stronger throughout the twentieth. From 1949 to the present, for every dollar the US spent on an African, it spent $250.65 on an Israeli, and for every dollar it spent on someone from the West outside the US, it spent $214 on an Israeli.[2] As Israel grows stronger the support becomes more solid. According to

[1] *Index on Censorship*, July 2003 published this in a shorter form. The full article appears here.
[2] The *Washington Report on Middle East Affairs* (www.wrmea.com). This expenditure continues: in Colin Powell's address to AIPAC on 30 March 2004 the Secretary of State said: 'While we deal with Saddam Hussein, we must not forget the burdens that the conflict with Iraq has placed on our Israeli friends. I am very pleased that President Bush has included in his supplemental budget request that just went to Congress $1 billion in Foreign Military Financing funds to help Israel strengthen its military and civil defences. And that's just for starters. The President is also asking for $9 billion in loan guarantees.'

Stephen Zunes, Chair of the Peace and Justice Studies Program at San Francisco University, 'Ninety-nine per cent of all US aid to Israel took place after the 1967 war.'[3]

In the United Nations the US has used its veto against thirty-four resolutions related to the Arab–Israeli conflict.

US support for Israel has involved turning a blind eye not only to Israeli flouting of international law, but to Israeli anti-American activities such as: spying (Jonathan Jay Pollard 1985 and David Tenenbaum 1997), selling arms to China (1990 onwards), espionage against American companies (cited in the *Wall Street Journal*, 1992) and attacks on the dignity and the lives of American subjects as in the bombing of the USS *Liberty* in 1967, the beating by Israeli police of David Muirhead who was working on an American-financed project to restore the main street in al-Khalil in 1997, the turning back of a US Congressional delegation from the Allenby Bridge in August 2002 and, in April, the Israeli army's shooting of peace activist Brian Avery in Jenin and its killing of Rachel Corrie in Rafah.

Washington matches actions with words. On 18 May 2000, the Democratic candidate for the presidency, Al Gore, addressing the powerful pro-Israeli Washington lobby, AIPAC, was able to say: 'The United States has an absolute, uncompromising commitment to Israel's security and an absolute conviction that Israel alone must decide the steps necessary to ensure that security. That is Israel's prerogative. We accept that. We endorse that. Whatever Israel decides cannot, will not, will never, not ever alter our fundamental commitment to her security.'

You might have thought support couldn't come much stronger. But the group now known as the Neo-cons, who became established in George W. Bush's administration, were waiting for a chance to demonstrate higher levels of commitment. The policies they dreamed of before coming to

[3] Remarks delivered on 26 January 2001, *Washington Report on Middle East Affairs* (May 2003).

power are well documented.[4] They were handed the opportunity to leverage these policies into action by the murderous
attacks on the Twin Towers and the Pentagon on the
morning of 11 September 2001. That day four major Israeli
politicians, Ehud Barak, Benyamin Netanyahu, Shimon
Peres and Ariel Sharon, took to the TV screens to assert
that the terror just suffered by the Americans was the
identical terror endured by Israel since its establishment –
to drive home the point Israel had been pushing for years:
that Israel's enemies were America's enemies.

But this was not always the case. Arabs (and some Israelis)
believe that without American support Israel would have
had to reach a just accommodation with the Palestinians
long ago. But since the Sixties at least the yardstick used by
the US to measure the acceptability/goodness of an Arab
country has been its government's stance towards Israel.
The softer the stance the more 'moderate' or 'friendly' the
country has been considered. It therefore came as a shock to
the US public that the nineteen hijackers who crashed
aeroplanes into the Trade Towers and the Pentagon with
such deadly results were from Egypt and Saudi Arabia:
countries regarded as 'moderate'. The true, albeit unpop-
ular, answer to this puzzle is that the more friendly (i.e.

---

[4] Back in 1996, several of them had presented a policy paper to the then new
Prime Minister of Israel, Benyamin Netanyahu, urging 'a clean break from the
slogan "comprehensive peace" to a traditional concept of strategy based on
balance of power'. ('A Clean Break: A New Strategy for Securing the Realm',
policy paper written under the auspices of the Institute for Advanced Strategic
and Political Studies). Its authors included Richard Perle, Douglas Feith and
David Wurmser, now all policy makers in or policy advisers to the Bush
administration. One of them, Douglas Fieth, now US Under Secretary of Defense
for Policy, was described approvingly by the Zionist Organisation of America as
'the noted pro-Israel activist'. (*Guardian*, 19 December 2002, page 20).

In January 1998, another configuration of Neo-cons wrote to President
Clinton urging him to attack Iraq for the security of 'Israel and our allies'.
Their view was that the road to a Middle East peace 'goes through Baghdad'.
Among the signatories were Elliott Abrams, Richard Armitage, John Bolton,
Zalmay Khalilzad, William Kristol, Richard Perle, Donald Rumsfeld and
Paul Wolfowitz.

subservient) a regime is to an America which so identifies itself with (an intransigent) Israel, the harder that regime has had to oppress its own people and to close off all their legitimate means of political opposition. This is possibly one of the most terrible effects the American–Israeli alliance has had on the Arab world: that most of the Arab men and women who could have played important roles in developing their countries' civil and political institutions have been de-activated. Some have ended up feeling that the only path left open to them is the path of extremism clothed in the robes of what is now called 'militant Islam'.

These processes are absent from any discussion of America's relationship with the Arabs. So, in *The New Yorker*, for example, Seymour Hersch can give a detailed analysis of the internal problems of Saudi Arabia without ever touching on *why* a 'nationalist' government in Saudi might be unenthusiastic about selling oil to America. This holds for practically all the mainstream media in the US. The support of America for Israel has been likened to the elephant in the drawing room; everybody sees it but nobody mentions it. Any discussion of America's relationship with the Arabs therefore has an elephant-sized hole at its heart. And pundits come forward to fill the hole with chatter about the 'innate hostility' of the Arabs to the US or the 'nihilism' of the terrorists or the 'fanatical nature' of Islam. Debate is reduced to 'they hate us because we are rich/free/democratic/unveiled'.

Most of the US administration's and media's information on the Arabs is now derived from the Middle East Media Research Institute (MEMRI), co-founded by Meyrav Wurmser, director of the Center for Middle East Policy at the Hudson Institute. According to the *Guardian*, MEMRI is connected with Israeli army intelligence and feeds the media and politicians with highly selective quotations from extreme Arab publications.[5]

[5] Meyrav Wurmser's husband, Davis Wurmser, heads Middle East Studies at Richard Perle's American Enterprise Institute.

The proposition put forward by the USA and Israel today is that they share common values – basically a commitment to freedom and democracy. American politicians are constantly upping the rhetoric on the indivisibility of America and Israel:

'. . . in war and peace, the United States has stood proudly at Israel's side. Our two nations and peoples are bound together by our common democratic values and traditions. So it has been for over fifty years. So it will always be.' (Secretary of State Colin Powell to AIPAC, 30 March 2003)

Next day: 'As always, there are some, here and abroad, who would drive a wedge between America and Israel. But to do so would be to separate America from its best self . . . our commitment to Israel grows from our duty to preserve the great heritage of liberty and democracy of which we are the most fortunate heirs and the most powerful defenders.' (Senate Democratic Leader Tom Daschle to AIPAC, 31 March 2003)

In this view America and Israel's love of liberty and democracy earn them the hatred of what prominent Neocons have called the 'uncivilised' part of the world. The only way to end this 'hatred' is through a 'civilising' mission; a process which the US has now started in Iraq. This can be seen as a logical move within long-term Israeli strategy. Israel has always sold itself to the West on the basis of the state's oppositional relationship to its chosen environment. Herzl assured the British Foreign Office at the end of the nineteenth century that Israel would provide a civilised bulwark against the barbarian hordes of Islam. Today, Israel's image is of a beacon of civilisation and, increasingly, America's only trustworthy friend in the region.

While some US policies (notably regarding the environment and trade) and the increasingly murky revelations about the links between corporate America and its government[6] make

---

[6] See, among others, 'Enron Used U.S. Government to Bully Developing Nations' Friday 30 May 2003 by the Inter Press Service www.ips.org, or on www.commondreams.org/headlines03/0530-01.htm.

much of the world deeply uneasy, America's unwavering support for Israel has implicated it in a whole range of behaviours which have brought its modus operandi very close to its protégé's. In the past two years the United States has joined Israel in:

- manipulating or sidelining international institutions
- ignoring accepted principles of international law (e.g. setting up Guantanamo Bay, sanctioning assassinations worldwide)[7]
- ignoring accepted principles of human rights (e.g. carrying out illegal detentions including the detention of children, condoning the use of torture)[8]
- adopting military policies to achieve its political ends, embracing a policy of 'pre-emptive' war
- moving to curtail the civil rights of its own citizens (e.g. the Patriot Act)
- encouraging the media to adopt government views and attempting to gag media which is not their own

Meanwhile the voice of the Christian right has moved in from the margins and the discourse of this movement and of members of the administration has become less guarded in its jingoism and its racism.

The US administration has now joined Israel in presenting itself as engaged in an existential war. Both states promote images of themselves as nations injured to a point

---

[7] The *Guardian* (19 December 2002) mapped the connection between Israeli advice and a new US sanction of worldwide assassinations: 'Israeli officials are proud that their country is "a laboratory for fighting terror" with tactics ready for export.'

[8] The United States was actually voted off the UN Commission on Human Rights in May 2001. The *Financial Times* suggested that Washington, by vetoing UN resolutions alleging Israeli human rights abuses, had showed its inability to work impartially in the area of human rights. Secretary of State Colin Powell suggested the vote was because 'we left a little blood on the floor' in votes involving the Palestinians. See later the *New York Times*, 'Lawyers decided bans on torture didn't bind Bush', 8 June 2004.

of no return – Israel by the Holocaust and America by September 11. In justifying the current war George W. Bush said it would be 'suicidal' of the US not to attack Iraq. The injury done them and the danger they are in justify putting aside institutions, concepts, ways of being that have taken centuries to evolve and from which they themselves – para-doxically – continue (in their own eyes) to derive their legitimacy. The paradox is accommodated in the image of the tough but reluctant fighter who takes up arms with a heavy heart because he has no other choice. Both countries evoke a national psychology which needs (for the sake of survival) to overcome a kind of wimpishness. For Zionism the wimpishness is that of the diaspora Jews – who finally 'allowed themselves' to be destroyed. For Americans it's the fallout from guilt over Vietnam.

Americans and Israelis also seem to share a view of themselves as a 'chosen' people. In Israel's case this is through the Covenant. In America's case a recent poll confirmed that 92 per cent of those polled believed that God 'personally and individually loved them'. To be Amer-ican is to be good. We now hear talk of America's 'manifest destiny' and of a 'shared mission' as in House Republican leader Tom DeLay's speech at Boca Raton (on the occasion of the death of space shuttle astronauts – among them the Israeli Ilan Ramon) in which he talked of a destiny shared by America and Israel and asked for divine assistance in protecting both.[9]

In this fight for their existence; the battle between good and evil, there are no middle grounds, no critical stances. You are either 'with us' or 'against us'. Americans who are not 'with' the United States' official policy are traitors, non-Americans are enemies. Jews who are not 'with' Israeli policy are self-haters, non-Jews are anti-Semitic. 'Enemies' and 'anti-Semites' are beyond negotiation or toleration; they have to be annihilated.

[9] *Newsweek*, 2 June 2003.

Americans on the whole appear genuinely uncomfortable being at odds with Israel. Israeli transgressions, injustices etc. cannot be discussed as freely as those of any other country. Indeed it seems almost in bad taste to express any reservations about the 'only democracy in the Arab region'. You can decry the absence of practical equality between black and white people in the US, or talk about the history and plight of the country's Native Americans, but it is a terrible faux pas to mention that Israel, by law, is not the same state for its Muslim and Christian citizens as it is for its Jewish ones.

It is possible that underlying this unease is the need to believe in the essential 'goodness' of Israel, a corollary of its 'moral' (as distinct from its de facto) right to exist. The intellectual inconsistency between deploring Israel's actions in the West Bank and Gaza today and applauding the even more extreme actions it took in the region in 1948 and the years leading up to them must be deeply problematic.

In this context one should note National Security Adviser, Condoleezza Rice's words in her May interview with Israel's daily *Yediot Aharanot*: 'I have a deep affinity with Israel. I have always admired the history of the state of Israel and the hardness and determination of the people that founded it.'

Any discussion of this issue feeds into the perception that the very existence of Israel is under threat. This is as patently absurd as the claim that Iraq under Saddam Hussein presented an existential threat to the United States. And yet it is the perception encouraged by the governments of both countries to mobilise their own people and to panic them. World media has carried pictures of Americans rushing to buy plastic sheeting and duct tape (to the financial advantage of one of the contributors to the Republican party) and Israelis in sealed rooms strapping gas masks on to babies' faces – with all the allusions to the horrors of the Nazi gas chambers that this must evoke.

This poisoned view of the world could not have been promoted without the collusion of the media. Yet now the protest movements within the US and Israel may be forcing parts of the media to re-examine their stance. *Ha'aretz*, in Israel, has for some time been providing a platform for dissident Israeli journalists like Gideon Levy, Uri Avnery and Amira Hass. A fledgling Berkley outfit called 'If Americans Knew' have just published a piece in the *Bay Guardian* showing that the *San Francisco Chronicle* is twenty times more likely to report on the deaths of Israeli children killed in the Israeli–Palestinian conflict than it is to cover Palestinian children's deaths.[10]

The US- and Israeli-professed love of liberty and commitment to human values, betrayed by the governments of both countries, is now demonstrating itself powerfully in the actions of their people and fuelling an important grass-roots dissidence. In two notable recent acts Professor Ilan Pappe of Haifa University has called for a boycott of Israeli institutions because of the increased restrictions placed on civil and academic freedoms; and William R. Brody, Dean of the College of Arts and Sciences at Johns Hopkins University, has used his Commencement Address to warn of the dangers to American society from the Patriot Act. But the most touching and heartening example is the movement of the Israeli soldiers refusing to uphold the occupation of the West Bank and Gaza. They now number more than 1,100.

Is it fanciful to suggest that the awakening of the world to the Palestinian–Israeli conflict has been – at least in part – an effect of the 'Likudisation' of the politics of the USA? And is it naive to hope that Israeli and American citizens with a true commitment to democracy and freedom may put a stop to this process before it destroys us all? And is it cynical to see more hope in this than in what is taking place now on the shores of the Red Sea?

[10] www.sfbg.com/37/35/news_chron.html.

For well over a century the statue of the Virgin Mary has stood in Bethlehem, before the French hospital, observing the endless procession of pilgrims to worship at the town's holiest sites. But last week it became one more casualty of Israel's undeclared war, hit by indiscriminate Israeli fire, the nose and hand blown off, the body of the statue left pockmarked ...
Al-Ahram Weekly, 21-27 March, 2002

The IDF's Military Police yesterday raided the 'Breaking the Silence' exhibit of photographs taken by soldiers during their military service in Hebron, confiscating a folder containing newspaper clips about the exhibit as well as a videotape including statements made by seventy soldiers about their experiences in the West Bank city. The four reservist soldiers who initiated and organized the exhibit also were summoned to interrogations today by Military Police. The army said the purpose of the raid was to uncover evidence of violence and vandalism conducted against Palestinians and their property. The reservists who organised the show said the army was trying to intimidate and silence those soldiers who gave evidence about brutality in Hebron and to silence any others who planned to give evidence about what they had seen there.
Haaretz, Wednesday 23 June, 2004

Bitter harvest in West Bank's olive groves

Jewish settlers wreck fruit of centuries of toil to force out Palestinian villagers

The annual olive harvest in the occupied territories has once again been rocked by Jewish settlers and their now routine assaults on Palestinian pickers to plunder their crop ...

Armed Israelis are systematically wrecking trees that have stood for hundreds of years and frequently provide the only livelihood for Palestinian families.
Guardian, Friday 14 November, 2003

The Waiting Game[1]

Sunday 19 October 2003, Allenby Bridge

Once again on the bridge. The first time I came here, three years ago, I recognised the wooden structure spanning the Jordan river from films, from photographs. Today I recognise nothing. The wooden bridge has disappeared and we cross the river on a stone and steel road. The Jordan, as far as I can make out, has run dry.

At Israeli immigration there is a queue for Palestinians and a queue for 'others'. My son and I stand with the six 'others': three Frenchmen, two Arab-Americans and a Spaniard. The Spaniard is a long-term resident of Israel. She waves her Spanish passport under my nose: 'Why am I being treated like this?' she demands of me. 'Why do I have to wait? I am not an Arab.' The glassed-off counter is manned by four young Israeli women soldiers. They joke and laugh amongst themselves. They eat. They dress each other's hair. They take three hours to process us.

Our driver, William, has been waiting for us. He is a Christian Jerusalemite. A graduate, trained as a tourist guide, he now he drives a cab because there are no tourists. On the drive to Jerusalem he tells us that his wife is from Bethlehem so under the new Israeli residence laws she is not allowed to live with him in Jerusalem. She lives with him illegally. She works in a travel agency and two or three times a week she gets picked up by the army and he has to go and beg for her release. At the weekend he takes her to Bethlehem to stay with her parents so she can feel 'normal' for a

[1] The *Guardian*, December 2003 published this in a shorter form. The full article appears here.

while. Bethlehem is about fifteen miles from Jerusalem but because they cannot go through the checkpoints they drive through dug-up dirt roads for about three hours each way. Now she's pregnant and long bumpy rides are not a good idea. What will they do? His church allows them a small house but the taxes imposed on it by the Israelis amount to 2,000 dollars a year. Other taxes and compulsory national insurance come up to another 4,000 dollars. That's 6,000 dollars he has to pay the state of Israel whether he works or not. The house next door has been bought by a Jewish neighbour who complains to the police every time William and his wife have a barbecue. The police are Palestinian since this is East Jerusalem. They say, 'Your neighbour's crazy but you'd best not have any more barbecues.' He believes the Israeli policy is to squeeze the Palestinians out of Jerusalem. He says Palestinians whose houses are worth maybe a hundred thousand shekels are offered five million, ten million, and help in getting residence in any country they choose. 'But we're not going,' he says. 'This is my city and there's nowhere else I want to be.'

I thought it was bad three years ago. Now the landscape itself is changed. New settlements spring up everywhere; more than sixty since I was here last. You can watch their metamorphosis from a handful of caravans, to some Porta-kabins, then basic bungalows and, finally, the bristling, concrete hilltop fortress that is an Israeli settlement. Hardly a Palestinian village is allowed to exist, nestled in its gen-erations-old home on the slope of a hill, without an Israeli settlement lowering on it from above. And everywhere there is giant construction going on – illegally: wide, Israeli-only highways to connect the settlements to each other, great mounds of rubble and yellow steel gates to block the old roads between Palestinian villages. And there are people waiting; waiting with bundles, with briefcases, with babies, at gates, at roadblocks, at checkpoints, waiting to perform the most ordinary tasks of their everyday lives.

All this, Israel tells the world, is in the cause of security. And in the cause of security. Israel has started the biggest construction project of all: the giant barrier that it is putting up between itself and the Palestinians; a barrier that does not follow the internationally recognised Green Line but twists and turns to grab yet another tranche of West Bank land.

Jerusalem al-Quds, afternoon

We go for a walk inside the old walls. My son is as taken with this city as I am. But three years ago the Israeli army stayed outside the gates of al-Haram al-Sharif. Today they sit inside the gates in groups of three or four, cradling their guns and checking passports.

As we walk through the quiet of the afternoon in the old rose-coloured streets we see a young Jewish couple walking together chatting and laughing pleasantly. They wear the traditional settler clothes, she with her hair tied up in a modest kerchief, he in white shirt and black waistcoat. And he carries, across his chest, the biggest assault rifle I've ever seen. The children playing on the street don't even look up.

Monday 20 October 2003, Jayyus

On this, our first morning here, we drive up through the West Bank to see Israel's 'security fence'; a monster barrier of steel and concrete that separates farmers from their land and refugees from their hard-earned homes. Brute technology hacking away at a living body of land and people. It rears up into a giant wall to block the sunset and the evening breeze from the people of Qalqilya, then spreads itself out to swallow great stretches of the land cultivated over hundreds of years by the neighbouring villages.

Along the half-constructed barrier we see a cart approaching pulled by a donkey. On it sits Muhammad Abu Khaled. His is one of the families now marooned in South Tulkarem between the security barrier and the Green Line, the area Israeli military edicts call the 'Seam Zone'. Behind him on the cart are piled up a television, some chairs and other household goods. We hail and greet across the barbed wire. We enquire after his family. His wife had fainted when the military order to evacuate the house came through and the family fears she may have suffered a heart attack. He smiles, says all is well and invites us to his home for tea. This is a man who does not have the money to put petrol in his car, who is clearly on his way to try to sell some of his possessions. He is no stranger to hardship and dispossession for he was brought up in Tulkarem as a refugee from 1948 Palestine. He has worked hard all his life and ten years ago was able to buy a few acres of land just outside Tulkarem and build his own family house on his own farmland. He will not leave. It has taken him a lifetime to get here and he is not going to leave.

At Jayyus the Israelis have built the barrier right up close to the Western side of the village. From the windows of the village hall you see it slide down the hill from the left, snake into a huge 'S' and vanish around the farmland to the right: a multi-tasked, fifty- to a hundred-metre wide swath of confiscated Palestinian land, sandwiched between two tall fences of coiled barbed wire. Running along the inside of the barbed wire is a deep trench. There's also a patrol road, a swept sand track to reveal footprints and an electronic fence with hidden cameras. Alongside this barrier at short intervals red signs in Arabic, English and Hebrew threaten that ANY PERSON WHO PASSES OR DAMAGES THE FENCE ENDANGERS HIS LIFE.

You cannot read the signs from here, from this window, but you can see them punctuating the acres that the mayor of this village has spent the last forty years of his life cultivating. From his office window he can watch – on his land on the other side of the barrier – his olive trees waiting to be harvested, his guava trees dropping their ripe fruit on the ground. In each of his three greenhouses, 40,000 kilograms of cucumbers are hardening. From this village of 3,000 souls, 2,300 acres have been confiscated for the barrier. And on the other side of the barrier another 2,150 acres with six ground-water wells are inaccessible, 12,000 olive trees stand unharvested, the vegetables in 120 giant greenhouses are spoiling; 3,500 sheep have been driven off the land – actually, 3,498. Because one man has lost two lambs. Three hundred families are totally dependent on their farms. Now their harvest is rotting before their eyes and they cannot get to it. They are feeding their flocks the husks from last year's planting.

There are yellow steel gates in the barbed wire but they are closed. Farmers are busy making phone calls, some are going to see the Israeli military to demand that the gates be opened. Eventually, soldiers arrive. Harvesting is a family affair so the soldiers face a crowd of men, women and children. What they do is this: first they collect all their identity papers. Then they call the people out one by one. Today they have decided that no male between the ages of twelve and thirty-eight will be allowed on his land. Also, no woman will be allowed unless she is over twenty-eight and married. So the majority of the farmers, men, women and teenagers stand at the gate, the Israeli soldiers and the barrier between them and the harvest that is their sustenance and income for the coming year.

Two men set off to try to find a way of infiltrating their own land. The rest make their way back to the village hall. On the mayor's desk lie some 600 permits that appeared in the village this morning. They are issued by the Israeli authorities and made out to individual farmers. About half of them are in the names of people who can't use them: babies, infants, a couple of men who've been in Australia for fifteen years. But that's not the point. The point is that the people know that if they use these permits they are implicitly accepting their terms: three months' access with no recognition of any rights to the land. They suspect that after three months Israel will start playing games with them, for permits like these were one of the mechanisms by which their parents and grandparents were dispossessed of their own land in '48. What should they do? Use the permits and try to salvage their crops and deal with the rest later? Boycott the permits? And starve?

The mayor is beside himself as he tries to get advice from the governor. One man tells me that his father, who is sixty-five, is talking of buying explosives. 'There will be no life for us anyway without the land,' he says. The fighters and the suicide bombers have generally come from the urban deprivation of the camps. Now they will come from the villages too.

On the drive back to Jerusalem we stop to look at Beit Amin-Azun Atme school. It was built with funding from the World Bank, stands on a hillside and looks well kept and pleasant. The headmistress tells us that the school had started building a toilet facility in its grounds when the settlement of Sharei Tikva was built on the hill overlooking it. The school was then told that for security reasons it could not complete the toilet building. She says the settlers of Sharei Tikva make a point of throwing their rubbish and their sewage down into the school yard.

And everywhere along the West Bank roads we see the names of Arab villages whited out from the road signs.

Jerusalem al-Quds, afternoon

Our friend, Dr Nazmi al-Ju'ba, comes to take us on a tour of the city. We tell him about Jayyus and I say I want to see the barrier in Jerusalem. The barrier built in the Abu Dis district cuts across a main road, turning a busy crossroads into a sudden dead end. It is still in the process of construction and takes the form of concrete blocks about two metres in height placed close together. Nazmi tells us that to walk around it you would have to walk about two kilometres. We watch children coming home from school scramble over it carrying their school bags. My son is taking photographs. Some Israeli soldiers sit at a table in the shadow of a house but they pay no attention. Then an elderly man carrying what is obviously a heavy briefcase starts climbing over. One soldier moves to the barrier, watches the man, and when he has completed his climb down to our side orders him up again. The man opens his briefcase, shows papers, argues. A young woman strides up to the soldiers at the table and demands that they remove other soldiers stationed at the door of her house. An army jeep comes screeching round the corner. It pulls up at the barrier and the Tannoy starts yelling out in Hebrew. We freeze. Its windows are black and we cannot see inside. The tannoy switches to broken Arabic and then to English: 'Come here! Come here!'

My son, who is between me and the jeep starts to walk towards it and I hiss at him: 'Come *here*. Come here *this minute*.' He stops, hesitates, and I move forward to place myself between him and the jeep. The door opens and a young soldier yells at me in broken Arabic. 'English,' I say, 'English.'

He points at my son: 'Come here!'

I grab my son's arm. He is nineteen, about the same age as the soldier. 'This is my son. What do you want?' The world has receded. I see nothing except the jeep. I know nothing except that these soldiers will not so much as touch my boy.

'Your son?'

'Yes. My son.'

'You not speak Arabic?'

'No. Only English.'

I have heard that they take young men away. Beat them up in the backs of jeeps. Drive them round for hours then dump them on some road to get back as best they can. Through the checkpoints.

'What are you doing here?'

'Looking.'

'Looking at what?'

'At this wall.'

'It is forbidden, forbidden—'

He is shouting and there are three more of them inside. I can feel my son brace up for an argument and I pinch his arm tight. I feel that my head is light, as though there were some great empty space inside it, then suddenly, there is a woman between me and the soldiers. I feel a comforting, almost motherly presence. She holds a clipboard, she is elderly and large and she speaks Hebrew to the young soldiers in soft, almost sorrowing tones. And she squarely blocks their view of us. They answer her truculently and she keeps up her sad reproach. Eventually they concede: 'You can go.' She takes my arm and leads me away to where her companion, another woman is standing. They both wear the uniform of activist women everywhere: the long floral skirt, the loose tunic top, the scarves. They are from Mahsomwatch, the organisation of Israeli women who try to monitor the barriers, the checkpoints. I tell her I'm writing about the situation and she gives me a copy of a very recent military order and begs me to get it published. It is the order on which the land permits we had seen at Jayyus are based. It states that the people who have the right to be in the Seam Zone without permits are Israelis or anyone who can come to Israel under the Law of Return. That is, any Jewish person from anywhere in the world. But in the Jayyus district alone Muhammad Abu Khaled and 11,550 Palestinians have their homes in the Seam Zone and now, it seems, they have no right to be there. 'It is Nuremberg all over again,' she says.

As we leave the area, Nazmi, who has been watching everything in an amused kind of way, says, 'You were scared.'

'Of course I was,' I say. In fact my legs are still trembling.

'If you were a Palestinian mother,' he laughs, 'you'd have been at their throats.'

Tuesday 21 October 2003, Jerusalem al-Quds

Our taxi driver says: 'The Israelis are clever. They build the wall and now everybody is talking about the wall. The wall is just a wall. It was built and it can be removed. The real questions are the borders, the settlements, Jerusalem and the refugees.'

My old friend, Albert Agazerian, says the situation is much worse than three years ago. We walk through the Armenian convent where he lives and I pick a tiny twig from the ancient olive tree in the grounds. He knows this city stone by stone. In the narrow alleyways he shows us houses where a sliver of stone has been hacked out of the top right-hand corner of the doorway. 'They come round in the night', he says, 'and chip a bit off the doorway. Then they claim there used to be a mizuza here and that makes it a Jewish house. Here,' he says, stopping by a stone doorway: 'this is the Qattan family house. It's been in the family for hundreds of years and suddenly there's this small chip in the top right-hand corner of the doorway. It's slight and maybe no one would notice it – but you should hear the Israeli tour guides telling the tourists that these chips mean that this was a Jewish house before it was taken over.' We turn a corner and I see a shop with a signpost that says 'The Third Temple'. Inside, there's an architectural model of the project for the Third Temple, literature, and boxes for donations.

The last time I was here the imam of the Dome of the Rock prayed for the safety of the Dome and al-Aqsa mosque. Today I know that the Christian right in the United States believe that the Second Coming cannot take place until the Third Temple of the Jews has been built on the ruins of al-Aqsa. It is their ambition that the Second Coming should happen in their lifetime. They form 18 per cent of the electorate in the US.

In al-Haram al-Sharif Israeli settlers are wandering around guarded by Israeli soldiers. The caretakers of the al-Aqsa and the Dome of the Rock have closed the doors to the buildings but they throw them open for Albert, the 'Professor', their Christian friend, and we go in and chat to the Egyptian restorers who are working on the decorations on the ceiling and pillars of al-Aqsa.

When we stop by the Church of the Holy Sepulchre we bump into another of Albert's friends: Dr Nuseibeh. The Church of the Holy Sepulchre is home to practically every

Christian denomination in the world. Hundreds of years ago, when the different denominations could not agree which one should have the supreme honour of holding the keys to the church and acting as its caretaker, they decided to ask a notable Muslim family, the Nuseibehs, to perform this task. Since then, the head of the Nuseibeh family acts as caretaker for the church. When we meet Dr Nuseibeh he is supervising the cleaning and arranging to receive the Patriarch's procession.

We climb some stairs and find ourselves in a courtyard above the city. From here we look down on the Wailing Wall and, beyond it, the golden Dome of the Rock. We can see over the rooftops of the houses of the old city. Where settlers have taken over a house they put wire fences round the roof, bar the windows and fly the Israeli flag.

Wednesday 22 October 2003, Bethlehem

It is Ramadan and less than two months to Christmas and the streets of Bethlehem are empty. There are no tourists, no pilgrims. On Star Street many of the shops are closed. The market where the neighbouring villages brought their produce to feed the town is deserted. The closures imposed by the Israeli army mean that farmers cannot come into Bethlehem and Bethlehemites cannot leave the town. The 'Monument to Peace' built to celebrate Bethlehem 2000 has been demolished by Israeli tanks. The International Peace Centre – built on land where Turkish, then British, then Jordanian police stations each stood in turn – was used by the Israeli army as its headquarters when it besieged the Church of the Nativity. 'They put up a crane with a box on top—' Yes, we saw it on television – 'with lights and a camera and an automatic sniper. And recordings. They played terrible sounds: explosions, animals, people screaming. All the time. Into the church.'

In the church today, an old priest dozes on a chair. Two Franciscan monks are silently busy about the Armenian altar. A young man – one of the beseiged 'gunmen' –

explains the Tree of Life mosaic to a group of schoolgirls, three young women in hijab sit in a pew reading. And Christ and the Madonna observe us from the walls.

Images of Mariam, the Jewish Arab girl chosen to bear the Saviour are everywhere in this town. Her head inclines sympathetically: a modest blessing. She lifts her hands in benediction above the courtyard of the Latin chapel in the Church of the Nativity. The Israeli soldiers shot her several times during the seige of the church – in fact they shot her everywhere they could find her – but she still stands, serene in her sorrow, the bullet holes adding poignancy to her almost unbearable grace.

Bethlehem keeps tapping you on the shoulder, gently directing your gaze. The symbolism never lets up.

Under the church, there is a whole structure of inter-connecting spaces: the small room where the young woman retreated to give birth in privacy, the alcove where she first laid her baby, the passage and the flight of steps she must have climbed, her child concealed under her cloak, to begin her flight into Egypt. And the crypt where, many years later, it is said that Saint Jerome completed the first Arabic translation of the Bible. On a corner near the ceiling some-one has chiselled out, patiently, in beautiful calligraphy, in Arabic and Latin: *al-majd laki ya Mariam ya mali'atan bil-ni'ma*, AVE MARIA GRATIA PLENA.

During the seige the young Palestinian fighters respected the priests' request that they not enter the holy grotto. They used one isolated crypt to store the bodies of their comrades picked off by the snipers; it was the crypt into which Herod's soldiers are said to have thrown the bodies of the slaughtered innocents.

The Israelis use Russian snipers now. They were hardened in Chechnya and are said to be more patient.

The settlements of Gilo, Har Gilo and Har Homa (Jebel Ghunaim) surround the city. Israel's military edicts are doing their best to strangle her. But Bethlehem will not lie down and die. The Peace Centre hosts an exhibition of

Nativity scenes sent in by schools from all over the world. Al-Nadwa, a new cultural centre, is buzzing with activity. The staff there are young and dedicated. Headed by the soft-spoken Reverend Dr Mitri al-Raheb, a gentle and impressive man, fluent in many languages with a beautiful and stylish wife, they run an exhibition space currently featuring a Norwegian artist, a gift shop which sells its merchandise on the Internet, a workshop where I counted twenty young men and women working on glass, pottery and ceramics, a state-of-the-art media centre and a theatre. A few days ago an Austrian chamber-music quartet was supposed to play here but the Israelis kept them overnight at the border then shipped them home because they refused to sign an undertaking that they would not go to Bethlehem. Today Mitri al-Raheb has been refused a permit to travel to a church meeting in Washington, DC.

Every road out of Bethlehem is blocked by mounds of dirt and a checkpoint. Imagine driving along as you've always done, between Hampstead, say, and Regent's Park, when you come upon a barrier of earth thrown up last night. Soldiers stand at the barrier in full battle gear, yelling at you in a strange language or a pidgin version of your own. They tell you to get out of your car; you're not allowed to drive here any more. If you're allowed to carry on you will do so on foot. They yell at you to line up and they take their time checking your papers, questioning you: Where are you going? Why do you want to go there? Prove to me that your daughter/best friend/dentist/music teacher lives there. A few yards away you can see the new highway that cuts across your old road. Cars are speeding along on it, driven by men and women of that other people, the people that the soldiers belong to.

An elderly French photographer is with us. He carries a battery of cameras and takes a photograph of every sheep we come across. He's not interested in shelled buidings or barriers or queues of people. When we come upon a young boy riding a donkey his face lights up and he lets out a sigh of pleasure as he adjusts his zoom.

We stand at one of the checkpoints, my son taking photographs of the pedestrians waiting to be allowed to walk to the next village. Two soldiers leave the checkpoint and stride towards us, raising their M16s to the level of our heads and shouting: 'No photographs! Give me your camera. You! No photos.'

An old hand now I am not so scared.

'Where's the notice that says no photography?' we call.

'Everyone knows. Give me the camera. I can shoot you. You take photo of me—'

'We took photos of the people waiting.'

'You took photo of me. I can shoot you—'

'I did not take photo. I think it is not allowed,' the French photographer says, *sotto voce*, to the soldier.

'Give me the camera—'

'What's the problem? Are you ashamed of what you're doing? Show me the paper that says we can't take photos.' This is Tony, our Palestinian guide. He's a film editor with an international press agency and has a US passport.

'I don't need no fucking paper. I can shoot you, that's my paper.'

'Show me the paper.'

'This is Israel, I do what I like. I can shoot you. Here I do what I like.'

'This isn't Israel. This is the West Bank.'

'West Bank? What is this West Bank?' The soldier turns to his friend questioningly.

My son starts speaking but I stamp on his foot; more testosterone we do not need.

'Look: in there, is Palestine. You do what you want. Here is Israel. In your country can you take pictures of secret soldiers?'

After a bit more of this Tony gets out his mobile and phones the army. The soldiers take off their shades and turn into unhappy young men: 'You think I like to do this? You think I like to stand all day wearing this, and this, and this? This I have to do so my mother is safe in Tel Aviv—'

We suggest it might be a happier situation all round if they did this on the Green Line.

'Green Line? They can creep under the Green Line. Look: we give them everything. They always want more. We give them land, we give them water, we give them electricity. They want more—'

'But you are stealing these people's land. What about the settlements?'

'That is for the politicians. We don't know about that. It is the politicians.'

They go back to the checkpoint. We keep the camera. Tony has to take our photos to the army censor for clearance within forty-eight hours.

Tony is the angriest Palestinian we meet on this visit. It's odd, because you can see that under this explosive anger he's a mild, thoughtful kind of person. He is deeply rooted in Bethlehem. His family's business is on Star Street, close to Manger Square. Four years ago he and his father pooled their savings and built a lovely, spacious family home on five floors: one each for Tony and his three sisters, the parents at the top. He is married to a diaspora Palestinian who has came back from Europe to live with him in Bethlehem. Two weeks ago his first child was born. I think that's what is making him angry; thinking about what kind of life his child will have here. Whether he should stay. Whether he can bear to leave.

On the walls in the street a poster of Edward Said has taken its place alongside the ones of Christine Sa'da, the ten-year-old girl shot in her father's car in March, and Abed Ismail, the eleven-year-old boy killed by a sniper in Manger Square.

Thursday 23 October 2003, Bethlehem

The atmosphere in Bethlehem University is happy and busy. The university is celebrating its thirtieth anniversary. Yesterday they held the annual elections for the student union and the posters are still everywhere. They have more girls than boys, facilities for the handicapped, and a number of mature students. They point out one of their stars: an older woman in a hijab, a mother of five who took her high-school exams and came out tenth in the province and is now studying English. They're very keen on languages and when we sit down to have a discussion they insist we do it in English.

Parts of the buildings have been shelled by the Israeli army. The university has carried out repairs but in the library and in two classrooms they have kept the holes made by the shells, covered them with glass and labelled them.

The main security concern of the staff is that many of their 2,000 students come from towns and villages around Bethlehem. The access roads between Bethlehem and its satellites are now all closed and manned by Israeli soldiers. Only one road is open for vehicles and no private cars or taxis are allowed on to it. University buses are often kept waiting at the checkpoint. They tell us that the previous night a bus taking students home had been kept at the checkpoint for two hours. They also tell us about female students being strip-searched at checkpoint while their male colleagues are made to watch and needled for comments.

'They're trying to divide between Christians and Muslims,' one young woman tells us. 'We were in the bus the other day at the checkpoint and they made us all get out. They took our identity cards and found that one girl was a Christian. "You go over there and sit in the shade," they told her. As for us they made us stand in the sun for two hours. When we got back on the bus she was weeping with embarrassment.'

But even though most of the students have to brave the checkpoints to come in, attendance, they tell me, is 100 per cent. We are served lunch by the young men and women in the hotels and tourism department, a department which became very popular as Bethlehem prepared to receive the world on the eve of the millenium.

'Look at it! Look at it!' The arc of Tony's arm yesterday

had taken in the brand-new conference centre completed in 2000 and shelled by the Israelis a few months later. The large hotel and leisure complex set up next to Solomon's Pools and also shelled by the Israelis. And then the Wall. Here it comes. Creeping up on the west of Bethlehem . . .

Saturday 25 October 2003, Birzeit

Three years ago Birzeit University was twenty minutes' drive from Ramallah. Now, on a good day, it takes over an hour to get there. The Israeli army has blocked the road at Surda and though today the checkpoint is not manned people have to get out of their transport and climb on foot over the rubble. I'm told that anyone attempting to remove rubble is shot at and that it is replenished from time to time by the army.

We climb over and proceed on foot for one kilometre till the next roadblock. Alongside the road a market has sprung up; stalls selling food, drinks and housewares. There are horses and donkeys for hire, mule-drawn carriages and small carts pushed by men. There are also some young volunteers from Dr Mustafa Bafghouti's NGO with wheelchairs for the infirm and elderly.

We walk along in the crush and I'm thinking of how one of the tasks of the occupation is to push people into more and more primitive conditions, but I am also thinking that this doesn't really matter, that it's manageable, that it's not the worst thing that can happen. Then I hear a low but spreading murmur: 'They've come, they've come' – and through the murmur the rasp of incomprehensible commands. The car is squat and broad and its windows are, as usual, completely black. It moves in jagged, erratic bursts among the crowd. People step quietly out of the way but no one looks up. This, in general, is how the people treat the Israeli army: by ignoring it as much as possible. But I can feel in my stomach and my spine that the Humvee is here to show us all who is master, who runs this road.

Getting to class here is an act of resistance and at the

university the Kamal Nasser Auditorium is full. No one wants to talk about the occupation. For three hours, these students and their teachers want to talk literature, theatre, music. And they want to do it in English.

But over lunch they tell me that earlier in the day the Humvee had parked across the university gates and the Tannoy had sputtered insults. 'Provocation. They provoke the students and hope one of them throws something, then they can begin to shoot.' One young man tells me that a few days before, when the checkpoint was manned, he'd been among some 200 students the soldiers had detained there. Eventually, as the students protested about being made late for class, one soldier had a bright idea: every young man who had gel in his hair could go through, he said. 'Today,' he said, 'gel will buy you an education.'

And yet I do not feel that the Palestinians hate the Israeli soldiers. It is more that they hold them in contempt: a bunch of kids hiding behind their weaponry and amusing themselves by playing dirty games with civilians. People point to differences in Israeli reservists, who 'on the whole aren't interested in being nasty. They just want to finish their time and leave.' I find I begin to tell the difference: something about the absence of swagger. That they don't always have their shades on. That they permit themselves small acts of kindness; when the crowd at Kalandia checkpoint passed a baby's buggy over their heads to allow the young mother to get to the front of the line, it was the young reservist who received the buggy at the end and set it down on the ground.

Sunday 26 October 2003, al-Khalil

The old town is still under curfew. Three years ago the Israeli army had taken over the city bus stop and the market. The market had moved into the main square of the modern part of the city. Now the army has emptied this too. The square is derelict, but the streets leading away from it are bursting with stalls, pedestrians and cars. A group of young men and boys stand about in the square. It is three o'clock.

Their homes are a couple of hundred steps up Shuhada Street but they're not allowed to go there because that's in the old city and the old city is under curfew. I can't see soldiers but a man tells me they're always watching. 'They'll drive up. You'll see,' he says. He says the soldiers tell them to just stand and wait: 'They say maybe we'll let you through at six o'clock.' He shows me his ID. He is a brigadier with the Palestinian police. He believes that adds to the Israeli soldiers' pleasure in humiliating him. His wife is Egyptian. She too has to run the curfew every day to get to work and back. Yesterday the soldiers had insulted her.

As we stand in the square the Israeli jeep screeches up. The usual black windows, the usual distorted voice through the Tannoy rasping out commands in barely intelligible Arabic: 'Come here! Come here!'

But who? Me? Him? Who? What's supposed to happen is that everybody approaches the jeep and then the soldiers open one of the doors and select the people they want to talk to. My son and I just stand there. The Palestinians approach the jeep demanding to be allowed to go home. Naji Da'na, the Palestinian photographer who is with us, lifts his video camera to his shoulder and begins shooting. Three years ago, as I stood on this spot being prevented by my driver and guide from going into the old city, a tall man had appeared at my side. He wore a grey cashmere overcoat and was obviously a figure of authority. People came up and greeted him and exchanged news. He shamed the men into driving me into the city by a back road. They told me his name was Mazin Da'na, a Palestinian photographer working with Reuters and seriously targeted by the Israelis. He was killed last June in Baghdad by an American soldier who said he'd mistaken his camera for a gun. Naji Da'na is his nephew. And he goes on filming the Israeli jeep as the soldiers close the doors and burn rubber away from us, hit the brakes, open the back doors, give us all the finger, then swerve to come round at us again. The Palestinian brigadier tells us to leave. 'This is when trouble starts,' he says. 'They'll carry on provoking these kids till one of them picks up a stone and throws it then they'll start shooting.'

Up, through the back roads, just like last time, breaking the curfew, no grown-ups on the streets, but kids everywhere, watching, playing, waving at us. Around one corner we come upon a company of Israeli soldiers sitting around on small camp stools by their jeep but they are so bored and dispirited they hardly glance at us. I am trying to locate the home of Hajj Ahmad al-Ja'bari whom I had met last time and – with the help of the kids on the street – I succeed. We show up on the man's doorstep: me, my son, my guide and driver, Naji Da'na and an Italian photographer. He clearly doesn't remember me but we proclaim ourselves guests and he lets us into his terraced garden, dusts off some chairs and asks his wife for tea. My son is wearing an England Rugby shirt with an O_2 sponsorship logo. A child points at the O_2: 'I know what that means, it means water.' They get to talking about rugby.

I ask Hajj Ja'bari how it goes. 'Anfas ma'douda fi amakin mahdouda', he says: a finite number of breaths in a limited number of places. He smiles: do we possess anything else? Yes, the Israeli observation point or sniper nest or whatever is on the roof next to his (indeed we can see it as we speak and I move a little into the shadow of the wall); yes, his passage into the Ibrahimi Sanctuary is still sealed off; yes, the Israelis came round and made everyone wear numbers on their chests and took photographs of them; yes, they are trying to strangle the city with curfews and closures and threatened demolitions. But the city finds ways of surviving, of fighting back. I show him a page in the dissident Israeli magazine, *News from Within*. It is a statement by the old Jewish families of al-Khalil dissociating themselves from the armed and militant settlers now occupying the heart of the old city.

'It's a known thing,' he says, 'they were our neighbours, our people. These settlers come from foreign lands.'

Sometimes, he says, on his walks, he sees young men rounded up by the Israeli soldiers. He stops to watch. 'What are you doing?' the soldiers ask. 'Watching,' he says. 'Do you like what you see?' they ask. 'No,' he says, 'I don't like it one bit.' The young Palestinians ask him to leave: 'Go home, father. We'll deal with it—'

Suddenly the tears are streaming down my face. I cannot breathe. 'Tear gas,' someone says and our host goes into his kitchen and comes back with a few small onions and a knife. He hands each one of us half an onion which we press to our noses. Whoever would have thought that onions can combat tear gas? Outside the kids seem unaffected, they have no need of onions as they cheerily wave us goodbye.

Monday 27 October 2003, Nablus

The driver taking us to Nablus is a Jew. An Arab Jew, a 'Samarian Jew', he tells me. His family have lived for generations in Jebel Jizzeen, the Holy Mountain. He can drive on the Israeli-only roads which makes our journey much quicker. He talks about the similarities between Judaism and Islam and ends up inviting us to his home where he shows us photographs of their latest harvest festival with himself dressed in his traditional costume: the costume of a Syrian farmer of the nineteenth century. His daughter tells us she studies at Nablus University. His mother looks familiar; I realise she looks like the photo of a friend and neighbour of my grandmother's in Cairo. And because this is the first day of Ramadan his wife gives us chocolates to take away with us and eat when we've broken our fast.

The University of Nablus has some 12,000 students, who mostly come from the surrounding towns and villages. Nablus is suffering from practically complete closure and movement has become so difficult that a large number of the students have moved into Nablus itself. Neither the university nor the city has the facilities to support them. They are living in hardship, compounded by the fact that they come from rural families already suffering from the effects of the closures and of the barrier and in no position to take on the added expense of a child living away from home. The women students are less likely to leave home and move into the city. The university provides buses for them. We were told of the many harassments they suffer at the checkpoints. They tell us that a few nights earlier the young women had been kept at the checkpoint till almost midnight then driven to a remote area and told to find their own way home. They had knocked on the doors of the nearest village and asked for shelter.

We go into a photographic exhibition set up by the students. Picture upon picture of young men blindfolded, wrists bound behind their backs. Shaheeds, funerals and demolished houses. Yet the place is buzzing with vitality and every single computer terminal in the large main hall of the library has a young person sitting at it busily working.

Tuesday 28 October 2003, Jerusalem al-Quds

Daphna Golan teaches Human Rights at the Hebrew University. She takes her students out to the 'field', the West Bank, to research specific topics. The right to education, for example. Today they have been south of al-Khalil. The settlers there have been terrorising children on their way to and from school. The kids' journey should take twenty minutes but to avoid the settlers they go by back routes which take them two hours. I ask how old the children are. 'Seven or eight. Today they went the short way because we were with them and the settlers could not harm them, but we could see that the children were very, very frightened.' I ask how the settlers terrorise them. 'They beat them. And they are armed. It is very strange,' she says. 'You know, these are not the settlers that you imagine. These are young people like hippies. Long hair, bright clothes, rasta hats. They grow organic vegetables. They carry their guitars and their guns and they are vicious.'

I ask her about the refuseniks, about the Israeli pilots who are refusing to drop bombs on West Bank cities. They are important, she agrees, but not important enough. Most of Israeli society cannot accept that what the army is doing is wrong. 'You raise your son and he is a fine young man and he is in the military. How are you going to believe that he is doing bad things?'

'What about the barrier?'

'Most people believe it's wrong.'

'But they're not out there stopping it.'

'No.'

She used to work in South Africa and believes that one day Israel will have to confront what it did to the Palestinians in 1948 and apologise for it.

'But it's happening again now?'

'Yes.' If she could she would just say 'Stop. Stop everything now, just for a while. And let us think.'

Chico Behar is a Jewish Israeli activist. He tells me of the danger and subterfuge involved in meeting his Palestinian comrades. He tells me he believes an essential purpose of the checkpoints and the barrier is to prevent ordinary Palestinians and Israelis from meeting lest they discover that they can actually live together.

How many stories can I tell? How many can you read? In the end they all point in the same direction; every Palestinian I meet (and many Israelis) tells me the same thing: What Israel wants is a Palestine as free of Arabs as possible. The settlers, when they properly understood the function of the 'Security Wall', demanded that it should secure the largest possible area of land with the smallest possible number of Arabs. They are planning to expand within this land. The illegal settlement of Zufim, for example, is planning to expand on land to be confiscated from Qalqilya and Tulkarem. It advertises on the Net its intention to grow from 190 families to 2,000 families and offers 'mortgages with grants and special loans' (www.tehilla.com/haut/bayit/List%20of%20Communities/zufim/htm). Meanwhile Israeli ministers accept that settlements are illegal but say that as long as Israeli citizens are out there they are entitled to services provided by the state.

This is the big push; the second instalment of 1948. Israeli policies are designed to make life unbearable so that every Palestinian who has a choice will go. The ones left behind – the ones with no options – will be a captive population, severed from their land, from their community, caged behind barriers, walls and gates. This is the labour that will work in the industrial zones Israel is already building near the barrier.

The Palestinians describe what is happening as ethnic cleansing. They also say that they have lived through 1948 and have learned its lessons: there is no way they are leaving.

Nazmi al-Ju'ba has the optimistic job of restoring old Arab architecture in Palestine. 'The Palestinians have many options,' he tells me: 'we can live in a bi-national state, we can live in a Palestinian state, we can live under occupation – but we will live in any case. And we will live as a collective; as a Palestinian nation.'

What hurts people most is the Arab governments. 'OK, Israel is the enemy,' the people say. 'What Sharon does doesn't surprise us. But the Arabs? They know and see what's happening and they are silent. What will it take for them to take a stand? And they fill their televisions with game shows, with singing and dancing. What do they have to sing and dance about?' When I say something about the Arab people I am told that the Arab people will have to change their governments.

Four weeks later

The farmers in Jayyus took the permits. Finally, they could not bear to watch their harvest die. And then the games began. Abdullatif Khaled, the engineer who runs the Emergency Centre at Jayyus, tells me he has just come back from a smallholding owned by four brothers. They are struggling to feed their flock of 150 sheep. Since the beginning of November they, like all the other farmers, have been dividing a day's food over five days. They are trying to slow down the process of starvation. Some of their ewes have miscarried and some of their lambs have died. They drive their sheep to the yellow steel gate in the barrier. They have their permits and the Israeli soldiers have no problem letting them through to their pasture. But they refuse to let in the sheep. They have no orders, they say, to let in sheep.

Khalid says that all the sheep owned by the village are going to starve, while their pastures lie across the Israeli security barrier. 'Can somebody intervene here?' he asks. 'You know when birds get stuck in oil slicks or whales get beached, everybody rushes to help them. Maybe helping the Palestinians is complicated. But the world could help the sheep. That should be simple.'

Shock new details of torture by US troops

Report tells how prisoners were threatened with rape

Chilling new evidence of torture and sexual abuse of Iraqi prisoners by American soldiers emerged last night ... Detainees were subjected to 'sadistic, blatant and wanton criminal abuses', according to a military investigation suggesting that last week's photographs of soldiers humiliating their captives may have been the tip of the iceberg.
Observer, Sunday 2 May, 2004

www.newsmax.com reported on Monday 24 May 2004 that it was believed that Israeli agents were involved in Abu Ghraib.

This Torture Started at the Top[1]

A man stands on an upturned box in a tattered black robe, his head hooded, his outstretched hands attached to wires. He triggers thoughts of the crucifixion, of lynchings and the Ku Klux Klan. Muscled, naked men stand in a line, a young woman in military uniform points at their penises, does a thumbs-up and laughs. More naked men are piled into a kind of collapsed scrum and again young women soldiers point and laugh. One man has the word 'raped' written across his buttocks. Apparently there are hundreds of similar images that have not been published: the American army in Iraq.

The images that these powerless naked bodies brought immediately to my mind were the images from the Nazi camps: groups of naked, Semitic people controlled by a small number of clothed and armed whites. There are differences: the Jews in the Nazi pictures are starved, emaciated; they have been in the camps for a while. The Iraqis are still well built; they are new to this torment. The Jews in the Nazi pictures look at the camera, make eye contact with the viewer, send their message of challenge, resilience or re-proach onward through the ages. The Iraqis are hooded, bagged. There will be some excuse about the dignity of the prisoner requiring his face to be hidden. But this is a joke. It was not the dignity of the prisoners that was being preserved in these photos. The hoods were ensuring that each man was isolated from his companions, that he suffered alone although the flesh of others was an instrument in his suffer-ing, that his individual humanity was denied and that he

[1] The *Guardian*, 5 May 2004 published this in a shorter form. The full article appears here.

was unable to identify his tormentors. We know what the Nazis thought of the Jews and what they planned for them. What do these pictures tell us of what the Americans think of the Iraqis? And how does that square with their declared purpose for being in their country? I have not come across photos of SS women officers laughing and pointing at Jewish genitals.

The media in this country is politely shocked. BBC1's newscaster (10 p.m., 29 April) says the pictures seem to have been 'merely mementoes'. That's all right then. The folks back home will not presumably ask their children/husbands/sisters what the hell they were doing in those pictures. They'll just have a good laugh and paste them into the family album. Where's the harm in that?

These pictures do have a pedigree, though. Their ancestors are to be found, for example, in the postcards sent home by the French from Algeria and Morocco in the first half of the twentieth century; photographs of prostitutes posing sullenly with bared breasts and skirts pulled up to their thighs, over captions like '*Le Harem Arabe*' or '*Fille Mauresque*'. The Americans have simply pushed it further, done one better: their pornography of occupation is at once more childish, playful, crude and sinister than that of old Europe. Also, we assume the prostitutes were paid.

BBC commentators and British politicians have also been reminding us that the soldiers' activities 'do not compare with Saddam Hussein's systematic tortures and executions' – a statement which draws the very comparison it pretends to deny. The greatest democracy of our world is being compared with the tyrant it invaded Iraq to overthrow. Saddam Hussein is now their moral compass. But Saddam Hussein never claimed to believe in democracy or human rights; he was a home-grown despot who used torture and murder to break people's will, to force them to cooperate with his regime, to ensure that he stayed in power. The Americans, on the other hand, would have us believe that they sent their troops across the seas to rid the world of his evil. What is their reason for using torture, humiliation, rape and murder on the people they are in the process of liberating? I remember one Iraqi saying that Saddam Hussein was a bad man but if you left him alone he left you alone. Iraq's citizens have no way of leaving these occupying forces alone: the soldiers patrol their streets, stop them at checkpoints, break down their front doors.

The media are fearful that these images will go down badly in the Arab world because 'they show Muslim men being humiliated by American women'. Again the not-so-subtle reduction of the Arab world to an entity that reacts only to religious prodding. Iraq has a large Christian community, and some Iraqi Jews continue to live in their homeland. How do we even know that all the men in the pictures are Muslims? The photographs have gone down badly in the Arab world because they confirm people's belief that the US and Britain are not there as an act of goodwill towards the Iraqis, and because it strengthens their suspicion that there is a deep racism underlying the occupiers' attitudes to Arabs, Muslims and people of the Third World generally.

It was only a matter of time. Over the last year the world has seen photographs of many Iraqis, stripped and with their wrists tied behind their backs with plastic cord. At first we could look into their eyes and bear witness to what was happening to them. Then they were bagged. At no point was there an outcry. We have grown used to seeing Arab men bound and hooded: in the occupied Palestinian territories and Gaza. Israel advises the US on how to control civilian populations and interrogate them. Ariel Sharon has made the Israeli army's rules of engagement available to the US military. The world notes the similarity between the practices of the US army in Iraq and those of the Israeli army in Palestine. There is evidence that scenes like the ones shocking the world today have been common occurrences in Israel's 'Facility 1391' (some say in other jails too) for a long time. We just haven't seen the photos.

It is no use for American spokesmen to talk about 'rogue elements' and how 'contractors' are not answerable to the military and how Army Reserve Staff Sergeant Chip Frederick had not been given the opportunity to read the Geneva conventions before he was put in charge of prisoners at Abu Ghraib. As though torturing people is what comes naturally to human beings unless they're informed that it's illegal. This abuse is going to turn out to be widespread. Amnesty International has already said it is systemic.

The acts in the photos being flashed across the networks would not have taken place but for the profound racism that infects the American and the British establishments' worldview. There have been reports of the troops outside Falluja talking of the fun of being a sniper, of the different ways to kill people, of the 'rats' nest' in the city that needs cleaning out. Well, soldiers will be soldiers, we might say. But that language has been used by Neo-cons at the heart of the US administration; both Kenneth Adelman and Paul Wolfowitz have spoken of 'snakes' and 'draining the swamps' in the 'uncivilised parts of the world'. It is implicit in the US administration's position that anyone who does not agree that all of history has been moving towards a glorious pinnacle expressed in the American political, ideological and economic system has 'rejected modernity'. That it is America's mission to civilise and punish.

I've seen a photograph of a young American soldier with two Iraqi boys. There is no nakedness or torture but it is no less nasty for that. The boys are holding up a cardboard sign. They and the soldier are smiling and doing a thumbs-up. He is pointing at the cardboard sign where he's written 'Lcpl Boudreaux killed my Dad. then he knocked up my sister!' Imagine the scene: Lcpl Boudreaux, a soldier on a liberating, civilising mission, asks the natives to pose for a 'memento'. They agree. He gives them the sign to hold. What was the lie he told them about what was written on it? 'Iraq is liberated'? 'Mission accomplished'? And who, in this scene, is the more civilised?

The one good thing in all of this is that there are soldiers in the US and British armies who could not live with what was happening and who blew the whistle. The world needs to see the photographs coming out of Iraq not as 'deviant' but as an authentic message from the heart of the thought system that is seeking to control our planet.

LITERATURE, CULTURE AND POLITICS

The Circus Comes to Town[1]

It is just after the fourth prayers of the day: the Sunset Prayers. As the men file out from the mosque to walk in small groups down the dusty lane, the loudspeaker on top of the stubby minaret starts summoning them back:

'O Citizens! Inhabitants of the Village of Zenein! Come to Your Mosque! A Religious Lecture of Import to You All. All Ladies Welcome. Ladies Particularly Welcome. There Will Be No Entrance Fee. No Tax. And No Collection of Any Type Whatever. A Valuable Free Gift for Everyone. Come to Your Mosque Now! All Ladies Welcome! We Particularly Ask the Ladies . . .' The Family-Planning Circus Has Come to Town.

It is a major coup on the part of the organiser of this event to be able to call his rally a 'religious lecture'. He has achieved this by discovering and roping in a rare imam who believes in – and is prepared to speak out in favour of – contraception. The promise of a religious lecture does not, as one might expect (as I expected, standing outside the mosque attracting hordes of small children repeatedly eliciting proof that I was indeed Egyptian), frighten people away; it actually pulls them in as nothing else would, except perhaps the promise of a free meal or clothing. But then they would suspect a trick. In religion there are no tricks. And so they flock to the mosque.

Family planning is the major social cause being campaigned for in Egypt today. To know the reason you don't need to read the statistics; you can see them at dawn queuing by the hundred outside unfriendly Arab embassies hoping

[1] The *Observer*, 28 June 1981.

for a contract; prowling the streets of downtown Cairo on Thursday night on the lookout for some action; squeezing like toothpaste out of the doors of weary, lopsided buses; spilling out of the windows of a university built in 1925 to house 6,000 and now holding 80,000 students.

With forty-two million people popping out a new baby every twenty seconds without fail, overpopulation is the single greatest threat to any hopes Egypt might have of actualising President Anwar Sadat's much publicised 'Age of Prosperity'. Sadat has repeatedly and rhetorically promised the parched populace of Egypt the 'Luxuries of Life'. He has committed himself, not to comforting vaguenesses, but to refrigerators and running hot water for everyone. But the millions who simmer behind the chic façades of modern Cairo, who occasionally erupt through the cracks in these façades, and who have so far been bludgeoned back in by the illiterate might of the Central Security Forces, are as far away from anything approaching the 'Age of Prosperity' as it is possible for human beings to be. They live twelve to a room, they eat stale bread, and they breed.

And herein lies the problem. The present government has flung open the doors of emigration, has even dangled financial carrots to encourage people to emigrate. But essentially, it must stop the breeding. And so the First Lady and various society ladies devote much of their time to the campaign. And so also, Western powers, anxious to consolidate what they see as a pro-Western, stabilising regime in the volatile Middle East, vie with one another to give funds, technical advice and contraceptives to the campaign. At least four major international agencies are currently financing a dozen separate projects with a strong family-planning element. Of course this is not done completely in a spirit of global altruism, but then the most dependable motives are, perhaps, selfish ones.

Foreign aid to developing countries almost always falls into the following structure: a certain sum of money is allotted to an area of interest (e.g., family planning). A foreign aid officer is in charge of this money, and various projects are presented to him. He allocates funds to projects he sees as viable. The spending of these funds is then in the hands of the local project boss. Except that where foreign goods or expertise are needed, they must be imported from the funding country. So, for example, the American AID (Agency for International Development) will fund only American consultants, American goods, etc. Thus a large chunk of AID money is fed back into the economy of the United States. The Big White Chiefs have helped the Natives. The natives have got their AID buses (soon to become lopsided), and the Big White Bus-Makers have made their Profits. Everybody is Happy.

But does it work? If it does, then it does so against the odds; for this microcosm is riddled with problems at every level: the unrealness of the *khawaga* – the foreigner – to the Egyptian peasant; the primness and rigidity of the central administration; the poverty and corruptibility of the infrastructure; and, finally, the psyche and the traditions of the 'target', the Egyptian poor.

General opinion is that the most powerful factor working against family planning in Egypt is religion. But the position of Islam on contraception can hardly be described as rigid. Quotes from the Qur'ān and the Hadith are used to argue both sides of the question. On the one hand God urges the faithful to 'increase and multiply' for the greater strength of the Islamic Nation. On the other, this very multiplication can be seen as weakening and the Prophet declares that 'a strong Muslim is more pleasing to God than a weak one'.

Muhammad also advised a man who came to him complaining that his wife's health was suffering from childbearing, to 'withdraw' from her. The possible interpretation of this advice as 'to keep himself from her completely' has largely been rejected as inconsistent with the Prophet's humane (some would say soft) attitude towards women and conjugal relations. The common interpretation, therefore, is that the man was permitted, even urged, to use withdrawal as a contraceptive technique. So, say the proponents of family planning, some contraception is allowed, why not use modern techniques? After all, were they not discovered by science, which Islam approves of? And, to crown the argument, could they have been discovered at all if God had not wished it?

At the root of the resistance, most often formulated in phrases like 'it is the will of God' and 'God will provide' is not, however, any structured theological attitude, but more the powerful and deep-seated sense of fatalism apparently inherent in the traditional Egyptian character.

People who live, who have lived throughout their history, at a level of deprivation unimaginable to anyone who has not actually come into contact with it, cannot conceive of an action that denotes assuming control of their own lives. They know when to plant maize and when to plant onions. They save a little, if they can, for the marriage of their daughter at the next cotton-gathering. But beyond these immediate acts, they are in the hand of God – and His representatives on earth. And His representatives on earth gather them in the mosques and the health centres and speak to them of things they do not comprehend.

The family-planning grapevine tells of the project in South-East Asia that was pushing condoms. For months the extension workers trudged the rice fields carrying sticks and showing their 'targets' how to fit the multi-coloured sheaths on to them. In stage two they visited the peasant homes where they were proudly shown, beside each nuptial mat, a sturdy stick planted in the floor and flaunting on its tip – yes – a coloured condom. And it is not as silly as it sounds; for the world which the 'target' inhabits, be he in Africa, Latin America or South-East Asia, is a world in which magic is a potent force, and as it is possible for a totem to cause fertility, so it is possible for another to prevent it.

Concepts have difficulty getting across. Women cannot see why they should take the Pill every night and not just when they expect something to happen. They take the Pill 'when necessary' and one of them gets pregnant. The whole village waits for the birth and the midwife swears that the baby arrived reproachfully clutching a fistful of yellow pills.

How can you be literal enough to avoid myth-making, yet sufficiently metaphoric not to offend? And offend whom? The project bosses in Cairo look with distaste at a 'pornographic' diagram of an erect penis. The women in the villages are round-eyed when I ask if they find it shaming. 'Oh Lady, let's have a laugh,' they plead, 'God knows we have little enough to laugh about. And besides, we're all women together.'

And here we come to another hurdle. There is no route by which a health worker can talk to a 'couple' about family planning; women can talk to women and men can talk to men; and whether the couple will actually raise the matter in the marital home is questionable.

In the mosque in Zenein the men sat on straw mats in the main body of the small building, while the women climbed up a wooden ladder to sit concealed on a hard mud floor in a gallery at the back. And even though they were concealed there were angry whispers when a young woman tried to peep through the curtains at the visual aids the male doctor was showing.

Two small girls, the only literate females in that gallery, giggled and nudged each other hysterically as over and over again they read the sentence 'that your life may be one long honeymoon' in the brochure given out as part of the Valuable Free Gift. The other part of that VFG was a condom. Most of the women did not know what it was, and one large, smiling lady blew it up and decided it was a ballon while an older woman who knew the score looked grimly on.

A huge appetite for comedy is an ingredient in the national character. Whatever happens to be going on – be it war, law reform, or riots – is voraciously seized upon and transmuted overnight into a hundred underground jokes sweeping through the valley and adding to a complex structure in which jokes cross-refer to other jokes, to proverbs and to catchphrases from famous televised plays.

One favourite butt of national humour at the moment is a project being funded and directed by Americans with an American approach to 'promotion'. Phase one filled the streets with posters exhorting the passer-by to 'Look Around You', presumably to see the problem. Phase two changed the poster to 'The Choice Is Yours', referring to types of contraceptive devices. The two legends were speedily combined in the national consciousness and sprouted scores of bitter, paradoxical jokes on the profusion but unavailability of housing, commodities, food, etc.

The poverty that makes such jokes possible, that makes these commodities so tempting yet so unavailable to the average Egyptian, is yet another hurdle in the path of the family-planning campaign. To succeed, the campaign has to depend on an extensive and efficient infrastructure. This infrastructure is, however, made up of underpaid and over-burdened health and extension personnel. In most projects they draw their meagre salaries whether or not they have worked for them. Some dream up their statistics sheets, adding what they decide is a reasonable number of 'new users' every month. One project tried to inject incentive: for every IUD fitted the health unit doctor would collect 70 piastres (about 45p).

One health unit constantly turned in perfect statistics – on time. Every month they met their maximum target and collected multiples of 70 piastres. The project boss thought he'd investigate. He dropped in, looked through the books and scanned the names of the clients. He found the names of all the Cabinet wives, the society ladies and the movie and media stars. The young doctor stood by his story. Various women had come in and had IUDs fitted. These were the names they had given.

He'd had his joke, indulged his fantasies, filled his books and collected his cash. No one could touch him. And why should they?

Many Flights into Egypt[1]

Thinking of all the 'foreigners' who come to Egypt for one reason or another, the images race through my mind. Earnest Belgians on bicycles doing socio-anthropological research, nostalgic Greeks sickening for Alexandria, motherly Italian nuns living honoured and loved amidst the criminal and the destitute. I don't know where to begin.

I decide, for no specific reason, to begin with the day when Hugo phoned me.

Hugo was in distress. 'Look,' he said, finally, 'd'you think you could come over? I mean – you could explain it to him. I know I've done this course and everything but I just can't seem to get through to Sayyed.'

The little white Honda whipped through the traffic. In the July heat every instant was vital.

Hugo opened the door. Behind him, across the hall and through the arched doorway to the inner part of the flat, I saw Sayyed, the Nubian manservant, advancing towards us. When he saw that Hugo had already opened the door he turned and vanished down the corridor, his white robes swirling around him.

Hugo kissed me hastily on both cheeks and pulled me into the drawing room. He was pale and the knot of his tie was halfway down his shirtfront. 'Right' he said. 'Will you – No – Look – I'll just go in and see where he is now and then I'll come back. You stay. Right?' He peered carefully round the door, then crept out.

I stood in the middle of the familiar pale-green room surrounded by the portraits of its owner's beloved birds. The

[1] The *Observer*, 9 August 1981.

panels teemed. There were detailed studies in ink, water-colours in the palest of beiges and browns; bold sketches in charcoal. Everywhere you looked you encountered the certain, dangerous stare of the falcon.

Hugo pushed the door open and beckoned. 'He's in the kitchen, watching over his damn freezer.' I followed him. Sayyed was standing at the end of a long table by the window, industriously polishing the silver. At the other end of the table, on a copy of the *Egyptian Gazette*, its eyes wide and piercing, lay a dead falcon.

Philip had left his precious falcons in Hugo's care while he went on home leave. Hugo was a newcomer to Cairo and glad of three months in the Ashbys' plush apartment complete with servants. Two birds were involved. One a large, grey female, newly captured and still untamed; the other a rare and perfectly trained peregrine. Small and fragile, it had the speed and accuracy of a bullet and it had taken Philip months of patient handling to tame the bird to his touch without dulling the sensitivity and nervous pitch that made it impossible for it ever to be at rest unless its hood was securely on.

Baqous, an Arab friend of Philip's, had turned up later and helpfully borne the birds off to his desert home. But he had had to return them a fortnight before the Ashbys were due back. And then it happened. Hugo went out one morning without feeding the birds. It was Sayyed's day off. Both birds were tied to their perches at opposite ends of the wide balcony. As the day and its hunger wore on, the powerful grey bird flapped and flapped and dragged its heavy perch closer and closer to the other. Finally, it attacked. Hugo returned to find the mangled and still-hooded peregrine dangling from its perch, while the wild one stood over it, immobile.

Hugo was horrified. He went inside and locked the balcony door. In the morning, Sayyed disposed of the mutilated peregrine and cleaned up the floor. But next day, Hugo was horrified even more when the remaining falcon refused to eat and refused to drink. It stood unblinking at its post and receded into a darkness of the soul. For three days and three nights it stood sickening while Hugo tried to coax its appetite with morsels of chicken, rabbit, pigeon, and, in desperation, cold cuts from the charcuterie round the corner. Sayyed went about his business shaking his head and clucking.

Finally, always retaining its fixed glare, the bird keeled over and died – and all that Hugo could think of was a grand interment in the freezer. So that Philip, returning, would find, if not two live birds, at least one dead one. And there he had come into conflict with Sayyed who could not see what use a frozen falcon could be to Mr Philip or Madame or any one else.

'He doesn't know about birds, 'Am Sayyed,' I pleaded. 'He thought it would be easy.'

'Easy? Looking after two falcons on a balcony in the middle of Cairo?'

'Well, that's what he thought. And he did try to save the second one.'

Sayyed shook his head sadly. 'How could she possibly go on living after she had eaten her friend?'

Caroline Ashby came home to a useless freezer. Philip Ashby came home to a glacio-Pharaonic burial: the falcon lay in the freezer, surrounded by enough little chicks to last it into Eternity. Whether he was touched it's hard to say, for he was into the 'Arab' rather than the 'Egyptian'.

Philip Ashby is as close as you can get to that British adventuring tradition which includes Burton and Lawrence. Born into the aristocracy, he fell in love with the Romance of the Desert and the Bedouin, and from the age of twelve practised falconry on the Sussex Downs. An unswerving course took him from Eton to the Foreign Office and a posting in Cairo. There, he came into his own: he spoke perfectly accented, pure Bedu Arabic and learnt the intricacies of Islam while remaining a firm Catholic. He brought up his baby son in a roomful of hawks and moved in a circle reminiscent of the *Alexandria Quartet*: wealthy, francophile Coptic ladies of a certain age, with Parisian Arabic, *déracinés* members of the intelligentsia, and the mysterious Baqous with his desert 'dacha' and his illegal black concubines.

To each his own reality.

There are some, a few, for whom the reality is nothing but a terrible chaos. An English lady publisher arrives on her first visit. Her agent takes her on a long walk through the old city. The streets are hot and dusty, the people elbow and shove. He checks her into a cheap hotel. The walls of her room are green with mould. She leans out of the window searching for some stray breeze, and sees a man being sliced by a tram. She packs her bags.

An American embassy staffer drives to work every day in a locked air-conditioned Cadillac, a black guard dog glowering on the back seat. She never unlocks her door or rolls down the window until she is past the armed marines and inside the embassy compound. She has never been attacked, she has no specific reason to be afraid. But she is. And Cairo is a good breeding ground for nameless fears, with its heat, its dust, its apparent muddle, its seething, expectant crowds with their babble of Arabic and their sudden eruptions into theatrical fights. It can be anything from bewildering to terrifying. And yet, there is a system, an order, a key to the code.

People come to Egypt in search of different things. The country is used to this; it's how she has been treated for centuries, and most of the time she obligingly turns towards her visitor with the face that mirrors his particular fantasy.

Some come in search of the oriental, the Islamic. Through the surface grime they feel the magic of the ancient souk, the narrow lanes, and see the fountained, secret courtyards. Some, like Ashby, come for the Sahara.

Sometimes it is hard to see why the fantasist bothered to trek all the way out to North Africa to act out his dream. On Roda Island stands an old palace which used to belong to a cousin of King Farouk: the old Prince Muhammad Ali. It boasts a colossal baobab tree which spreads over the entire grounds. Paved pathways run through it, lit on either side by torches. After the revolution it was turned into a museum. Today – with the open-door policy – it has become the Cairo Club Mediterranée.

One of the pathways leads to a large hall with a marble floor and a white silk canopy flowing tent-like from the ceiling. On either side of the hall there is a raised dais and on it are glowing braziers, oriental rugs and clusters of low couches draped in striped cream satin. In various postures lounge the French *gentiles touristes*. Some are in black robes with gold-encrusted swords or jewelled daggers at their sides; some are in brilliant *Arabian Nights* pantaloons; some are in fake leopard-skin salopettes; some wear stage make-up. It's not a party: just another holiday evening. They preen and stalk and eye each other and the air is as dangerous with unspoken malice as any medieval oriental court.

The open-door policy does not work for the natives. Egyptian guests are strongly discouraged by the management. They would ruin the Middle Eastern atmosphere.

There is another road which leads to Egypt. Tradition has it that the young and kohl-eyed sons of the Egyptian poor hold an attraction for certain Western gentlemen. But, as with most things, there are forms to be observed. An Englishman who came to Egypt early in the century bought a house from a Maltese in one of the old districts and peopled it with his 'boy-servants', lived there happily and died of old age. Indeed, the house is now a museum bearing his name. Its centrepiece: a portrait of a young turbaned Nubian valet of peculiar and fine-boned beauty.

Modern equivalents exist. Men who go out to society parties with a girl on their arm but always end up in their own bed with their resident gardener/houseboy/cook. They live untroubled. But a trendy gay who mistakes this tradition for a true acceptance will find life difficult. Sandals and a pair of baggy brown trousers tied round the waist with a necktie go unnoticed in London but will certainly be commented upon in a Cairo street and perhaps discriminated against in a Cairo hotel.

Conformity is the rule. And different types of it are required. You must conform, not to an Egyptian ethic, but to the image that the Egyptian expects of you. A British person, therefore, is expected to be punctual, polite, hardworking and honest. He is expected to be a gentleman. And if he chooses to employ five olive-eyed manservants or to hang whips on his bedroom wall, well, these are his little foibles – and even breeding hawks on a downtown balcony is merely to be clucked over.

But should he turn out to be deceitful or lazy or rude he would be dismissed as 'not British at all'. But then, what is he? An intolerable puzzle, making it impossible for him to remain in the country.

An expatriate in Egypt has to get along with two quite distinct sets: Egyptian society and the supporting world of servants, shopkeepers, plumbers, etc. But the approval of both is earned in roughly the same way: by fulfilling what are seen as your national characteristics. Provided, of course, they are agreeable ones.

The Russians, for example, won nobody's approval even though they had no preconceptions to fight against or live up to. Apart from the October celebration when vodka flowed freely in the gardens of their embassy on the western bank of the Nile, they kept to themselves, employed a minimum of servants and acquired a reputation for being solemn, excessively hard-working killjoys, curt and tight-fisted.

Americans, on the other hand, are seen as open, warm, generous, pleased with themselves and perhaps a trifle foolish because they talk so loudly and laugh so easily. Americans are very much in evidence in Cairo these days and their variety brings many aspects of Egypt into focus. There are the officials rolling around in their Cadillacs with the now-powerful CD 79 prefix on the number plates (the Russians are still CD 1!) They hand out the AID greenbacks and venture every weekend into the nearer margins of the desert to practise their horsemanship on the thoroughbred Arabs in the riding schools. There are the 'American marginals', wives and dependants of embassy staff, mostly engaged in organising 'events' such as motor rallies and treasure hunts. There are the big-boned oilmen who hit Cairo after having been out on Red Sea rigs for six weeks solid. They erupt with dollars and take their companions to the most expensive, uncomfortable restaurants: 'You sure look foxy, honey-babe. Here, let me show you a snap of my old lady and the kids back home,' and on the porch steps is revealed a plump, uncertain woman with her blonde hair still carefully curled upwards at the tips in mid-Sixties style. There are the speculating businessmen being entertained by small-time local operators who want to set up 'joint ventures'. 'I have four son, two of them daughter. How many you have of child?'

There are the eternal students, doing course after course of Arabic or Islamic Studies at the American University in Cairo, hanging out in one another's pads and smoking the excellent and illegal resin hashish that can still be bought simply and cheaply through 'contacts'.

There are the freaks, the California kids who come over to worship the Sphinx (literal translation from Arabic: the Awesome One), gyrating before him in the moonlight, hands clasped high above their heads in approximations of scenes from the walls of Pharaonic tombs. Or the pale, withdrawn lady with the long Burne-Jones locks who hired a felucca and then made the boatman unload a Wagoneerful of flowers into it. As the baffled man sailed her out into the middle of the river, she set up a low chanting and started to strew the August waters with flowers. The felucca sails caught the breeze and they sped downstream where her solitary pagan revival gathered strength and she scattered gladioli and bird of paradise flowers in huge sweeping armfuls, her song rising in pitch and in volume. The boatman was mesmerised. Soon the river police were upon them. The lady was a 'crazy American' tourist so she was merely accompanied back to her hotel, while the boatman – who had no licence for craziness – was taken in for questioning and the obligatory beating. It's a risky business consorting with foreigners.

These lithe, brown boatmen – usually from Upper Egypt – have built up a mythology of rich European or American women who sailed with a mate of theirs, 'fell in love with him, married him and set him up with a villa and an import-export business'. Each one of them is waiting for it to happen to him.

American and European women. Their Egyptian mirror is constant: 'you are the fairest of them all', it says again and again. Whatever her rating among her own race, her fair skin and hair, her coloured eyes and the legend of avail-ability surrounding her will make her beautiful to the Egyptian male. Some 'wise up' early and decide on celibacy while in Egypt; some don't, and pick up a reputation for being 'easy', which then makes their stay intolerable; and some, a lucky few, find a man whose fantasy complements their own and settle in to marry and breed sons and out-native the natives.

But, of all the nationalities that flow and recede over Egypt, the closest to the heart of the ordinary man are the British. This is odd. Not too long ago the British were the tyrants, the oppressor. The generation that is now in its fifties still remembers the riots and demonstrations against the British occupation and the indignities and cruelties inflicted by that occupation on its unwilling subjects. And yet it is the Englishman who has the least prejudice to combat and who is most easily forgiven for not being Egyptian.

Perhaps the Englishman's Egypt is not too remote from the Egyptian's Egypt. He certainly seems to come closest to sensing the central, multi-layered metaphor of the country. To accepting that the white lines are only there because – well, because modern traffic systems have zebra crossings. But they have no function other than as a formal constituent of a modern traffic system. The Fiats zooming past the stranded tourists are not conscious of having wronged them.

And no traffic policeman would dream of booking a driver for not stopping at the white lines.

No. The real system, the one which functions, is one in which cars and pedestrians coexist simultaneously on the road. If you have to cross and there are no traffic lights, you set out on a slanting, zigzag path across the road. You slot in with the cars and don't hesitate or vary your pace. They'll see what you are doing. They'll make room for you. You'll almost certainly – whoever you are – get to the other side safely.

Passing Through[1]

William Golding, *An Egyptian Journal*

About ten years ago, on a previous visit to Egypt, William Golding arrived at a simple truth: that Egypt is a complex country of more-or-less Arab culture and it is outrageous for the uninformed visitor to confine himself to dead Egyptians while the strange life of the valley and the desert goes on all around him. This time, therefore, it was going to be different: the Goldings would hire a boat on which they would live, proceeding up and down the Nile, stopping off at such places of interest as Oxyrhynchus and Abydos; and mingling light-heartedly with live Egyptians instead of dead ones.

The boat, the Nile, the places of interest, but most of all the Egyptians fail to fulfil these idyllic expectations. The boat is old and keeps kaput-ing, the Nile is often 'exactly like the Thames' or is a 'muddy ditch' and 'disease ridden' into the bargain, the places of interest are OK as far as such things go but are better looked at in books. Worst of all are the Egyptians; they stare (be it benignly) at the traveller, they build their houses at wrong angles and heap up rubble in village streets, they play Arab music and they pepper their talk with proverbs. Far from mingling light-heartedly with them, Mr Golding appears to spend most of his trip trying to avoid catching their eye. He is at his most imaginative and sympathetic when contemplating phenomena or events conspicuous for their emptiness of natives – live ones, that is – and the pervading feeling is that Egypt is too good for the Egyptians. A true Egypt would be depopulated: an Egypt of historical, geological and botanical interest, where the king-

[1] The *London Review of Books*, 3 October 1985.

fishers and mock-ibis hunt their patches of the river and donkeys gambol happily on the shore, their backs for ever unburdened.

Here I must come clean and admit that one of the Egyptians frustrating Mr Golding on his trip up and down the Nile is very close to me; Ala Swafe, the Goldings' 'minder', is my brother, though he chooses to transliterate his name differently. I myself had, I confess, a hand in setting the whole disastrous thing up when Faber, having first tried to arrange the trip through a travel agent, decided they were getting nowhere and asked if I could help. The author of *Free Fall* had been one of the heroes of my sixteenth year. I now read his essay on Egypt in *A Moving Target* and liked it. Two weeks before it was announced that Golding had won the Nobel Prize, Faber arranged for me to meet him and Mrs Golding at their home in Wiltshire. I took to them both and agreed to help. Faber nervously brought up the 'question of, uh, recompense', but I, foolish Egyptian, waved it aside: it was a gift.

I spoke to my brother, about whom a couple of words are now necessary. Ala is an electronics engineer who had been working for two years with a multinational oil service company. He had just resigned because he had hated the life and the ideology of the industry. He wanted to live in Egypt among Egyptians and he wanted to do something which 'mattered'. So he was in the process of setting up a small, radical publishing house. He had, of course, read *Lord of the Flies*, and now its author was interested in Egypt. Interested, moreover, in the 'right' kind of way: in the forty-two million live Egyptians etc. Ala was willing to take six weeks to escort Golding and show him the country and the people. We agreed that although the deal was a commercial one it was still a 'good thing' and therefore he would charge Faber only the standard courier daily fee plus expenses. Everything else (which was plenty) would be freely given.

The rest of the story is in the book. Even though I must say I do not recognise the brother I've known for twenty-eight years in the *Journal*'s minder. I don't recognise his syntax or his attitudes, but above all I don't recognise the man whose 'Egyptian Limbs' Mr Golding believes must have 'quaked with an apprehension as old as the Pharaohs' upon being ushered into the presence of the secretary-general of a provincial governorate. Mr Golding himself, naturally, is above taking titles (and Egypt abounds in titles) seriously, yet he assumes that everybody around him believes in them to the point of 'quaking' in their presence. Assumes this upon no basis whatsoever. Except, of course, that he has a stereo-type Egyptian in mind, one of whose traits is abject servility to authority. Another is the possession of an extended family.

In the *Journal*'s description of the day of sailing we have the Goldings mysteriously 'taken with their suitcases to the boat', where people start to turn up. Among these people are 'the females of Ala's apparently extended family'. Well, maybe Ala does have an extended family. But if he has, Mr Golding certainly hasn't seen it. There were two females in this instance: myself and Soheir, Ala's fiancée. The reason we were both there was that it had taken both our cars to get Goldings and suitcases from the Giza Sheraton to the Ma'adi Yacht Club. Far from turning up to gape at them, we had put aside concerns of our own to drive them to their boat through the Cairo rush-hour traffic.

At one point in the *Journal* Mr Golding says: 'the trouble with a storyteller is he can't even grieve without watching himself grieving. Why expect truth from such a creature?' But this is not a story book. It's a journal, a travel book, and the trouble with travel books is that their subjects/victims don't normally get to read them, much less to give their version of what things were like.

There is, of course, a tradition of travel writing that wishes to find itself at odds with its subject; to highlight the subject's weirdness by insisting that the only normal behaviour is that of the author and – incidentally – his readers. But that is not the task that Mr Golding overtly sets himself. He sets out to 'get to know', to understand. From the beginning he is touchingly aware of the difficulties of his situation. He quotes an earlier author: 'English go their way . . . with their habit of looking "through" persons who do not interest them, and of waiting for friendship rather than going to seek it . . . the British are the most foreign of all the foreigners in Egypt . . . Prevented . . . by their temperament from assimilating themselves to the life of the country . . .' And finds himself in agreement:

'It was true. I could feel a lifelong experience of being a particular sort of Englishman building up in me like a wall. It was more impervious than a wall of language. It was assumption and custom. And I was the one who had hoped that my book would not be about temples but about people.'

And, naturally, one feels sympathy, admiration, even compassion for the elderly English gentleman, the distinguished author, the ex-naval officer and teacher, marooned, as it were, on the *Hani* with a crew who do the work as it comes up rather than in definable shifts and a 'reis' who advises him to 'weave his sails of patience'. Marooned also in what he feels to be a false position: as well as being an experienced sailor, Mr Golding is a teacher, at one time by profession and perpetually by temperament. The *Hani* is not being sailed as he would have sailed her and, even as he watches, things go wrong. He is unable to assume the position of either captain or teacher because he speaks no Arabic: 'This put me in the position of being a passenger,' he complains, 'a position in a small boat to which I was not accustomed.' And if one were to be uncharitable, one might ascribe a lot of the chauvinistic sourness which informs this book to simple pique.

Both chauvinist and sour it surely is. Consider the tone of the following: Reis Shasli's 'face was black as the Nubian's. It was well enough featured but mud-coloured from heredity and exposure.' And on the same page: 'Ma'adi is a nondescript suburb of Cairo.' 'Nondescript' here must mean that Mr Golding is not willing to take the trouble to describe it, since anyone who has been to Cairo knows that in a dusty and over-built city, Ma'adi is a small paradise of trees, lawns and villas.

And yet chauvinism and sourness alone do not quite account for the complacency with which he delivers his off-the-cuff pronouncements. Upon seeing shrubs growing in painted kerosene tubs on the deck of a cargo boat, Golding remarks that 'Egyptians don't often go in for private gardens'. How does he know? By casually glancing round the Sheraton area in Cairo? But Cairo, we are obliged to say again, is over-built, overpopulated. The very few people who live in houses do have private gardens as, for example, in Ma'adi. The rest of us manage as best we can; we 'go in for' plants on balconies, stairs, living rooms and kitchens. The meanest hut, the type that sits alongside a railway track, usually has some sort of trellis with ivy and bougainvillaea.

I may seem to be making a big fuss about a small point, but this sort of idle condescension ambles through the book; when one of the crew suffers a (recurring) kidney attack, Mr Golding kindly suggests that he should be put 'in a train for Cairo, where we would get as proper treatment as was possible in Egypt'. Not quite up to the standards of Mr Golding's local cottage hospital perhaps, but it would have to do. When he witnesses the spectacle of a young man returning to his village loaded with Western-type goodies after a stint working in an Arab oil country, Mr Golding comments on the 'historical process which is remaking not just Egypt but the whole Arab world in one way or another, possibly for the better, it could not surely be for the worse'. These throwaway summations sit uneasily next to the studied carelessness with which Golding, seeing a face wordlessly opening and shutting its mouth on a TV screen, 'thinks' it is Mubarak. The observant eye of the travelling journalist has somehow failed to notice the posters and portraits of the President plastered on every wall, so that, coming across him on TV he cannot quite – oh yes, it's probably Mubarak!

Apart from all this, there is an inconsistency of attitude on the part of Mr Golding which is the fatal flaw at the heart of his expedition. Early on in the trip, the travellers come across an island; Fisher's Island. Enquiring about its history they are informed that an Englishman, Mr Fisher, was given the island as a gift by its Egyptian owner whom he had insulted by refusing to eat with him. Mr Golding ponders this and decides that while 'the Egyptian was a dislikable fool, Fisher was just dislikable'.

One need have neither sympathy nor respect for the Egyptian who gave away his island in return for an insult to see that throughout this trip Mr Golding has played the part of Fisher: he has accepted – even solicited – gifts which he does not value or even acknowledge. This is not a reference to the numerous clumsy objects of bamboo or clay that people keep embarrassingly pressing into his unwilling hands.

One of the variety of Egyptians that Mr Golding wants – or thinks he wants – to meet is the peasant. Not formally, but in as 'natural' a way as possible. This, of course, is not easy to arrange, but towards the end of the trip, when the Goldings are back in Cairo and a trip to the Delta is being planned, Ala learns that one of his friends is having domestic problems and is intending to visit his family in their village. The friend agrees to let Ala and Golding accompany him. How does Mr Golding view this? He considers that 'Ala has killed two birds with one stone. I needed to have a glimpse of the Delta and the Doctor needed to see his family' – he, in effect, sees himself as giving 'the Doctor' a lift home. He does not see that the man has done him the supreme courtesy of allowing him into his parents' home to witness the family at a moment of crisis. And why? Out of friendship for Ala and out of respect for Golding the writer, because the friend is himself a man of letters, a teacher, a writer and critic. But of course that's in Arabic and doesn't count. Anyway, Mr Golding has nothing to be grateful for since he got nothing out of the visit. He sums it up: 'The patriarch and his piles, a grandfather wounded in his self-esteem by his grand-daughter. The mother more bitter than anxious, the father no more concerned than the others, the educated son, smoothing things down and persuading everyone to do nothing.' He has missed the entire point of the domestic crisis surrounding a threatening police visit to the family because their daughter has taken part in a student demonstration in Cairo. And he fails to do justice to his host's mother: 'tiny in black, with wrinkled yellow face', who 'shared her kitchen with a goat' and managed to say, after almost two thousand years of oppression: 'We shouldn't make too much fuss about it. It's really rather honourable to take part in a protest.'

Blind to what is right there before his eyes Golding ignores what must have been his best opportunity to 'meet the Egyptians'. He had on the boat a crew combining as representative a cross-section of Egyptian society as he could ever have hoped for: Rushdi: cook, musician, comedian, teacher of invented hieroglyphics and improviser of verses, a graduate of the faculty of commerce waiting to be called up by the army; Said: the old Nubian who had served with the British and hated them but was won over by a joke and ended up saying, 'English troubles all long past'; Reis Shasli: the old Minyan with two wives and a conjugal feud on his hands; Faroz: the young man of the star-sprinkled tracksuit and the resplendent robes; Ahmad: the engineer about whom we learn nothing at all and whose name is consistently mis-spelt 'Akhmet', possibly because it feels more Pharaonic that way; and Ala.

Mr Golding is busy keeping his distance from rather than getting close to his subject. He confesses that 'the fact was – and I here put it down in black and white – I was shy'. This is quite engaging. It is followed by a discussion of whether an exact equivalent of the word 'shy' is to be found in any other European language. A discussion from which Mr Golding concludes that shyness is a peculiarly English trait. It never occurs to him to ask – or even to wonder – whether Arabic contains a word for shyness. (It does.) And whether people might therefore have understood his predicament.

Towards the end of the *Journal* Mr Golding ruefully accepts that 'whatever I wrote would not be about Egypt, it would be about me, or if you like, us middle-class English from a peaceful bit of England, wandering more or less at will through infinite complexity'. This is honest. And had Mr Golding been true to himself and stayed with Pharaohs, the archaeological formations, the wildlife and the marvel of sailing, we would certainly have got a much more informed and informative book.

It is only fair to say that having received Ala's detailed comments on the manuscript, Mr Golding removed some of the more blatantly offensive material. But what remained was bad enough for my brother to withdraw his photographs from Faber. He could not, honourably, ask for his name to be deleted, even though he is now vulnerable to attack from the more severe of our compatriots for having opened doors and smoothed paths which have only led to our being made the subject of yet another wrong-headed and patronising account by a Western passer-through.

Goat Face[1]

Diana Athill, *After a Funeral*

Waguih Ghali's excellent novel *Beer in the Snooker Club* was published by André Deutsch in 1964. It attracted attention and enthusiastic reviews. The same happened when it was reissued in the Penguin New Writers series in 1968. On the night of Boxing Day that year, Ghali wrote in his diary:

> I am going to kill myself tonight . . . The time has come. I am, of course, drunk. But then sober it would have been very very very difficult. (I acknowledge the drunken writing myself.) But what else could I do, sweethearts? loved ones? Nothing, really. Nothing.

He swallowed 26 sleeping pills 'sneaked' from a friend's medicine-chest:

> And the most dramatic moment of my life – the only authentic one – is terrible let-down. I have already swallowed my death. I could vomit it out if I wanted to. Honestly and sincerely, I really don't want to. It is a pleasure. I am doing this not in a sad, unhappy way; but on the contrary, happily and even (a state of being and a word I have always loved) SERENELY . . . serenely.

Waguih Ghali had good reason to love this state of being which had eluded him throughout the forty years of his life. Born a Copt in predominantly Muslim Egypt and into a wealthy class at a time of socialist revolution, and educated at

[1] The *London Review of Books*, 3 July 1986.

an English school at a time of national revival, he was also the one penniless member of a very rich family. 'Ram', the protagonist of *Beer in the Snooker Club*, has a very similar background and biography to those of his creator. He is a character full of contradictions, poor, but living rich on his family: 'The fact that my aunts were very rich but not my mother, never occurred to me. I drifted on that rich tide. I was as well-dressed as the other [children] and went to the same school.' Steeped in English culture, he engages in anti-British activities: demonstrations against the occupation – 'shouting "Evacuation" like everyone else, without precisely knowing why evacuation was so important' – develop into excursions to Suez to harass the troops stationed there. He is financially dependent on his family, but abhors the means by which their wealth is made. To an old family friend who asks if he is 'in business now', he replies that he has 'discovered a brand new way of exploiting the fellah. All I needed was capital.' 'You mustn't joke about such things, dearie,' she says. He cannot joke too much because he has the addiction to the good life which has been planted in him by family and upbringing: a taste for well-cut suits, for drink and for gambling. And yet when the revolution comes in 1952 he takes to it 'wholeheartedly and naturally, without any fanaticism or object in view . . . socialism, freedom or democracy . . . yes, that's what the Egyptian revolution was; everything good was going to be carried out by the revolution.' At the same time, his education at one of the Cairo English schools, and his prodigious reading (which is where he differs essentially from his class), have made him restless.

The world of ice and snow in winter and red, slanting rooftops was beginning to call us. The world of intellectuals and underground metros and cobbled streets and a green countryside which we had never seen, beckoned to us. The world where students had rooms and typists for girlfriends, and sang songs and drank beer in large mugs, shouted to us. A whole imaginary world. A mixture of all the cities in Europe; where pubs were confused with zinc bars and where Piccadilly led to the Champs-Elysées; where miners were communists and policemen fascists; where was something called the 'bourgeoisie' and some-one called the 'landlady'; where there were Grand Hotels and Fiat factories and bull-fighting; where Americans were conspicuous and anarchists wore beards and there was something called the 'Left'; where Christopher Isher-wood's German family lived, where the Swedes had the highest standard of living and where poets lived in garrets and there were indoor swimming-pools.

This world Ram describes here is the one visualised, longed for and sought out by large numbers of Western-educated Egyptian 'intellectuals' from the beginning of this century until 1956.

Suez does not by itself disillusion Ram: it completes a process begun in the waiting rooms of the Home Office:

> We said this isn't 'cricket', and didn't smoke with our school blazers on because we had 'promised' not to do so. We had been implanted with an expectation of 'fair play' from the English. This stupid thing of expecting 'fair play' from the English, alongside their far from 'fair play' behaviour, was a strange phenomenon in us. Perhaps in our subsequent outcries against the English, there was the belief that if they knew that what they were doing wasn't fair play, they would stop it. In spite of all the books we had read demonstrating the slyness and cruelty of England's foreign policy, it took the Suez war to make us believe it. Of course the Africans and the Asians had had their Suezes a long time before us . . . over and over again.

His answer was not to pack up and go home as so many others did, but to stay in London and join the Communist Party: 'If . . . someone has read an enormous amount of literature . . . and he is just, and he is kind, and he cares about other people of all races, and he has enough time to think, and he is honest and sincere, there are two things can happen to him; he can join the Communist Party and then leave it, wallowing in its shortcomings, or he can become mad.' Ram left the Party, did not wallow in its shortcomings, and returned to Egypt, thinking he 'could do something useful. Teach or something like that; even help in villages and things.' But he finds that 'life here is exactly as it used to be . . . I mean how can I go and work in a boiling village when he is travelling about in Farouk's yacht which costs a million just for upkeep? And all this nationalisation business makes me laugh . . . the money goes to that useless army. Even the Aswan Dam; by the time it's completed we'll have increased by ten million.'

Ram joins an undergroud cell. His job is to procure photographs of torture victims from the concentration camps and pass them on to the national newspapers. The papers, censored, never publish them and Ram has a terrible insight that 'some of the pictures wouldn't be so gory if we didn't pay for them'.

Ram surrenders in 1958. He marries the rich and beautiful Didi Nackla, who has always been in love with him. With her, he finds 'a peace which someone of my type hardly ever comes across or even knows of'. He wants her, he says, to endow their house with 'serenity'.

In 1958 Ram's author left Egypt for the second time. His family, being wealthy and well connected, were probably tipped off that he was about to be picked up for subversive activities. He came to England, which, despite his political reservations, remained the only country he could imagine living in besides Egypt – the only other country where he felt he could belong. But when his passport ran out he was in trouble. The Egyptian authorities – as they do in such cases – would refuse to renew it and would only furnish him with a 'carnet' with which to return to Egypt. In Egypt he would probably be sent to a concentration camp.

Ghali chose not to return, and the British authorities – as they do in such cases – refused to let him stay in Britain. The Germans, in the middle of their post-war reconstruction programme, were not so fussy. He found work on the Hamburg docks and started writing his novel. But the Germans were uncongenial. His Egyptian-style wit and resourcefulness and his personal code of honour had no place there: 'The winter he finished his novel he lived in an unheated cellar – unheated until he discovered a way of leading a wire from the next-door house's electricity supply into his room . . . the heater he improvised, of which he was proud', was a 'spidery coil of wire between two structures of brick. After he had sold his book he rang at the neighbour's door, told them what he had done, and offered to pay – and they called the police.' In 1961 he entered into correspondence with the publishing house of André Deutsch. Diana Athill was to become his editor there. Her book *After a Funeral* takes up the story when, in 1963 on a brief visit to London, Ghali comes to a party at her house.

Miss Athill sets the tone from the first page. She patronises the author even before she has met him: 'A German acquaintance had described him as a "modest, tender and gazelle-like being" . . . I was a sucker for oppressed foreigners, and an oppressed foreigner who was a gazelle-like being and who could shrug off hardship in order to look at things with the humour and perceptiveness shown in his book was one whom I would certainly like . . . he would be a friend.' Soon Miss Athill is debating whether or not to fall in love with this new 'friend'. 'It would be impossible for me to love little goat-face better than I loved Luke' – her resident lover – 'but "falling in love" has little to do with love'. The question is resolved by 'little goat-face', who 'answered warmly to my friendship but . . . made it clear that he wanted nothing more.'

Over the next two years Ghali's emotional stability and mental health became more and more precarious. He is convinced that this is because of his life in Germany and that if he 'could be in London for three months or so I'm sure I could get round this work permit thing and find a job and then I'd be alright. This place is killing me.' Miss Athill gets him an entry visa and scrupulously records that she had landed herself with 'more than I had bargained for, but I had to admit that *I* had landed *myself* with it. Didi' – her alias for Ghali – 'once he felt he could trust me, had grasped eagerly at what I was offering, but he hadn't forced it out of me, he had only accepted what I wanted to give.' The visa, however, does not carry a work permit and Ghali has to content himself with 'odd jobs – translating, baby-sitting, decorating', these were jobs for which he could be paid 'without the Home Office being any the wiser'.

Needless to say, he finds this kind of job demoralising and hard to do, and the money is never enough to support him, let alone his by now compulsive drinking and gambling. Soon he has cadged his way into debt and disgrace. Living off family and friends had been comparatively easy in Egypt: a tab was left in Groppi's or at the Club and was discreetly picked up later. Here money had to be explicitly asked for and there was no real hope of returning it. What was left of Ghali's self-esteem sank lower and lower. That he felt his financial position to be degrading, that till the end he wished to be the 'vrai gentleman' he had been taught he should be, can be seen from the meticulous accounts he kept and his expressed last wish that any money which accrued from his writings after his death should go to settle his debts. That these amounted to less than £1,000 makes his situation all the more pitiful.

After the war in 1967 Ghali decided to visit Israel. His diary states only that he had made the decision and had, astonishingly, been granted a visa. There is a hailstorm of exclamation marks after the statement, and the explanation that 'it will be an "Egyptian interviewing the Israelis" gimmick'. He sold the idea to *The Times*, which put up money for his journey against articles to be written. The pieces he wrote were reasonable and balanced – too reasonable to win him favour from either side. And he had now closed the door for ever on any possibility of going home. Visiting Israel – indeed entering an Israeli embassy anywhere in the world – was treasonous according to Egyptian wartime law, and punishable by death. It was also an act that would have gone competely against popular feeling in a country suffering the aftermath of a terrible defeat. It is the one thing which has stayed in the minds of the very few people who remember him today in Cairo.

Ghali had found the two articles extremely difficult to write. He must have known he would never finish his second novel, would never get a work permit, would never be able to earn a living. He was humiliated and defeated. He could never go home. Aged forty now, he saw no way out.

When I first read *After a Funeral* I was puzzled as to why Miss Athill had written it. On this showing, 'Didi' is simply not worth having a book – albeit a bad book – written about him. She shows us an obsessive drunk, an egocentric who battens on people, hurts and reviles them, and who bores them, and us, beyond all permissible limits. The saddest thing about this sad book is that, for all Miss Athill's protestations about her subject's charm, intelligence, courtesy, wit and attentiveness, these qualities never come through.

In order to place any value on this short life, one has to turn away from Miss Athill's 'Didi' to the self-portrait in Ghali's now out-of-print *Beer in the Snooker Club*. Why does she choose to conceal her friend's identity? Why does she choose the diminutive 'Didi' – the name of the rich girl Ram marries in the novel – for his alias? It is all part of a belittling attitude, of the 'not taking him too seriously' which constantly appears in phrases like 'poor little Didi', this 'poor little demented creature', 'I could have spanked him', and which must have been apparent to him during his years with her. Doubtless this has to do with the frustrated maternal instinct which Miss Athill analyses at length, and which he can only have found undermining. She 'takes him on', he lives in the lodger's room in her house. It is an uneasy situation: they would both like him to pay rent but he can't – and this is added to his debts. Nor is he ever quite sure that her threat to fall in love with him has lifted. Miss Athill, though, has settled for a maternal role.

One cannot blame her for being immovably English and middle class, but one can see how her responses would affect the volatile, disturbed, lonely Easterner in her care. When, after almost two years, she asks 'Didi' to leave (she will rent another room for him), 'the truth of the situation' emerges and she receives the long-awaited confirmation of her role: 'He stood up and turned his head sideways, his chin up, his eyes hooded – a forced moment of intense and haughty composure and then, without warning, he stumbled across the room, threw his arms round me, and was sobbing with his head on my shoulder . . . The "child of eight" was crying hopelessly in my arms. The truth of the situation had emerged.' She deals with this by going to make a pot of tea, while he sits 'waiting for it in trusting docility, all defences down'.

It is of course possible that it is 'Didi's' 'commitment to emotion' which pushes his mentor further and further into such stolid sensibleness. 'Didi's' is 'a family which expresses the feelings violently . . . a strong feeling is justified by its strength'. She 'learnt gradually that his control is a balancing trick. He admires self-control but in fact often abandons himself to the force of gravity with defiant relief.' But was that not part of his initial attraction? Although he was fond of her (in his last letter to her he says she is 'the person he loves most'), how heavy he must have found her personality, and since, as she stresses, she was physically unattractive to him, how distasteful must have been the murkiness of her maternal feelings: 'Having never had a son I cannot be sure to what extent sex would have coloured motherhood, but judging by the extent to which motherliness now colours sex in my relations with young men whom I find attractive, I suspect that it would have done so strongly – that I might have been quite a Jocasta, given the chance.'

The chance finally arrives: a drunk 'Didi' finds his way into the bed of an equally drunk Diana Athill. She tolerates him with amused selflessness, generous and in control, motherly to the end: 'My drunkenness had been restricting the range of my consciousness, but hadn't been distorting it. Now, as activity gradually widened the range of what I could perceive, it was my ordinary self perceiving it and I knew that it would be a pity to spoil what was happening by letting it go on too long. Tenderness would soon be counteracted by the weariness of my unaroused body, so I had better end this love-making by faking a climax and bringing Didi to his.' The episode was never repeated. But why did it happen? Why did 'Didi' – after politely skirting it for four years – land in his benefactress's bed? What was the significance of that act in his process of self-destruction? Miss Athill does not address these questions, even though she has read the passages in his diary where he describes his physical loathing of her – passages which she all too readily holds up for our inspection:

I have started to detest her. I find her unbearable . . . my reactions to Diana are sparked by my physical antipathy to Diana. I find it impossible to live in the same flat as someone whose physical body seems to provoke mine to cringe. This has led me to detest everything she does, says or writes. I am trying hard to understand the monstrosity of my attitude and I can really only explain it by accepting the fact that I am diseased, abnormal, sick.

I'd be sitting in my room watching a stupid thing on telly and annoyed with myself for not switching it off and working. In her sitting-room her typewriter would go tick tick tick tick. 'Christ,' I'd tell myself, 'there she is, hammering away at that bloody mediocre muck, dishing out one odious stupid sentence after another, and thinking – no, pretending it is writing.' And this mood would seize me.

Then I would remember all she has done and is still doing for me, so I knock on her door, 'Cupa-tea, luv?' I say. She's so engrossed (pretending) she hardly hears me. Finishes a sentence, looks at me – very much 'unaware of her environment', so taken up she is by her 'art'. 'I'd love a cup, luv.' Afterwards I go back to my room. 'What a bastard I am,' I keep whispering, 'what a bastard I am.'

He may have been a bastard, but he could write. And, what's more, he was correct in his assessment of his editor's prose style. There might have been some point to all this if focusing on 'Didi's' many delinquencies had resulted in a better book. But despite the (superficially) lacerating self-examination, the relentless stockpiling of detail, *After a Funeral* can almost be quoted as an exercise in how not to write narrative. 'Soon after we had sat down to the meal someone said something more interesting, which related directly to the speaker's experience, and instantly the sardonic goat-face changed. The eyes actually appeared to light up, melancholy gave way to animation. He began to describe something which chimed with what had been said, and he was funny.' The book reads like a cliché-ridden paraphrase, an abridgement. Events, feelings, are all made simple. 'Didi's' position abroad is briskly described as 'exiled by Nasser': this is to draw a blind over a world of equivocation and deception. All 'Didi's' problems are reduced to a frustrated need for mother-love: this is to ignore all but a fraction of his character and history, while providing an excuse for Miss Athill's supply of the commodity. She claims that 'this record was written for him and for people who are going to have children'. He would probably have liked it better if she had edited his diaries.

In the Beggars' Cell[1]

Nawal el-Sa'adawi, *Memoirs from the Women's Prison*
In early September 1981, Anwar al-Sadat, angered by the
Egyptian intelligentsia's consistent refusal to support his
agreement at Camp David or to cooperate in 'normalising'
relations with Israel, frustrated by the militancy and the
anti-Western ideology of the Muslim groups he had initially
nurtured as a buffer against the left, and fearful of the
disappointment of the masses with his much promised
'Egypt of Prosperity', launched what was in his own words,
a 'purge'. He ordered the arrest of some 1,500 people and
slammed them into 'precautionary detention'; others found
themselves moved from their jobs or simply ordered to stay
home.

Nawal el-Sa'adawi, already at odds with the regime for
her publicly stated liberal and nationalist opinions and her
frank treatment of women's problems, was one of fourteen
women who found themselves sharing the hastily emptied
'beggars' cell' in the women's prison at the Muhammad Ali
Barrages in the fork of the Nile Delta. Her *Memoirs from the
Women's Prison* spans the eighty days after her arrest on 6
September.

Her tale begins dramatically as a knock on the door inter-
rupts her grappling with a recalcitrant new novel. The state
security men break down her door (she refuses to open it
without seeing an official warrant) and within a couple of
hours she is in the newly named 'political' cell in the Barrages.
She chronicles day-to-day survival in her new world; the cell
and its adjoining dirt enclosure, the times of despair and the

[1] *New Society*, August 1986.

times of hope, the jubilant rejoicing on 6 October when Sadat was gunned down, the following weeks of doubt and apprehension until her release on 25 November.

Dr Sa'adawi is a novelist (as well as an essayist, lecturer and physician) and the non-political prisoners capture her imagination. Without apparent strain she spins threads that connect these women to memories of her aunts and grandmothers. She conjures up scenes from her village past: a wife who refuses to mourn her unloved husband but tightens a belt around her belly and saves piastres towards her son's education; a grandmother desperately offering her own dried-out breast to her orphaned and screaming grandchild; and the author's own mother, bewildered to the end by her own unceasing reproduction.

The 'criminal' prisoners assume mythic stature: Dhouba, the gentle, black procuress; Sabah, the mad, prophetic beggar; Fathiyya-the-Murderess, who struck her no-good husband with a hoe when she found him 'on top of her nine-year-old daughter'. These prisoners and their Shawisha (Sergeant) Nabawiyya come to life under Sa'adawi's touch.

What is curious is that the same can't be said about her treatment of her own cellmates: Latifa al-Zayyat, influential critic and author of a novel which has become a landmark in the progress of the women's movement; Awatif abd-el Rahman, an MP for the opposition; Shahinda Miqlid, propelled to the front of the national struggle by the murder of her husband; Safinaz Kazim, a free-living journalist who astounded everyone by assuming the veil; Amina Rashid, a French-educated aristocrat now actively involved in leftist opposition; and others. All of them are distinguished, fighting, articulate women who – with the exception of Bodour, the Muslim extremist, and Fawqiyya, the Communist organiser, obviously set up as two polarising extremes – are here reduced to the role of a chorus providing backing for Sa'adawi's courageous outspokenness.

There is no doubt that Sa'adawi is courageous or that she is outspoken – these qualities have cost her her job in the

Ministry of Health, but have won her a reputation and a place on the international feminist platform. One would have wished, however, that she were a little less outspoken in her own favour. Her novelist's light touch deserts her when it comes to devising vehicles for self-promotion: Sa'adawi's daughter writes to her that 'there's been a major international campaign in your support'; I'tidal, who is being recruited to spy on the women, only has to mention 'Dr Nawal' and that satisfies her interrogator; the shawisha's niece briefs her aunt on a page-full of the doctor's brave revolutionary activities.

So far, one assumes that what these statements lack in taste they make up for in accuracy of information. But when Nabawiyya hints that Jihan el-Sadat was driven to get her husband to act against Sa'adawi because 'she gets jealous of any woman who's more beautiful or more intelligent than she is', then that really becomes too much – even for a non-admirer of Mrs Sadat – to take. This sort of self-advertisement (better left to the publisher's blurb) detracts from what is essentially a fearless and important book and coloured my response even to its more poignant human moments.

Marilyn Booth has crafted a stylish and precise translation – no simple feat when working from Arabic to English. She preserves the exoticism of the quotations, proverbs and idioms and retains the humour of the jokes while keeping the narrative easy and natural. There are problems, as when Sa'adawi finds herself in the cell: 'Have I fallen to the bottom of a well? Or sprung on to another planet? Or returned to the age of slaves and harems? Or was this a dream? Was I asleep?' This can work in a certain rhetorical Arabic style – but in English?

Similarly, I found the far-fetched and illogical nature of some of the imagery – similes mainly – irritating and distracting. Here is Sa'adawi following the warden into the jail for the first time: 'On one shoulder, raised higher than the other, a black stripe perches like a black feather on the head of a mythical bird or legendary beast of ancient times. The keys in her hand, though, give her more than the appearance of a gang leader whose band haunts the forest or deserted wilds.' Huh? And what – apart from everything else – would a gang leader do with a bunch of keys in the 'forest or deserted wilds'? This is not at all to detract from Booth's achievement. Rather, I suppose, it raises a general question about the role of the translator and whether a bit of editing might not be permissible in some cases.

The one and only inaccuracy in the translation is in the depiction of Dhouba delousing Nabawiyya: when the person doing the grooming finds a louse on the square, white, narrow-toothed bone comb, it is customary to crush it with the nail of her thumb, not her big toe. However, that is nit-picking. What matters in the end is that the louse is dead.

Heroine of the Operetta[1]

Jehan Sadat, *A Woman of Egypt*

My grandfather used to visit the shrines of the saints. Walking with him one night to the festival of a favourite, we came upon a rickety old tumble-down shed with a padlocked door. To this door was nailed a notice and on it a semi-literate hand had painstakingly drawn the words 'Institute of Typwritting. Biggest Institute in the East'. The lone and level sands stretched far away – or would have if this had not been a muddy dead-end alley among the back streets of Cairo.

A Woman of Egypt reminds me a lot of that self-proclaimed and obviously ill-fated edifice of 'Typwritting'. Jehan Sadat never builds a hospital, it is always hospitals, her agricultural reforms cause crops to increase their yield tenfold, the Wafa wal Amal (her controversial charity for war veterans) boasts – among other things – 'a factory for manufacturing artificial limbs which was so advanced that doctors from all over Africa and the Arab world came to study our methods and to be trained in amputee physiotherapy'. It could be said that this transparent sort of exaggeration is harmless and possibly even rather endearing, but spread over 465 pages it becomes tedious, and as a way of recording history it is less than reliable.

Predictably, this hyperbolic trait is most apparent in Mrs Sadat's self-portrait. The book starts with the shooting of Anwar al-Sadat on 6 October 1981. In Maadi Hospital the doctors declare him dead. Leaving his bedside, Jehan makes her way to the waiting room where she addresses Vice-

[1] The *Times Literary Supplement*, 1987.

President Hosni Mubarak: 'Mr President . . . Anwar Sadat is gone . . . Now it is you who must lead us.' Mubarak sits silently: a man dazed. Ministers try to persuade him to come to an emergency Cabinet meeting but give up and leave without him. Then Mrs Sadat speaks again: ' "Go away from this place now. Your duty is to save Egypt." And finally, Mubarak stands.' This story is representative of the book on three counts. First, it casts Mrs Sadat in a heroic role to the detriment of all those surrounding her. Second, it does not (so far as I know) occur in any other account of the event described. And third, if it is true, then she behaved incorrectly; before his death her husband had changed the law so that he was not automatically succeeded by his Vice-President but by the Speaker of the People's Assembly, Sofi Abu Taleb. Mubarak was voted in as President later by a 'referendum'.

The question of factual correctness crops up repeatedly. Even inconsequential details strike a jarring note: Mrs Sadat tells us that as newly-weds she and 'Anwar' were so fond of the open-air cinemas in Cairo that they would often go for the three to six o'clock show and stay on for the six to nine o'clock. But open-air cinemas don't have three-to-six and six-to-nine shows. If they did the Egyptian sun would render the film invisible and would inflict a massive sunstroke on the audience. Wisely, therefore, these establishments open their doors at around eight o'clock. Well, maybe that doesn't matter. But building up to her first meeting with 'Anwar', Mrs Sadat tells us that he was a hero to her, that in Ramadan (which fell in July) of 1948 she was constantly following the news of his trial (for the assassination of the pro-British Cabinet minister, Amin Osman) in the papers. The suspense builds up and finally, on the day following the trial, 'Sadat Acquitted, the headline read'. In July 1948 the Egyptian newspaper headlines were full of the war being lost in Palestine and there is no mention at all of the Amin Osman trial until Sunday 25th when, on page six of *al-Ahram*, there is a report on the judgement. Sadat was indeed acquitted but his name occurs as number fifteen in the list of twenty-five accused.

The portrait of Sadat that emerges from his wife's auto-biography is a curious one. The adjective she most commonly applies to him is 'frustrated' and he is often seen as blocking his wife's reforming and liberating efforts. And so we find ourselves back with the now near-mythic character of the First Lady of Egypt: petitioners queue at her door. Couples ask her to intervene in their marriages. The native wit of simple women invariably expresses itself in compliments on her slenderness, her beauty. She is the only person who dares to disagree with Nasser at the dinner table. She starts cooperatives and charities and builds student housing. She is a support and a fount of wisdom to all. Among those who constantly seek her advice are Farah Diba; Empress of Persia, Queen Alia of Jordan, Safiyya Qaddafi, the Sheikhas of the Gulf and the Princesses of the House of Saud. In air-raid shelters she scolds hysterical women and forces them to behave reasonably. She holds a spoonful of rice to the lips of a soldier on hunger strike and, behold, he eats. She rescues Yasser Arafat's brother and sister from an automobile accident. Her efforts cause a 'new respect' to be shown to women. Indeed, she prophesies the revolution in Iran and if only 'Anwar' hadn't told her to mind her own business she would have warned the Shah and Khomeini would never have stood a chance.

Mrs Sadat is without doubt a remarkable and outstanding woman. She is clever, beautiful, ambitious, gracious and possessed of a powerful will and enormous energy. Yet there is a truly naive quality in all this boasting, and naive too are the attempts to tackle the minor issues for which she and her husband were criticised. The 'special uniforms he [Sadat] had had designed', with their invented medals which became the butt of many a local joke, were apparently intended to 'stress the pride and importance he had always felt serving as an officer in the Egyptian Army'. The three hours of prime-time television devoted to Mrs Sadat's defence of her MA thesis – a scandal which brought lasting disgrace on all who had to do with it at Cairo University – were intended to 'encourage other women to educate themselves'. This glibness – which ultimately insults the intelligence of its audience – was, of course, the trademark of the Sadat era and so it is no great surprise to find it here. And it is always 'for Egypt'. But where is Egypt? What Egypt is this 'woman of Egypt' showing us? It is a land where the President's wife – in order to fit in with the peasants of his home village – dresses up like an arcadian fallaha in a long gown and 'a colourful scarf which I fixed to my head, as they did, with a band of flowers'. It is a land where the populace is in the habit of expressing its approval of the President by spontaneously choreographed outbursts of piping, drumming and dancing in front of the presidential residence. Where, when this same much approved-of President is finally shot and killed, the Minister for Social Affairs sits herself down on the ground outside the hospital and 'in a mourning ritual that had been passed down from the days of the Pharaohs . . . [starts] beating her chest with her arms and crying out to God'. In other words, it is the Egypt of some American-produced operetta. And it was, of course, this vision, this pandering to some facile semi-educated Western notion of Egypt, that became the most repellent characteristic of the Sadat regime and the one that led ultimately to its downfall.

Mrs Sadat's American friends and publishers are fulsomely thanked in her acknowledgements. Perhaps it was on their advice that her autobiography was fleshed out, not to say made corpulent, with 'Basic Egypt' lectures? The geography of Egypt, Islam, the Pilgrimage, Al-Azhar, shopping, marriage customs – nothing is spared the banal run-through. Even as her slain husband is being laid in his grave, the bereft widow takes time out for an aside on burial rituals. So much for dramatic structure. Where was the advice on linguistic detail? Is it to preserve an authentic second-language tone that we get – among many others – 'he have been watching the parade', they 'shined their light in my face'? The members of the twelve-man Council of the 1952 Revolution are constantly referred to as 'revolutionist'. And later – when 'Democracy' takes hold – we get both 'oppositionists' and 'oppositioners'. The one (unintentional) bit of wit is provided by the translation of an Egyptian proverb into 'The man is a river, the woman is a dike.'

Doing Something[1]

Diane Johnson, *Persian Nights*

Deborah Moggach, *Smile, and Other Stories*

Jayne Anne Phillips, *Fast Lanes*

Three or four years ago, a friend of mine was asked to illustrate a teaching-English book for the Ministry of Education in Cairo. He was (is) an Egyptian, but an Egyptian from outside officialdom – a cartoonist. He painted a series of charming and instantly recognisable street scenes: stacked greengrocers', lemonade vendors, decked-out taxi cabs, dust-carts pulled by donkeys. The Under Secretary flew into a rage: Who *is* this man? An Israeli? Why has he drawn everybody with kinky hair? Doesn't he know selling lemonade on the street is unhygienic? And where did he get all these donkeys? *There are no donkeys in Cairo*. We want representations of the real Egypt. Eventually the commission went to an artist who had apparently suffered a time-seizure somewhere in Hampshire in the mid-Fifties and the Ministry got its real Egyptians: blazered schoolboys with satchels and freckles and cute, short-dressed little girls with blonde pony-tails.

I was reminded of this incident when, early on in *Persian Nights*, Chloe, the protagonist, innocently asks a colleague at Shiraz University about the veil.

> 'The veil? The veil?' cried Mrs Reza. 'There is no veil. The Shah has outlawed it. It is over, the vestige of a bygone day.'

[1] The *London Review of Books*, 1 October 1987.

213

Chloe anxiously tries to reconcile Mrs Reza's statement with the vast numbers of chadored women she is constantly observing. Being foreign means, among other things, having no access to the underpinnings of 'reality'; no tools with which to interpret what you see. So when Chloe finds a man lying face down in the shade of a bush she has no way of making out whether he is dead or merely sleeping. This question of perception is, of course, where a great deal of the humour in writing about foreign places comes from – and Diane Johnson uses it to good effect. When Chloe finds herself in a bathroom with her Iranian friend Noosheen, she is amazed to find that

> she had no pubic hair. Chloe tried not to stare but it did make a person look strange, statue-like. She could not tell if Noosheen was naturally this way or if she shaved herself. Chloe was not so conscious on herself of that little fat pad of flesh over the pubic bone.

Noosheen, I might say, would have been appalled at the thought that shaving was her chosen method of depilation. This is in the best 'East meets West' tradition and brings to mind the bemusement of the eighteenth-century Turkish ladies on discovering Lady Mary Wortley-Montague's corsets and their conviction that these corsets were a kind of over-all chastity belt into which her husband had padlocked her before he allowed her to leave England.

Ms Johnson has plenty of good 'foreign' stuff: the humbly born Minister of Education who comes with his collection of slides to address the American wives: 'My father had seven donkeys and a camel and many goats. Therefore we were rich, yet I could not read, nor could my parents.' The finale of his show is a slide which shows 'tribespeople dancing, made happy by literacy'. Then there is the hotel – in this case it is the Cyrus – with a 'Western-style bar where people hung out like expatriates in a movie'. There, you can meet the foreigners and the 'Westernised' locals and listen to the expat know-all pontificate to the over-courteous native:

> 'They think of women as property, all these Arabs do. No offence, as the kids say.'
>
> 'I'm not offended. I agree completely. Although, you know, we in Iran are not Arabs.'

The expats, the telephones, the typhoid/cholera, the literacy campaigns, the stray dogs, the vibrant rugs, Westernisation vs. Islam, the gold-braceleted women; the problems, the images and the jokes are the same the Third World over.

Persian Nights is not merely a funny book: it is a serious tale, a tale of altered perceptions and of moral responsibility. Emblematic of the problem at the heart of the book is a scene where the principal dramatis personae sit around in the sunshine discussing the imminence of revolution and wondering whether it would, in fact, better the peasants' lot; 'a company in tennis whites, at leisure amid the tangled thicket at the edge of the courts, bare legs in view, easy and laughing, while the peasants in question trudged by in their somber draperies'. Diane Johnson, unlike many writers on the Middle East, maintains a curious and amused but even-handed and respectful stance. She knows the distance cannot really be bridged; her heroine, although she can just about get to within an amulet's throw of the veiled peasant women, cannot, in the end, think their thoughts.

Chloe Fowler is an American who by accident – or is it treacherous design? – finds herself alone (that is, without husband or children) in Iran for a few weeks. She is a pretty, good-natured, scatty, conventional doctor's wife, 'more given to idle reflections than to purposive thought', susceptible to attacks of guilt about her children: 'sometimes she caught herself thinking of nothing at all and would hurriedly think of her children, to atone'. She is mildly irritated by her husband and tolerantly critical of herself: 'Chloe did not know why she was not spiritual. She believed in a general way that people should be spiritual, it was just that she was not. She hoped she might have natural piety.' Her view of the world, and of herself in it, is essentially a comfortable one: she believes that love affairs are harmless but divorce is bad, that people are basically friendly, that good generally prevails. This is at the beginning of the novel. Is Chloe going to learn? To adjust to being a woman alone? To being in foreign territory? Is she, in sum, going to grow up? Halfway through the novel there is Chloe, sweet as ever, and still believing that the US general who says they should have gone in and nuked 'Nam is only kidding and that he would have done something 'more sympathetic' with his life if only someone had told him that war was wrong. And at the very end, Chloe, arm in arm with her lover, Hugh Monroe, ecstatically greets the spectacle of little boys skipping amid the hordes to the rhythm of 'Death to the Shah!': these are the people bringing a tyrant down simply by marching, the people having 'power over their lives and the course of things'. *Persian Nights* is a story about the limits of change – and, finally, its impossibility.

The non-Iranians in Diane Johnson's novel are mainly good guys. Not, for example, your common-or-garden entrepreneur looking to make a quick profit through ruining some small, thriving industry. No. They are doctors escaping from a bit of tedium or a tangle in their American lives and seeing in Iran a chance to 'do something'. But to do what? What is it they can do in Iran? For Iran? Iran on the eve of revolution is like the lapis beads Chloe wears round her neck: 'if you were bad it made you worse, if good better. It intensified your qualities.' Richard Dare, a normally ambitious archaeologist, is transformed by greed and opportunity into an arms smuggler and a thief. As for the good guys, they appear, as usual, to be better on perception than action. Dick Rothblatt, a dermatologist, sees that 'here was a chance really to do things, something to be done, a need surpassing the mere acne and drug reactions you got at home in America. Here huge horrible things swelled up on people

. . . Here you could die of impetigo or typhoid.' Chloe, too, reflects that in the life she's lived 'you seldom get to do anything you believe in. She thought of people in lifeboats, deciding which one to eat.' The comparison between life in the US (standing in for the West) and life in Iran is maintained over the course of the novel. Discussing Matthew Arnold with Noosheen, Chloe says that Empedocles represents the ennui and spiritual desolation of the nineteenth century: 'he is a symbol of Western man'.

Noosheen Ardeshir is a kind of Irani equivalent of Chloe: married – reasonably unhappily – to a doctor, with two young children, she has spent two years in Cleveland and now struggles with her identity and her domestic problems:

> The washing woman looks at me with scorn because I am so Westernised, I know, but the pity is I am not so Western I do not mind the stares of certain old women. I suppose they remind me of my grandmother . . . If I had a washing-machine I think I could control my life much better. Another woman to deal with, it's just too much. An ordinary Maytag, like any American woman, it's not much to ask.

She is engaged in decoding Arnold (as Chloe intends to try to read Hafiz and Sa'di) and 'Dover Beach' moves her to cry out: 'It is so beautiful. The man and the woman against all hollow change and worldliness.' Chloe is amused and sympathetic. She diagnoses Noosheen's yearnings as romantic and imagines her in love with the handsome and tragically widowed Abbas Mowlavi: 'She thought of the affectionate glances between Abbas and Noosheen and could imagine Noosheen's beautiful body, blue like the body of a goddess in a miniature painting, entwined with Abbas in the act of love, his the heavy penis of a sultan, the two as one, emblem of sultry sexuality, in an arched pavilion cooled by the waving fans of servants who have been blinded so as not to behold this inspired copulation.' The compulsion to do something about something, however, is not exclusive to foreigners in the Third World: indeed it is a desire often most keenly felt by the children of this world themselves – or at least by the good guys among them. Noosheen eventually finds her vocation in adapting Arnold's verses to the cause of the Ayatollah.

Ms Johnson's Irani characters are sympathetically detailed and (despite Chloe's attempts) not romanticised. Abbas Mowlavi, prey to the same thirst for meaningful action, but hampered by having an avowedly revolutionary brother living in Paris, goes for long walks, unobtrusively trying to discover the contaminated well that might be causing the officially non-existent typhoid. He consoles himself with the Qur'ānic verse that extols the 'doing of righteous deeds in shadow'. The moment of truth comes – for himself and his foreign guests – when, on a visit to the ruins of Persepolis, they come upon another emblematic scene. Massive carved heads are being winched into a waiting aeroplane which has just disgorged the barter – crates of guns now lying in the desert sand. As Abbas realises what is happening all his dilemmas are resolved: 'His dismay intensified along with a feeling of moral correctness that verified it; he was right to feel this patriotic, this admirable dismay. Foremothers shrouded in veils murmured from the sky . . . joyous in his release from some self-preoccupation, some tense and Western inwardness. Here was something he could do something about.' The last anyone sees of Abbas, he is running towards the aeroplane, arms waving, just as some troops arrive and a battle breaks out.

As the battle rages, Chloe watches a boy soldier, apparently dying in the full glare of the sun, the flies already clustering at the corners of his eyes. 'It is her duty to prevent them. She has the notion, brief and incomplete, that this is as much as she ever could do, and that she will not have another chance, ever, to be heroic.' Under gunfire, she drags the boy into the ladies' toilet and bolts the door. Minutes later, a voice outside whispers: 'Chloe, help.' Is it Abbas? Is it a trick? Is it a new danger to the life she has just saved? She does not open the door. Has she misjudged her moment? Later, on the plane out of Iran with Rustum, the mongrel puppy she has tamed, Chloe mourns the fact that 'we're just going back to America, where I'll never have another chance to be good'.

In America, there is the small matter of Chloe's marriage to be sorted out. Away from her husband in Iran, Chloe had, infrequently, but with the standard exasperated wifely fondness, thought of him, and each time she's done so we've learned something disagreeable: Jeffrey is ill-mannered, he is bad tempered, she had looked inside him 'once or twice and found only crossness and clutter'; his grievances are petty, his physique is puny. And yet she is resigned to being married to him, even though she realises that in Iran she is enjoying 'something of the fun and power of being a man, being far away, on her own, working at something, sleeping with someone she won't mention to the person at home'. I won't give the denouement away – except to say that the story of Chloe's marriage could happily – inappropriate term – fit into Deborah Moggach's new collection. *Smile* is mostly about people out of communication with each other and therefore, to a large extent, about unhappy marriages. In fact, the only 'good' marriage – in 'Snake Girl' – is one where the allowances and sacrifices that need to be made are of such magnitude that they almost become the point of the marriage and the husband attains the rank of some sort of idiot saint. 'In marriage you learn to be silent,' says the bride in 'Horse Sense' and that dictum is followed by Anna in 'The Wrong Side', who navigates her husband through a tour of France while trying to remember when they were last happy, when she had last not been nervous. But it is not just women who are the victims in *Smile*: Frank, in 'Making Hay', has just learned that he has leukaemia and can't bring himself to tell anyone, least of all his childless, highly strung Hungarian wife, Dorizia, who would 'smother him in her arms and soak him with her tears'. In a field, he is set upon by a young CND marcher and they make what he calls 'love' and she calls 'despair'. He thinks he might tell *her*, but so intent is she upon the plight of the world that she marches off without learning anything about the plight of the man she has just held in her arms. The best thing about Deborah Moggach is the irony, the wit, of which she and her characters – in their dreadful situations – are capable. And this is where she most differs from Jayne Anne Phillips, whose world is simply, lyrically sad.

Fast Lanes inspired in me the same sort of feeling that I imagine Iran must have aroused in Diane Johnson. This is a foreign land, a land where people have names like Danner, Thurman and Kato, where, in the normal course of things, they take mescaline and coke, share houses with TM instructors and have lovers who have dropped out of Harvard Law School to become carpenters. And yet, is it so strange after all? It's still a land where men get lost at sea, where women talk to their unborn babies, where brothers and sisters love each other as only brothers and sisters can and where people are, on the whole, out of communication. The first story in the collection is an unremitting monologue: Mickey, the young, aspiring rockstar-cum-gigolo talks nonstop while his older lover contents herself with very occasional asides to the audience describing his appearance and his actions. From the rockspeak of 'How Mickey made it' to the elegiac *fin de siècle* 'Bess' to the surrealistic 'Bluegill', Jayne Anne Phillips moves with assurance and charm. She creates haunting landscapes out of snow, summer woods, a girls' changing room and, occasionally, the odd, arresting image: 'something dead was out there, yellowed like the dust and lacy with vanishing'. Deborah Moggach's world is made sad by betrayal. What is it that makes Jayne Anne Phillips's world so sad? Maybe it's because there, the enemy is not marriage or men or the Shah or any particular person or thing, but the same old Empedoclean ennui – as Shinner Black in 'Blue Moon' says, 'people can't live in this world'.

Lovers and Terrorists[1]

Oriana Fallaci, *Inshallah*

Now what have we got here? We have a-parable-for-our-times, we have a panoramic-view-of-a-city-at-war, we have tough-talking-soldati-made-human-by-an-eye-for-a-woman-and-a-soft-spot-for-a-kid. And look who's coming round the corner. Why bloody dick of a dick superdick it's the-Saigon-journalist and in a minute we will see just what it is she is carrying in her knapsack – and if you're longing for this to stop, well, too bad: it goes on for 599 breathless pages.

In her knapsack, the Saigon journalist who believes that 'man is much funnier than the other mammals and more touching than any other animal', carries a mathematical formula $(S = K \ln W)$ that is supposed to provide the 'intellectual' underpinning for her book, a list of weapons with their specifications, a cast of sketched-in Italian soldiers meant to correspond to the heroes of the *Iliad*, a clutch of 'verses' that achieve the feat of being embarrassingly bad even in Italian, a couple of images (bands of stray dogs plus a white mare) intended to carry a mighty symbolic charge, a cliché post-modernist trick whereby the reader is made to observe the writing of the book, a whole rabble of unwashed Ayrabs who can't even speak their own language properly and a range of curses and insults which, it must be admitted, have more resonance in Italian than in English.

But swear words do not a character make, nor do lists of squadron numbers and positions add up to a slice of life; and as for subtlety, you're more likely to come across it in an episode of *Thundercats* than in *Inshallah*. Here is our

[1] The *Washington Post*, 13 December 1992.

introduction to Ninnette, the Lebanese who bumps into the 'Hamlet-like' Angelo in a bookshop in the Eastern Zone: 'Long and sleek chestnut hair which waved in glitters of gold, disquieting violet eyes that inflamed all the world's desires, harsh and fiery features of a barbarian queen, and a body that took your breath away'. For two months she shows up at the barracks in 'a dress so tight that at first glance she looked naked' pleading 'Let us make love, let us make love' and eventually she hands the disdainful Angelo a condom. A vote for safe sex?

We might excuse this kind of thing by reminding ourselves that Ms Fallaci's literary reputation is not principally in the field of fiction; she has built her renown on her dispatches from international trouble spots like Vietnam and Latin America. And, to be sure, she seems reasonably trustworthy when it comes to naming numbers of battalions and listing the items that go to make up a field hospital. But when it comes to people, the way they feel, speak and act, there is in the book's factual stretches the same residual contempt for authenticity, for simple truthfulness, which infects its fictional components.

Take the Arabic language, for example. Every time an Arab speaks we are given – before the English – the utterance in transliteration, and almost invariably it is wrong. 'Tawaffi' the rabble yell when they want to say 'Death to you', 'kaofa aktòl' seems to signify 'I'll kill him' (note the meticulous – and misplaced – accent) and 'Hal tas ma'wai la'im?' is apparently how an Arab says 'Do you hear me, you sheep?' Even the call to prayers, repeated five times a day and containing the basic creed of Islam, is quoted madly, hilariously wrong. And why are the 'Isha (Evening) prayers in *Inshallah* mysteriously conducted at midnight when everywhere else they happen at around eight p.m.?

But underlying this contempt for the real, a further contempt operates, a contempt which we have already caught glimpses of in Ms Fallaci's introductions to her interviews with Yasser Arafat (1972) and with Sheikh

Ahmed Zaki Yamani (1975); it is a contempt for Arabs – and particularly Muslim Arabs – as a whole. And what makes this so repellent is its insidiousness; the non-partisan 'I am speaking for all humanity' stance adopted overtly by the author of *Inshallah* and denied by its text. For the Arabs in it are denied their humanity: they are represented mainly as a hysterical, changeable, murderous rabble and when they are given an individuality it is as caricatures seriously deranged by lust, grief, hatred or greed.

It is hard to mount a critique of this sort without going into more detail than a short review allows for, but the magnitude of error here is of such an order that one is moved to ask what if an Arab were to write a book, call it 'Arrivederci', set it in Genoa and fill it with Italians who spoke a language no Italian would recognise and who behaved in ways unfathomable to any ordinary Italian? Italians who existed only to be outsmarted, screwed and generally pushed around by a squadron of Arab soldiers? Surely there would be a hue and cry and at the forefront would be those who spoke for a common humanity. All I can say is, hasten the day when we Arabs can take such arrogance for granted and hope to get away with it.

Women: The Battles That Have Not Been Won[1]

Susan Faludi, *Backlash: The Undeclared War against Women*

Marilyn French, *The War against Women*

The statistics in Marilyn French's *The War against Women* make grim reading: women do between two-thirds and three-quarters of the work in the world. They also produce 45 per cent of the world's food. But they are granted 10 per cent of the world's income and less than 0.01 per cent of the world's property. The sex-tourism industry in Thailand, the Philippines and South Korea was first planned and supported by the World Bank, the IMF and the United States Agency for International Development. Its revenue still figures as part of those countries' GNP. Eighty per cent of the poorest people in the United States are women and children.

Looked at in conjunction with the fact that women still get paid less for doing the same job as men, the continued absence of state provision of childcare for working mothers in most countries and the current move in the United States to repeal the law giving women the right to abortion, it is hard to see why there should be a general feeling that the fight for equality has now been won; that the Eighties have ushered in a new era in which it is no longer cool to be perceived as a 'libber'.

Susan Faludi's surprise bestseller presents an analysis of the 'post-feminist' stance: the *Backlash* of the title. This backlash, in the United States particularly, manifests itself

[1] The *Sunday Telegraph*, 29 March 1992.

in a measurable slowing-down of progress on 'women's' issues such as the Equal Rights Amendment, moves to go back on victories gained such as the Abortion Law, a sharp rise in physical violence against women, and media sensationalisation of scare stories about the Man Shortage, the Rise in Infertility, the Working Woman's Depression, the Executive Woman's Burnout, Abuse of Children in Day Care, etc.; stories which play on women's insecurities, which carry the message 'Liberation is bad for you' – and which, in all the cases Faludi cites, turn out to be based on faulty statistics or confessedly 'general' impressions. The agents of the backlash are the United States' government which during the Reagan administration aligned itself with the New Right and the new Fundamentalists, recanting men who once supported the cause, recanting 'sisters' like Betty Friedan and Erica Jong, and 'the Contenders': a significant population group of young men 'median age thirty-three, disproportionately single, who were slipping down the income ladder – and furious about it'.

The impetus behind the backlash as Faludi sees it, is not that women have achieved equality but the perception that they are getting close – too close for the industries that have a vested interest in keeping them on lower wages, for the corporations that fear reductions in 'woman-type' consumption, for institutions (like the military) which see women's interests as opposed to theirs, and for men – who have suffered an erosion of their sense of 'maleness'.

An American poll that has tracked social attitudes in both men and women for the last two decades found that the leading definition of masculinity by a huge margin was being 'a good provider for his family'. Faludi concludes that it is not surprising that the backlash developed during the Eighties when the 'traditional' man's real wages shrank dramatically and the traditional male breadwinner was to be found in less than 8 per cent of all American households. It is also not surprising that the feminist drive for economic equality is felt by 'the breadwinners' as a direct threat.

A 1980 mental health study reported husbands of working women suffering higher levels of depression than husbands of housewives. In 1982 a Michigan study of 2,440 adults found depression and low self-esteem among married men was closely associated to their wives' employment. In the same year a study of 3,000 singles found that women earning high incomes are almost twice as likely to *want* to remain unwed as women earning low incomes. A 1986 survey concludes that 'dual earning may be experienced as a downward mobility for men and upward mobility for women'. In 1987 researchers from the Universities of Michigan, Illinois and Cornell observed that men's psychological well-being appears to be significantly threatened when their wives work. But apparently men can't just turn their backs on marriage: data chronicled over the last forty years show that the suicide rate of single men is almost twice that of married men and that single men suffer from nearly twice as many severe neurotic symptoms and are far more susceptible to nervous breakdowns, depressions and nightmares. So it would appear that men need to marry – and need to (courteously or otherwise) subjugate their partners in marriage in order to fulfil their own maleness. US government demographer Paul Glick estimates that 'being married is about twice as advantageous to men as to women in terms of continued survival'.

Both Faludi and French cite data to support also the converse of this remark: a study which tracked women for thirty years reported in 1990 that 'traditional' married women ran a higher risk of developing mental and physical ailments in their lifetime than single women.

Married women report 20 per cent more depression than single women and three times the rate of severe neurosis. Married women have more nervous breakdowns, heart palpitations and inertia and other afflictions including insomnia, trembling hands, dizzy spells, unhappiness with their physical appearance and overwhelming feelings of guilt and shame. A twenty-five-year longitudinal study of college-educated women found that wives had the lowest self-esteem, felt the least attractive, reported the most lone-liness and considered themselves the least competent at every task – including childcare. A *Cosmopolitan* survey of 106,000 women found that single women make more money than their married counterparts, have better health and are more likely to have regular sex. In 1972 family sociologist Jessie Bernard warned that 'Marriage may be hazardous to women's health.'

It follows that among divorcing couples we find that less than a third of divorced men say they were the spouse who wanted the divorce while 66 per cent of women claim they are actively seeking it. Post-divorce statistics show 60 per cent of women reporting increased happiness after one year, growing to 80 per cent after ten years, while the number of men who report increased happiness remains static at 50 per cent over ten years.

Finally, the majority of women killed or battered by their partners are attacked after they have initiated or completed divorce or separation proceedings.

Since the institutions that govern the way the world is run are controlled by men, this image of the beleaguered man fighting for his manhood is surely one that has to be taken into account if women are to progress further – or indeed to hold on to the progress they have already made. And surely the combative polemic of both books is not helpful here. It must be said though, that of the two it is French who goes over the top with statements like 'Because women are mothers and men are not, men feel lacking without a center' and, sadly were it not also funny, 'The real ground of [men's] upset may be their knowledge that the clitoris is the superior [to the penis] organ.' Can it be that after centuries of being told that a man is superior to a woman because he has a penis we are going to climb our soap boxes to proclaim the superiority of the clitoris? Surely this type of statement is the mirror image of the ignorant and abusive language which has for so long been used against women and which we should by now have learnt to be wary of? Surely also this kind of discourse and the whole 'philosophy' that underlies it is not 'cohesive' or 'nurturing' or any of the other life-enhancing qualities we claim for ourselves. And surely too, it is not in our interests – not in the interests of our children and of the human race which we see ourselves as the champions of – to alienate even those men (and there are some) who are trying to accept re-education and to find ways of living with women as friends and companions.

In a 1976 review of Susan Brownmiller's *Against Our Will*, Germaine Greer put forward a plea for 'men and women [to] express without brutality the hostility that is a permanent part of the spectrum of their relationship'. Perhaps that is indeed the most that we can – at the moment – strive for.

Intimately Egyptian [1]

Amitav Ghosh, *In an Antique Land*

It is a habit of certain Jewish (and indeed Islamic) communities to preserve everything they have ever written. This is done in special chambers and its aim is to protect any written form of the name of God from inadvertent mistreatment. Such a chamber (a 'Geniza') was attached to the Synagogue of Ben Ezra in old Cairo; members of the city's Jewish community from well before the tenth century until the end of the nineteenth deposited all their writings there. The story of how the Geniza Collection came into the possession of Cambridge University Library is, sadly, the story of so much of the heritage of our so-called Third World: a fragment finds its way into the hands of a Western scholar – in this case Solomon Schechter, reader in Talmudics at Cambridge – who then, armed with embossed letters from the 'protecting' country, heads East – or South. Schechter arrived in December 1896 to an Egypt presided over by Sir Evelyn Baring and soon 'the Chief Rabbi of Cairo and Joseph M. Cattaoui Pasha [head of a prominent and wealthy family of Egyptian Jews] came to a decision that seems little less than astonishing in retrospect. They decided to make [him] a present of their community's – and their city's – heritage; they granted him permission to remove everything he wanted from the Geniza, every last paper and parchment, without condition or payment'.

In the winter of 1978, Amitav Ghosh, a twenty-two-year-old student with a scholarship to do research in social anthropology, comes across S. D. Goitein's *Letters of Medieval*

[1] The *Times Literary Supplement*, 15 January 1993.

Jewish Traders in a library in Oxford. In it he finds the English translation of a letter from one Khalaf ibn Ishaq in Aden to his friend Abraham Ben Yiju in Mangalore. The letter is held in the Geniza Collection, is dated AD 1139 and conveys – among other matters – greetings to Ben Yiju's Indian 'slave and business agent, a respected member of his household'.

'The reference', writes Ghosh, 'comes to us from a moment in time when the only people for whom we can even begin to imagine properly human, individual, existences are the literate and the consequential, the wazirs and the sultans, the chroniclers and the priests . . . But the slave of Khalaf's letter was not of that company'. This is not strictly true, for the lives of many slaves from the medieval Middle East have been recorded and imagined: from Bilal, the sweet-voiced black slave who was among the earliest to embrace the new Muslim faith and became its first muezzin, to 'Anan, the poetess who won literary contests for her master, the list goes on. That a slave, from a society in which slaves were often scholars, should be mentioned in a piece of writing is not in itself an extraordinary thing. But this willingness to be astonished is a part of Mr Ghosh's stance. Which is not to say that he is wrong to be captivated by this fragment; by the distances (both geographical and cultural) that it implies and travels.

In 1980 he sets out to learn Arabic by living in a small village in the Nile Delta. *In an Antique Land* interweaves the story of his Egyptian sojourn with a reconstructed account of the life of Abraham Ben Yiju. And if the direct links between the two are somewhat tenuous (Ben Yiju spent a portion of his youth in Cairo, and he returned to it for the last years of his life), we are still willing to suspend disbelief while we wait for more profound connections to show themselves.

The book invites us to see parallels between the lives of the people in the village (given the name of 'Lataifa') and the life of Ben Yiju in Aden and in Mangalore. Thus, talk of a blood feud in Lataifa leads to speculation about why Ben Yiju left Aden and might it not have been because of a blood feud? The wedding of 'Ali in Lataifa leads into the (possible) marriage of Ben Yiju to his freed slave Usha. The death of Sheikh Musa's son prefigures the death of Ben Yiju's, and so on. But what does this tell us other than that love, anger and death have always been components of life?

Both in Egypt and in Mangalore Ghosh is told the story of a local holy man: how his tomb resisted the spades and bulldozers of developers and eventually forced them to reroute the road they were building. When Ghosh told his driver in Mangalore that he had heard a similar story in Egypt, the man 'nodded politely but disbelief was written all over his face'. I am not sure what we are meant to make of this story. Of course the people who believe in their saint will believe, *need* to believe that he is unique. But of course also we on the outside know that miracles tend to be repetitive; that saints have, as it were, a limited repertoire.

Mr Ghosh, as I've said before, is willing to be astonished; a professional anthropologist, he plays the 'innocent abroad' pretty well. Maybe he knew that in the idiom of national characteristics, 'Hindi' (Indian) in Egyptian Arabic carries the connotation of 'fool' – as 'Saudi' means 'rich with no need for his money (so to be ripped off)', or 'Berberi' means 'hot-tempered and half-crazy', etc. In any case, he does his best to let his characters speak for themselves and the result, in the Egyptian village sequences, is some lively and authentic scenes. Whether they add up to 'an intimate biography of the private life of a country, Egypt, from the Crusades to the Gulf War' as the publicity for the book suggests is, I think, questionable. He ought also to have got the Egyptian word for nargila or hubble-bubble right – given that it occurs nine times throughout the text: write out one hundred times 'shisha'.

Various odd little red herrings are strewn in our path. For example, describing the matrilineal hierarchy of the society to which Ben Yiju's (presumed) wife (presumedly) belongs, we are told that it is the mother's brother who would 'play Laius to the Oedipus' of her sons. One, legitimately I think, expects this to be followed up with some tragic family event – but it never is.

It is as though, while instinctively in accord with the book's general theme, that change and 'progress' often bring limitations and loss, one can also see that the evidence it offers doesn't quite add up. A story as sad and as 'big' as that of the decline of two major civilisations should surely not need padding out with set passages on 'the rituals of Ramadan' and 'the meaning of slavery in Sufism'.

For all that its heart, for this reader, anyway, is in the right place, its attitudes fair, its spirit generous and its motivation apparently worthy, *In an Antique Land* leaves behind it a feeling of incompleteness, of not having quite delivered what it promised.

Daughter of Persia [1]

Sattareh Farman Farmaian, *Daughter of Persia*

Many years ago when I was a student at Cairo University and my mother took the Shakespeare class I sat on my bench and fretted at the sudden divide that had opened up between us. Once, as she walked up and down the aisle, she paused and rested her hand on my desk while she talked to another student. I looked at that hand I knew so well; my mother's hand, now my professor's, and then I moved my fingers slightly and surreptitiously touched one of her nails.

If she registered my touch she gave no sign. I felt a pang of recognition, therefore, when the seventeen-year-old Sattareh Farman Farmaian, daughter of Abdol-Hossein Mirza Shahzadeh, one of the last of the warrior princes of the Qajar dynasty, quietly touches the fingernails of her sleeping, eighty-year-old father, 'lightly brushing each yellow ridged surface with the tip of [her] finger', trying, in this way, to bridge the distance that always lay between him and herself; the fifteenth of his thirty-six children.

It was not the only time during the course of this remarkable book that I felt such an affinity. In other depictions of people and of feelings there is much to stir a collective Middle Eastern memory. And in the clear-eyed narrative of her country; in its transformation (I will not say progress) during this century from Persia into Iran, with all the now-familiar components of that narrative, there is a version of the history of the entire region.

Sattareh Farman Farmaian's story is closely linked to that of her country. In 1908 her father, having acquired a new

[1] The *Sunday Telegraph*, 1993.

German machine gun to use against the Ottoman Turks, picks from among his soldiers an illiterate but strong and brave sergeant. He promotes him to officer and gives him the heavy machine gun to carry. The soldier's name is Reza Khan. In 1921, with British backing, Reza Khan accomplishes the coup that will transform him into Reza Shah Pahlavi.

From then on the Farman Faramians' history is one of persecution: their properties are confiscated, the father is placed under house arrest, eventually his eldest son is imprisoned and murdered. One day the compound on which they live is razed to the ground to create a road linking the Shah's palace to his accounting offices. Throughout all this, the young Sattareh is sustained by the resolution (formed during a visit to the slums of south Tehran) that she will grow up to 'help the people'. Against huge odds she makes the journey to the University of Southern California and a degree in social work and returns to found the first School of Social Work in Iran. She fulfils her plan to 'help the people' until February 1979 when, denounced by her students to the new Islamic Revolution, she flees to the United States.

There, a refugee, writing her memoirs, displaced, disillusioned, and in her sixties, Farmaian displays the sterling qualities that have helped her shape her life – and notably absent among them is humility. Her book suffers from the well-known defect of any 'star' autobiography: reading it you get no sense that anyone, anywhere else in the country was working along parallel lines. And yet there were people: Farrokhrou Parsa for example, Minister of Education and the first woman Cabinet minister in the Irani government, had made radical steps towards emancipating women before Khomeini had her executed in December 1979 for 'warring against God'. But *Daughter of Persia* has room for only one heroine. An aristocrat to the last, Sattareh Farman Farmaian brings to mind the more well-meaning of the members of the *ancien régime* at the time of the French Revolution; she displays wit, style and humour, love for her country and her own people, compassion for her deposed enemies, and tolerance towards her oppressors, yet never a glimmer of awareness of that inbred arrogance which (one assumes) caused the beneficiaries of her good works to turn her in to the Ayatollah.

In the dark outer courtyard of Khomeini's improvised headquarters, waiting through the freezing night for her interrogators, her mind keeps 'turning over the stones of my past, trying to find beneath old mistakes and faults an explanation (for being there) that made sense, as though guilt were a priceless jewel I had mislaid'. And as she walks in the hills above her old home, waiting for the visa that will take her into exile, she finds the jewel: her fault had been to work within the system, rather than to throw herself into the political process of opposition to the Shah. Her fault was that she – and others like her – did not 'sacrifice ourselves, our careers, our cherished dreams, to protest what the Shah was doing to us . . . And unlike us, the mullahs had had guts . . . They had let themselves be beaten, tortured and killed to destroy the Shah. They had had no plan, no program and almost nothing positive to suggest – only "The Shah must go!" But they had been brave.'

If this is the fault, it is shared by thousands in the Middle East today. And if history repeats itself, then the subtle, the open-minded, the ironically equivocal, will always go unheard. And tomorrow will inevitably belong to those who are called fanatics and who are loud and certain – and brave.

Muslim Queens [1]

Fatima Mernissi, *The Forgotten Queens of Islam*

When the Prophet Muhammad settled in Madinah in the first year of the Hijrah, one of his first acts was to build a mosque. Adjoining it, he built three rooms, and the room opening on to the mosque was his own. In the mosque, the Prophet taught his followers the principles of the new religion and led them in performing its rites. He adjudicated in their disputes, held political meetings, and planned strategy in times of war – all these activities taking place in the company of women as well as men. This ideal image of the mosque has been central to all discussions of political Islam since then; it posits a centre for the communal life of a group of believers, and a wise leader, accessible to those who have freely chosen to be ruled by him, and indeed, bound by the same laws that bind them: the laws of God Himself.

From the time of the accession of the third khalifah, 'Uthman ibn 'Affan, in the twenty-third year of the Hijrah, until the present day, practically all Muslims have believed that the Islam practised upon them by their rulers is at variance – and even at odds – with the Islam established by the Prophet fourteen hundred and fourteen years ago. How the religion was diverted from its true path, and how it should return to it, are the subjects of the violent and often murderous disputes that the Muslim world has been witnessing ever since.

In her latest book, *The Forgotten Queens of Islam*, the noted Moroccan sociologist, Fatima Mernissi, brings together two issues central to the current debate: the nature of govern-

[1] The *Sunday Telegraph*, 1993.

ment; by what authority and what process does a ruler rule? And the position of women in an Islamic society, specifically: is a woman allowed to rule?

The traditional ruler of ummat al-Islam (the Muslim nation) is a khalifah (Caliph). The title derives from the Arabic root *khalafa*: to come after, or to leave behind [in a certain capacity]. The khalifah is 'left behind' by the first leader, the Prophet, to act in his stead for the greater good of his people, both in this world and the next. The spiritual dimension of the office is demonstrated on a daily level in the khalifah leading the ummah in prayer. But since opinions vary on the legitimacy of a woman leading men in prayer, it follows that the office of khalifah (despite the curious feminine ending of the word) is not open to women.

But the main function of the khalifah since the middle of the fifth century of the Hijrah was to rubber-stamp the legitimacy of the growing number of local chieftains who declared their independence in terms of earthly power, but needed his spiritual imprimatur. And among those local chieftains were a number of women. The question then becomes: Can a woman, in Islam, exercise temporal power? How many women applied for the khalifah's endorsement of their rule? And to how many was it granted?

Mernissi traces the history of twenty-two women who have ruled in Muslim countries. Four were jawari (female slaves) who had captured the hearts and minds of their kings and were content to exercise influence through them – and through their sons after them. Three Indonesian, six Mongol, four Maldive and two Yemeni princesses were Queen Consorts who ruled with and after their husbands. Two Turks, Shajarat al-Durr of Egypt and Sultanah Radiyyah of Delhi, were powerful women who seized power in their own names and were brought to tragic ends through sexual passion. One, Sitt al-Mulk of Egypt, ruled instead of and after her insane brother, al-Hakim bi-Amr Allah (unaccountably referred to throughout as al-Hakim ibn Amr Allah). All their stories are ablaze with drama and intrigue.

And in all cases the Caliphate steadfastly opposed and undermined them.

Mernissi places the opposition of the Caliphate to women rulers in a political context that is wider than that of gender. For her, as for many other thinkers, the history of political Islam has been a history of growing distance between the idea and the actual, between the ruler and the ruled. Mu'awiyah, the first Umayyad khalifah, having seized power in 41 Hijrah after the civil war that split the Muslim world into Sunni and Shi'a, led the prayers accompanied by armed bodyguards. Later, a courtier with the title of hajib (literally 'veiler') was appointed to act as a barrier between the khalifah and his subjects. And shortly after, Harun al-Rashid (d. 193 Hijrah) delegated the very public function of leading the Friday prayers to an imam. This ever-increasing distance, Muslim intellectuals across the ages have argued, facilitated the growth of despotism, and made easier the systematic disenfranchisement of all those outside the circle of power: the adherents of other religions, women, and al-'ammah (the populace) in general.

One of the things this fascinating book shows is how things could have been different: 'We might have seen the birth, in the heart of Islam, of a democratic practice founded on a neighbourhood mosque/local assembly. The Prophet left everything in place for moving in that direction. A parliament could have been created without arguing about it as a satanic Western importation. We would have given to the world . . . the ideal which inspired the Prophet and his whole strategy: a group led by . . . an arbiter.'

Islamic Perplexities [1]

Jan Goodwin, *Price of Honour*

Nanny Suad sat on the floor of the kitchen stuffing vine-leaves. As she worked, she chatted to her young charge, my five-year-old niece. But she was not just chatting – she was teasing; winding the child up. As the little girl got angrier and more violent in her replies the nanny smiled up at me easily. 'I'm sharpening her,' she said, 'so she'll never be afraid of anyone.' An Egyptian peasant-woman, who could neither read nor write, was administering a course in self-assertion to a girl-child.

This memory sprang to my mind in response to the following lines from Jan Goodwin's *Price of Honour*: 'From the time a girl is five or six [in the Muslim world], preparation for the only acceptable role for her – wife and mother begins. She is groomed to be a good wife: docile, obedient and self-sacrificing.' [. . .] 'The birth of a girl . . . is invariably a time for mourning' – 'invariably' no less.

Fortunately, the book does not much deal in general wisdom. It is mainly a survey, based on interviews, of Middle Eastern attitudes to political Islamism – the 'extremist' wave sweeping the Middle East with its call for the abolition of secular government and the establishment of the Islamic state. Many of Goodwin's interviewees are women and several of them are not in the least docile or self-sacrificing. Goodwin covers ten countries and her research exhibits courage, determination and fairness; qualities which sometimes (as in the excellent chapters on the occupied Palestinian territories and on Iraq and Kuwait) lead her away from

[1] The *Sunday Telegraph*, 5 February 1995.

the question of religion into an examination of the daily problems and struggles of women's lives.

Some of the interviewees are predictable: Egypt's Nawal el-Sa'dawi pops up yet again, Jordan's Tujan al-Faysal (recently to be heard lecturing at SOAS) complains of being barred from work (since this book was written, however, she has been elected to Jordan's parliament where she had a fight with a male colleague who threw a hole-puncher at her).

But most of these self-portrayals make good reading – small close-ups of lives that are a good deal more sensible and complicated than the book's publicity makes them sound. The 'sixteenth wife of a sheikh', for example, turns out to be the fifty-year-old Dr Su'ad al-Sabah, author, publisher and philanthropist who, by her account, lived contentedly with her loving and encouraging husband for thirty-two years until his death.

Who writes these blurbs – and why? It is as though a rather thoughtful book on, say, *Childhood in Britain in the Late Twentieth Century* were to be heralded with 'The land where ten-year-olds stone toddlers to death – where fathers rape their daughters then butcher them – where small country churches are settings for scenes of ritual satanic abuse.'

Price of Honour tells a tale full of sound and fury, signifying – as if we didn't know it – that the Middle East is in turmoil. The rapid changes undergone by the area in this century have left people disoriented. They see themselves hurtling towards a Western model which they do not choose to adopt fully; they want to hold on to their own culture, their identity, while remaining part of the world community in the twenty-first century. Political Islamism announces it can enable them to do that.

It can't of course. What it offers, at best, is cheap (if biased) education and health care. At worst, it provides examples of loony-fringe thinking such as the injunction to males travelling on Cairo buses not to use a seat vacated by a female until the heat imparted by her bottom has vanished – ten minutes is the estimated time – injunctions which would be laughable were it not that people get killed for laughing at them.

Again and again, in these interviews, women state that they are happy living within their traditions, that tradition is amenable to change, gradually, from within. They protest that political Islamism is 'political greed', that it is used to 'create antagonism between compatriots', that it is a 'trivialization of a great religion'. They perceive it not just as a threat to themselves, but as a threat to Islam itself.

All this is reassuring, and not just to Middle Eastern readers. Westerners also like to be told that things out there are moving slowly. But they too should beware. As Jan Goodwin points out, the West is dangerously dependent on Middle East oil and on Saudi and Kuwaiti investments in the US. Miss Goodwin wants to know if this state of things is advisable given the volatility of the region? The answer seems to be no – but in spite of her 'humanizing' case histories, she suggests no alternative. Political Islamism may be moving slowly, but it is moving bit by bit.

What then is to be done? The interview with the distinguished Egyptian jurist Muhammad Sa'id Ashmawi goes some way towards providing an answer. Is anybody listening?

A Mistaken Return to Tehran [1]

Cherry Mosteshar, *Unveiled*

Cherry Mosteshar was two years old when she left Persia in 1959. She returned from time to time for family holidays and despite appearing to fit in quite nicely with the court set, she 'came to despise a way of life that called for designer clothes and prestigious marriages'. Thus, when the revolution came, she believed she was ready for it, and when in 1980, it seemed that she was losing her homeland, 'the urge increased to go and become part of its future'.

Unveiled is Mosteshar's account of the ensuing years, as she tries to live and work in Iran. At first, it's pretty much what you would expect from a pampered child of privilege, whose Farsi is comically broken and whose quixotic notions of 'helping to make things better' are sharpened by an ambition to see her name in bold above her dispatches to the *Independent* and the *Financial Times*.

The combative journalist seems an absurd, exasperating presence as she blunders through Tehran putting her life – and the life of whoever is unlucky enough to be with her – in danger. As the book progresses, however, it turns into a gripping account of daily life in a world fallen apart. And as Mosteshar battles through this world, struggling with her bad back, her nervous stomach, her slipping headscarf, her broken Farsi, she gradually wins us over. Call her stupid, infuriating, snobbish: she has already called herself all these things and more.

Besides, it seems inappropriate to require reasonableness

[1] The *Sunday Telegraph*, 1995.

when life becomes a kind of tragi-farce. When you pick up your phone to be abused by a distraught woman's voice for – yet again – not being a hospital, when you are poked and prodded and made – for the sake of decorum – to change from thick coloured cotton socks into sheer, black knee-highs before an interview, when your neighbour – turned amateur prostitute – begs you to take on one of her clients, when your relatives are dropping dead or killing themselves all around you, the quality you need most is doggedness, and that Mosteshar has in plenty.

In *Unveiled* people exist in a sort of limbo: the old way of life has been swept away, but no new way has evolved. Government agencies have Orwellian names like the Foundation for the Oppressed and Life-Sacrificers. The *ancien régime* drugs itself to death behind closed doors. The women grit their teeth and scrub and polish and serve tea. The men mostly are total bastards.

The best chapters in this strange and absorbing book are the most personal. Mosteshar, the Oxford-bred aristocrat and career woman, hears her biological clock ticking ever louder in the loneliness of her Tehran flat and so becomes the second wife of a boorish, parasitic, ultra-conservative, petty officer of the revolution. The marriage breeds loathing, but also guilt. When her stomach turns as he spits through the car window she castigates herself for snobbishness, when she finds out that he's been making a percentage on bribes she's had to pay, she wonders whether she has a right – having never known poverty – to be angry at someone who's always been poor.

There are harrowing, hilarious scenes as, back in Oxford, she tries to act as a buffer between her self-righteous husband and her incredulous family, as she tries to persuade him that not every chador-less woman on the city streets is a whore. Finally, he finds fault with her home: ' "It's not as grandiose a home as I had imagined. We will have to find somewhere newly built to live," this man, brought up in half a room with fifteen other people, said as

243

he jogged round the acre of garden that surrounded Mummy's six-bedroom home just five minutes from the centre of Oxford.' In the end, we are truly glad to see him board the plane for Tehran. And so is she.

Land of Stone and Thyme [1]

A Land of Stone and Thyme: An Anthology of Palestinian Short Stories, edited by Nur and Abdel Wahab Elmessiri

If Hemingway were alive he would have gone to the West Bank or Southern Lebanon and joined the Palestinian resistance. If he'd survived, he would have told a tale as compelling as any he told of the Spanish Civil War – and possibly more harrowing.

The Elmissiris (father and daughter) have chosen these stories to lead us through the Palestinian experience. From displacement, to disbelieving exile, to alienation and despair, to a fulfilment (of sorts) through resistance; the collection tells its own story.

The problem, though, with this kind of structuring, is that what emerges in the end is fairly uneven. Rashad Abu Shawer's 'A Green House with a Brick-Red Roof', for example, reads like a ten-year-old's attempt at describing the random horror of war: a bomb falls on a boy and girl who've just been playing together. The two children's heads fall, roll, then settle 'side by side . . . like two wilted oranges'. While Rasmi Abu Ali's 'Kurza', in which a group of villagers thrown off their land try to decide where to go, is a small gem of subtlety.

The stories also vary hugely in their literary antecedents. There are the allegories, like 'And They Confiscated Joy in My City' by Mohamed Ali Taha; the Kafkaesque: Ghassan Kanafani's 'Nothing'; the Lyrical/Tough – the story which made me think of Hemingway – Yehia Yakhlaf's excellent 'Norma and the Snowman'. The effect is of a nation trying to

[1] The *Times Literary Supplement*, April 1996.

find the form that expresses its suffering. For my money, the more straight the telling, the better the tale. Liana Badr's 'The Trellised Vine' tells of a woman, exiled in Lebanon, surreptitiously picking some vine-leaves to make a Palestinian dish celebrating the coming of spring.

In their 'Note on the Politics of Translation', the editors state their intention to adopt a 'non-fluent strategy of translating'. This is supposed to show the reader that 'Arabic writing . . . cannot so easily be appropriated by, or naturalized and domesticated into English. It resists.' They call this 'err[ing] on the side of the text' rather than on the side of the reader. But surely the text is best served by assuring it a fair and accurate representation in the target language?

To take just the opening paragraph of Liana Badr's 'A Land of Stone and Thyme', (the story which gives the book its name):

> Last night I dreamt that we walked together. He always visits me in my dreams. We were walking near the martyrs' cemetery. No sooner had I seen him than he left me and went under. Just leapt down and went among the graves.

This is 'non-fluent' indeed. But it is also inaccurate and doesn't make sense. The reader has to wonder, if 'no sooner had she seen him than he left her' – how come we've just been told they were walking together? And surely he 'went under' means he was submerged? Drowned? A closer translation of Badr's opening paragraph would, I think, be: 'Last night I dreamed we walked together. He always visits me in my dreams. We were walking on the road by the martyrs' cemetery when, suddenly, he left me and went down. He jumped and went down among the graves.' It seems to me that being fair to the text is being fair to the reader.

We all know that a great deal is lost in translation. But sometimes translations can misrepresent the text. This is particularly dangerous when a reader believes he/she is gaining some insight into the consciousness of a people. When a story is read, as these stories must be, as testimony rather than completely imaginative fiction, and when the reader is 'the West' and the stories are 'the Palestinians', then a truly serious responsibility falls on the translator.

So, read this book, and read it as testimony. But remember that the English text you are reading is a reflection, not just in the normally fogged and speckled mirror of translation, but with the added quirks of a fairground glass.

The Sands of Timelessness [1]

Susan Brind Morrow, *The Names of Things*

Egypt, more than most countries, tends to be regarded as a free-for-all; its heritage common to all comers, and every season now brings a crop of new books about it, written by American women. Well, Egyptians have long been used to foreigners poking around in their lives. Nevertheless, these books always occasion a flurry of questions among members of the studied species: Who is this book useful for and how will it be used? What is its hidden agenda? What yardsick are we being measured by? Can 'they' ever really get 'us' right? And if this sounds paranoid, well, it's not pleasant being the pinned-down frog – or scarab.

I'll say at once that I think *The Names of Things* reads as though it was written in good faith. Even so, I found the passages about the squalor of Cairo overdone, and the quick rejection of its relatively clean districts as being 'not Egyptian' unfair. On the other hand, Susan Brind Morrow looked with a more sympathetic eye than most visitors; she saw that although 'in Western terms [Cairo] . . . did not work . . . yet . . . [it] did work. There was a structure, but it was hidden, internal, because the people . . . were adaptable, resourceful, compassionate.' And after all, it was not the city she was interested in, but the desert.

The Names of Things sets its sights beyond the merely contemporary – or even historical; what it's concerned about, what it's author is concerned about, is timelessness. And by the Red Sea, she found what she was looking for: a timeless desert, a land of mythical dimensions, where a cave

[1] The *Washington Post*, 6 July 1997.

held the ten-thousand-year-old 'fur, bones, and teeth of twenty-seven leopards preserved by the salt and heat'.

Brind Morrow is the post-colonial, post-Sixties, American female child of the European adventurer-travellers: Burton, Doughty, Thesiger, et al. Drawn to Egypt originally through its heiroglyphs and its press in the classics, she first goes on a dig at Dakhleh Oasis in 1980, then to the Eastern Desert (on a Crane–Rogers Foundation grant) in 1988. *The Names of Things* is a record of an intermittent journey – a toing and froing between home (Seneca on the Finger Lakes) and Wadi Halfa and the Eastern Desert.

The book also aims for another kind of map – an impressionistic chart of the commerce between world and word. In the early sections it is enchanting in its wondering discovery of hieroglyphics. At Dakhleh, for example, Brind Morrow comes across the arm of an ancient child: 'It was a grace note, a trace of some lovely polished thing lying on the ground. The outstretched arm that held – was it a piece of bread? – in its curled hand. The hieroglyph to give.' The moment is emblematic of what is best about the book: the clarity of observation, the sympathy with objects, the creative linking of language and the world.

That arm stretches through the narrative: in the fierce sun of Midan el-Tahrir, an old man pushes the traveller out of the path of oncoming cars; a woman in the Aswan train motions her to join the children in a meal of chips and pickled turnips; soldiers, seeing her distress after a phone call to her husband, give her cigarettes; a Sudanese bookseller, on the boat to Wadi Halfa, offers her a song. They all do 'that intangible, freeing human thing: giving something priceless . . . to a stranger, for nothing'.

All, I feel compelled to add, except the author's American friend Liz who, because she cannot sell her car when she leaves the country, pushes it into the river: 'Easiest way to get rid of it,' she says.

Where the book takes on Arabic it doesn't do so well. Brind Morrow clearly learned enough of the language to get by, but not enough to transcribe it correctly: Why is '*am* (uncle) constantly written *Om* (mother)? Abu Shnab becomes Abu Shendab, Shatarang becomes Shararang. We are told that *naama* [sic] means light, when it means smooth. These are details, but they point to a handicap which makes it impossible for her to pick up clues vital to her mission.

She tells us, for example, that in hieroglyphs the word for death is the word for mother: mut. She does not tell us that in Arabic too, the word for death is *mut*.

Similarly, Brind Morrow's main quest in the Eastern desert is 'the Elba massif . . . the central feature in the tribal territory between Egypt and Sudan . . . there is a legend that the mountain is a place of origins, is itself a living being'. She tells us that the Elba massif is on the Galala Plateau. She does not tell us that *galala* is majesty, attributable, for Muslims, only to the living God.

For someone searching for 'the threads that run throughout language' it seems a fairly large blind spot.

Becoming Edward Said [1]

Edward W. Said, *Out of Place: A Memoir*

'Regard experiences, then,' Edward Said wrote in the conclusion to his *Culture and Imperialism*, 'as if they were about to disappear: what is it about them that anchors or roots them in reality? What would you save of them, what would you give up, what would you recover?' *Culture and Imperialism* was published in 1993. In September 1991 a routine blood test had revealed to Said that he had chronic lymphocytic leukaemia. His response – aside from finding the brilliant doctor in whose care he has been ever since – was to lever a new and enormous task into his already teeming schedule. The task, in effect, of answering his questions as applied to his own life. In 1992 he returned – for the first time in forty-five years – to Palestine. The following year – also after a long absence – to Cairo. In May 1994 he started his 'archaeological prying into a very distant and essentially irrecoverable past'. The memoir, *Out of Place*, is both the process and the result of that excavation. The 'experiences' it digs for have of course disappeared, but so also has their context, their location; the writer's only resource is memory.

We are all dispossessed of our childhoods; we return to a remembered or imagined scene to find at best frayed edges and faded colours. I say 'at best'; for many of us the changes are more than the forgivable effects of time and an altered consciousness: in Cairo flyovers overshadow beloved streets, elegant old buildings are pulled down and monster towers raised in their lieu. In Baghdad one can only guess at what a

[1] The *Journal of Palestine Studies*, spring 2000.

returning Iraqi might (not) find. But nowhere, of course, are the changes more sweeping, more radical than in the cities and towns of Palestine. And of Palestine Edward Said has been twice dispossessed.

His father, Wadie Ibrahim, a self-invented and dedicated businessman, found his home town, Jerusalem, too small for his ambitions and, in 1929, branched out with his Standard Stationery Company to Cairo where he became phenomenally successful. In 1932 he returned to Nazareth to marry Hilda Musa, the Baptist minister's daughter, and although their son, Edward, was born in Jerusalem three years later, and the new (nuclear) family would frequently – until he was twelve – visit the old (extended one) in Jerusalem and Safad, their workaday life was lived in Cairo:

> As we increasingly spent time in Cairo, Palestine acquired a languid almost dreamlike aspect for me. There I did not feel as acutely the solitude I began to dread later, at eight or nine, and although I sensed the absence of closely organised space and time that made up my life in Egypt, I could not completely enjoy the relative freedom from it that I had in Jerusalem. I recall thinking that being in Jerusalem was pleasant but tantalisingly open, temporary, even transitory, as indeed it later was.

So although '[Palestine] was a place I took for granted, the country I was from, where family and friends existed . . . with unreflecting ease', it was also 'transitory' and 'dreamlike'. Lost, one might say, already.

And lost again when, having spent most of 1947 in the old family home in Talbiyah, and enrolled in St George's School where his father (and possibly his grandfather) had studied and where he 'very quickly felt totally at home; for the first and last time in my school life I was among boys who were like me. Nearly every member of my class was known to my family', the twelve-year-old Said left Jerusalem in December with his father, mother and sisters, never to return.

In Cairo it was from a position of wealth and seeming security that he was 'a scarcely conscious, essentially unknowing witness' to the start of the Palestinian diaspora. Family and friends began to arrive in the city, people like Sbeer Shammas, Wadie's cousin, 'a patriarchal figure of authority and prosperity in Jerusalem [who] now appeared in Cairo as a much older and frailer man, always wearing the same suit and green sweater, his bent cane bearing his large slow bulk as he lowered it painfully and slowly into the chair where he sat in silence'. And it was through his aunt Nabiha, in whose Talbiyah house he had lived in Jerusalem, that Said first experienced Palestine

> as history and cause in the anger and consternation I felt over the suffering of the refugees, those Others, whom she brought into my life. It was also she who communicated to me the desolations of being without a country or place to return to, of being unprotected by any national authority or institutions, of no longer being able to make sense of the past except as bitter, helpless regret nor of the present with its daily queuing, anxiety-filled search for jobs, and poverty, hunger and humiliations.

Aunt Nabiha ran a kind of one-woman aid centre for her compatriots and, over fifty years later, her nephew faithfully records her efforts and those of the family doctor, Wadie (and later his son, Farid) Haddad and the driver, Osta Ibrahim, who helped her. He also places on record the names and circumstances of family and friends (Michael Marmoura, Munir Musa, Shafeec and Lore Mansour, Yousif Beidas, etc.) exiled from Palestine and fated to live out their fractured lives in Toronto or Wisconsin or other towns whose principal significance for them was that they were places of refuge.

It was, presumably, Said's account of 1947/48 that was the intended target for the spoiler launched by an American-Israeli lawyer, one Justus Reid Weiner, in the pages of

Commentary a few weeks before the book's publication in the UK last September. Weiner's sleuthing had yielded the information that the house in Talbiyah was not registered in Wadie Ibrahim's name but in the name of his cousin and business partner, Boulos Said, Aunt Nabiha's husband. Ergo, Said had falsified his history 'to strengthen his wider ideological agenda – and in particular to promote the claims of Palestinian refugees against Israel'. Weiner later admitted that the contents of *Out of Place* were '100% true' but speculated that Said might have 'caught wind of his investigation and, realising the jig was up, hastened to correct himself in print' (*New York Magazine*, 27 September 1999). The sheer preposterousness of the attack and the follow-up speculation would waft them off together to the realm of the absurd were it not for the unseemly and uncritical glee with which they were taken up by various papers in the US and the *Telegraph* in Britain. For Palestinians particularly, the episode demonstrated once more that process by which they are required over and over again to 'prove' that they are indeed Palestinian; that they exist. Said himself, despite his evident anger, conducted himself with his accustomed poise: 'I'm not into victimhood, it's not my style. All that is made absolutely clear in my book . . . I never suffered the fate of a wretched refugee.'

But didn't he? A refugee he technically wasn't; after all, he held American citizenship through his father who had served with the American army during the First World War. But wretched he mostly was, wealthy father and loving mother notwithstanding. A different and difficult only son with four sisters, a (sometimes crazily) dominant father and an elegantly manipulative mother, a Christian Palestinian in Arab Muslim Egypt, an Arab child in a colonial British school in Cairo and then a supposedly American child with an Arab surname and a British schoolboy's clothes in an American school also in Cairo, an Anglophone in a Francophone community, the list goes on and on. His account of the first two decades of his life, wedged firmly out of place by his family's position and leanings, must surely touch even the most neutral reader.

And I am not a neutral reader; Edward Said is my friend. But there was something other than friendship in the emotional charge this book had for me, and other too than a reader's sympathy for living characters or a lover of literature's delight in a well-wrought book. There was, on page after page, the pleasure of recognition, the discovery of a shared perspective, and the sorrow of a common loss.

An example: he describes the corner building in Zamalek where, above Vasilakis' grocery, his aunt Nabiha received the many dispossessed Palestinians who from 1948 onward came to her for help. That corner is the corner of the street where I grew up, Vasilakis' is where we bought our groceries and in the same building was the studio of Salah Taher where I went many times in 1971 to have my portrait painted: Taher's gift to me for my twenty-first birthday. Now the studio is in disuse, Aunt Nabiha and her refugees are long since gone and Vasilakis' itself has been replaced; cheap, gaudy shoes substituted for the soap and yoghurt and cheese that formed – as we say – the flesh on our shoulders. Crossing the golf course of the Gezira Club, hearing one's name called at dusk as you played in the rock hideaways of the Fish Garden, family excursions for tea at Mena House or picnics at the Barrages, the father of the family briefly liberated into exuberant playfulness, American films at Cinema Metro, tennis at the Tewfiqiyya Club – Said is there, just ahead of me. And other things too: the life lived simultaneously in English and Arabic, the imagining of oneself into the comics or novels we read, the response to the different and authentic energy in the conversation and company of maids and drivers, the cherishing of 'the sounds made by the orchestra's pre-performance tune-ups' on the radio, and then his description of himself in New York doing what I did years later in the north of England: parcelling up memories of life in Cairo, rationing them, pulling them up to help one fall asleep in one's loneliness. Words written from the heart strike at the heart. And underneath it all, the gradual shifting of literature into central position, the dependence on it, the almost belief that it can save us.

But my childhood was a happy one, my family (and therefore I) essentially in place: Egyptian, Muslim, the new forward-looking professionals and academics of revolutionary Egypt. In 1942 Said had been forbidden to speak Arabic at the British Gezira Preparatory School, in '58, barely 500 metres down the road, I walked to school in a uniform that carried the proud emblem of Amun, God of Ancient Egypt. The seismic shifts that settled my people comfortably into their space in Egypt finally dislodged his from their (albeit borrowed and provisional) space in it.

Yet Said and his mother (and presumably other members of the family) were emotionally and morally drawn to Nasser's project, more or less siding with it against the interests of their class and sect. Once again, I find myself thinking that a major fault of the Nasser regime was that it did not, in the end, believe in itself enough; it had enemies, yes, but perhaps not as many as it thought. Farid Haddad, the gentle physician son of Said's family doctor and my uncle's comrade was not its enemy. Yet he was killed by the 'reception beating' he had to have when he was picked up by the police for suspected Communist activities in '59. My parents, like Said's, distrusted politics and where Said's parents kept silent on Palestine mine did not discuss (in front of me) their reservations about certain aspects of Nasser's policies. And then 1967 caught up with us all. Said describes a chilling scene in December of that year when he visits Charles Malik (married to his mother's cousin and former Lebanese ambassador to the UN and Washington) in Rabiyé, north-east of Beirut, with the vague idea of 'getting him to come out, to speak and help guide the Arabs out of their incredible defeat'. He is stunned by Malik's cold dismissiveness, astonished that what he 'had assumed was a common need to resist and rebuild' was not shared by a man whose ideas and commitment he still had faith in.

Malik was, in fact, in the process of turning himself into the chief ideologue for the anti-Palestinian Christian right whose eventual collaboration with Israel resulted in – among other things – the Sabra and Chatila massacres.

That December was about the time when we teenagers in Cairo started putting up posters of the PLO 'freedom fighters' as they were then. 'The children of '48,' the slogan ran, 'are the commandos of '68.' There were posters of Che also, and we boiled and foamed out of the universities demanding that the leadership be brought to trial, demanding the right to have a say, the right, indeed, to fight. 'A common need to resist and rebuild.' In a *Guardian* interview last year, Said restated what he has said for years: that it was precisely because he was not living in a refugee camp, because he was in a position of privilege, that he felt the need and the obligation to identify himself as Palestinian, to make the Palestinian cause his cause. By doing so he moved from being a professional, a specialist, a professor of comparative literature and founder of post-colonial studies, to being a public intellectual. In the Reith lectures, delivered in London in 1993 and later published as *Representations of the Intellectual* (1994), he describes the functions of this role, and chief among them is the critical analysis of received opinion and the paramount duty to intellectual truth; the necessary stand for the intellectual is a moral stand and the natural place is in opposition. *Out of Place* locates some of the earliest foundations of this view.

Example: At Victoria College, Cairo, Said is caught throwing stones during lunch break. This results in a severe caning, ordered by the weak, ill, colonial headmaster, J. G. E. Price and administered 'with neutral efficiency' by his secretary, Mr Lagnado, a Europeanised Eastern Jew whom Said had previously heard admonishing an Armenian boy who was dipping his bread in his gravy: '*Ne mange pas comme les Arabes.*' Smarting with insult and injury the fourteen-year-old Said vows 'to make "their" lives miserable, without getting caught, without allowing myself ever to get close to any of them, taking from them what they had to offer entirely my own way'. And if this smacks of Stephen's famous vow in *A Portrait of the Artist as a Young Man*, why that confirms the lived reality of Dedalus' and Said's experience and the porousness of the boundaries between literature and life.

Of school at Mount Hermon:

> I soon discovered that I would have to be on my guard against authority and that I needed to develop some mechanism or drive not to be discouraged by what I took to be efforts to silence me or deflect me from being who I was rather than becoming who they wanted me to be. In the process I began a life-long struggle and attempt to demystify the capriciousness and hypocrisy of a power whose authority depended absolutely on its ideological self-image as a moral agent, acting in good faith and with unimpeachable intentions.

That 'deflect me from being who I was' is crucial; for Said did not yet know who he was. He knew who he wasn't: the 'Edward' that his father, his mother, his schools, in effect everybody was trying to make him into and who, therefore, never matched up, was always a disappointment, always in trouble. He suspected he was someone else, someone different and special and, at times, his mother seemed to have this knowledge too. She, more than anyone, seemed able to give him access to his secret self – but he could never quite rely on her. The slow and painful discovery/formation of this self and its relationship to Said's other selves, in short the question of identity, is central to the process of *Out of Place*. At an early point, in reaction to his 'colonial' schooling, and chafing at his father's acquiescing in being designated a 'khawaga' (a European) in Egypt, Said notes his 'emerging consciousness of [himself] as something altogether more complex and authentic than a colonial mimic'.

A couple of years ago, writing a short notice for Said's

Peace and its Discontents, I noted that from his 'difficult situation as a Palestinian in the United States and an American in the Arab world he addresses East and West with even fairness and vigour. In the articles written for the Western press he speaks of shoddy American deal-making, of Israel's imperialism and racist policies. In the Arab press he writes of the compromises of the Palestinian leadership and the brutality of its security apparatus. To Arabs eager to canonise him as an implacable foe of Israel he writes of the need to establish dialogue with dissident Israelis like Israel Shahak and Danny Rubenstein.' (*TLS*, December 1996) Perhaps the role of the public intellectual is the only one that will allow (perhaps necessitate) Said's fluid identity; the only 'place' where he can be not out of place. Just as his advocacy of the Palestinian cause is the closest he can come to regaining the homeland he never had.

This memoir is essentially a record of the emotions. The plot has been determined by others: fate, history, politics, his parents; it is to describe and understand his own moral and psychological development as a character in this already written 'text' that Said deploys his literary critical arsenal in this excavation of memory. And he does it with sensitivity and courage. Three times in the course of an almost 300-page book he refers to his illness. The first time is in the preface. The second time is briefly at the end of the first third of the book, in a chapter that outlines his discovery of music and its central importance in his life. The third is at the beginning of the last third of the book, at the beginning of a chapter of painstaking self-analysis he describes how *Out of Place* was written in 'counterpoint' to the leukaemia and the treatment he was undergoing. This is in no sense special pleading, rather the ongoing (and clearly urgent) need to place everything in context, to trace 'the pattern in the carpet'. Cancer is, it seems, part of the legacy inherited from his parents. What of the rest of that legacy? His father battled to mould him, to create the 'Edward' he imagined as his only son. Yet, by forcing his extremely unwilling departure to Mount Hermon at fifteen, later engineering his exile from Cairo for fifteen years and supporting him financially throughout his student years, he made it possible for him to shake free of that very mould, to discover his hidden self. His mother, simultaneously cherishing and undermining him, was yet the foundation for the sustaining passions of his life: language and music. Throughout the book Said examines their characters in detail, generously trying to see and represent them as their own selves, linked to but apart from the personae they were as his parents. In effect, while his body and his blood are subject to the most detailed medical analysis and procedure, himself and those he holds dear are subject to the most detailed psychological and historical analysis. And how it all must have hurt.

But he has come through; continues to come through. This wonderful book has been written, and, nine years after his diagnosis he is still fighting. His list of acknowledgements, most particularly the loving message to Mariam, his wife, and Najla and Wadie, his children, are witness to the people who are grateful for that. For myself, I have been sustained by Edward Said in person for the last nineteen years, and by the idea of Edward Said for longer. As with Gorky on Tolstoy: I sleep better knowing that Said is alive in the same world.

Golden Child [1]

Christine El Mahdi, *Tutankhamen: The Life and Death of a Boy King*

When Christine El Mahdi was seven she happened to pick up a book about Ancient Egypt. Next day she persuaded her father to take her to their local museum in Bolton, England. 'Here', she writes, 'I could see a mural through the fanlight of a door, but I could not get into the gallery as it was not finished.' Over the following months she 'devoured' everything she could find about Ancient Egypt and started to teach herself to read hieroglyphics. By the age of nine she was certain she wanted to be something nobody she knew had ever heard of: an Egyptologist.

This little story on the first page of the foreword to *Tutankhamen: The Life and Death of a Boy King* highlights characteristics demonstrated on every page of this remarkable book: El Mahdi's passion for her subject, her determined pursuit of material in Egypt and in what seem to be all the museums of the world, and her insistent return to original sources; to what the Egyptians themselves wrote, carved and drew.

And of course seeing fragments through the fanlight of an incomplete gallery is an apt metaphor for Egyptology itself. Tutankhamen himself may be regarded as a tiny fragment in the four thousand or so years that make up the history of Ancient Egypt. In fact, I don't believe I had heard of him until I came across him in the West. Egyptian history in Egyptian schools tends to concentrate on Pharaohs who *did* things: Mena who unified Upper and Lower Egypt in 3200

[1] The *Washington Post*, 24 December 2000.

BC, giving us the Egypt we know (and giving his name to the hotel in Giza where Churchill, Roosevelt and Stalin signed the end of the Second World War), Khofu who built the Great Pyramid, Sesostris who cut the first canal joining the Nile to the Red Sea, Akhenaten who proclaimed the worship of the Aten, the One God, and so on.

Tutankhamen is the young king who reigned for a mere nine years after the death of Akhenaten. Not much at all is known about him, but piecing together his story El Mahdi takes her readers on a wonderful journey of discovery. She places her fragments (stones, mummies, historical data, circumstances of a particular excavation, other people's scholarship) meticulously on to a map of Egyptian history, custom and belief. In doing so she dismantles the most widely received ideas about Akhenaten. She shows how his religious ideas were not a new heresy but a crystallisation of the beliefs of his father, Amenhotep III, and his grandfather, Tuthmosis IV. She undoes the spin put on him thousands of years ago by Horemheb, the army general who took power shortly after the death of Tutankhamen and – more recently – by Egyptologists keen to portray the Ancient Egyptians as irredeemably 'pagan' and resistant to the idea of the One God.

Her tools are what appears to be an exhaustive knowledge of the scholarship, fluency in hieroglyphics, logic, common sense and the absence of an agenda. And so she draws the reader with her into a detective story, one of the most attractive features of which is her hands-on brand of Egyptology: 'If you go to the temple at Karnak at around three in the afternoon on any day, when the rays of the sun fall obliquely over the walls, you will see images carved lightly on Amenhotep's third pylon. These images are invisible at other times of the day, and are indeed only clearly visible for a period of around thirty minutes.' These lightly carved images provide a crucial clue to when Akhenaten's reign started; a point which itself is crucial to what comes next in the story.

El Mahdi's close engagement with her subject is everywhere to be felt. Describing Amenhotep III marrying (over and above his Great Royal Wife Queen Tiye) a foreign princess, then apparently marrying his own daughter and having a child with her, El Mahdi comments, 'From a personal point of view, one cannot but admire a woman who took all of this in her stride, and still managed to support her son [Akhenaten who was setting up his independent court] as well as running foreign state affairs.'

Tutankhamen: The Life and Death of a Boy King is more than what its title suggests. It is a survey of ancient Egyptian beliefs and a history of one of the most powerful Pharaonic dynasties. It is also an object lesson in painstaking research, in independence of mind and in sympathetic reconstruction. 'Scholarly work on the whole, finds a limited reading market, while wild theories, usually based on nothing but intuition, reach a wide readership,' El Mahdi justifiably complains. Let's hope that – in this instance at least – she's proved wrong.

Al-Jazeera[1]

The first time I happened on al-Jazeera was in a hotel room in Cairo. I was channel-hopping at two in the morning and suddenly there was a channel, speaking in Arabic, but in a way I had only ever heard people speak in private – away from the censorship and the various state security services that dominate our public discourse. This particular debate was between two Algerians: one a dissident (and exiled) journalist, the other a representative of the government. It was ferocious. They were naming names, citing incidents, quoting figures. It was live – and alive. Then, wonder upon wonder, there was a phone-in. People called from all over the world to ask questions, express views. I wondered if what I was watching was a play, or a hoax; the theatre is allowed a little more leeway than reportage. I phoned my mother, my brother: 'That's al-Jazeera,' they said, 'isn't it amazing?'

Back in London I had a dish installed and I was in touch. When the current Palestinian Intifada broke out a year ago I became hooked. In a way, even though the images we saw on al-Jazeera were far worse than the ones presented on British television, it was a relief to see them straight and hear the interviews from the ground rather than getting reports from the British TV point of view.

Al-Jazeera interviewed Sheikh Hasan Nasrallah (of Hezbollah) and Ehud Barak (then Prime Minister of Israel), Sheikh Ahmad Yaseen (spiritual leader of Hamas) and Itzhak Rabin (now Israeli Foreign Minister). It was the first time any of these people had been interviewed on Arab

[1] The *Guardian*, 9 October 2001.

TV. Nasrallah and Yaseen have never to my knowledge been interviewed on Western TV.

In the current crisis al-Jazeera's reporting has been straight and sober; a welcome relief from the flag-waving and rhetoric of CNN for example. Sunday night, when the US and Britain started bombing Afghanistan, the gale that was blowing over London blew away my satellite reception. I was so bereft I found myself staring at the black screen, trying to stare through it to what al-Jazeera might be transmitting.

Within the Arab world this channel has made censorship of news and of opinion pointless. For us outside it provides the one window through which we can breathe. It also provides reassurance against the negative or partial image of ourselves constantly beamed at us every day from the media of whatever country we happen to find ourselves in. It's not that we want to hear our own opinions, rather we want to hear a variety of opinions of which ours is one. The titles of some of their most popular programmes speak for themselves: 'Against the Current', 'The Opposite Direction', 'One Opinion and Another' and so on.

Perhaps the most poignant example of the unique work undertaken by al-Jazeera is a two-part documentary on Egyptian prisoners of war killed by the Israeli army in 1967. An Israeli journalist and an Israeli academic presented their research. Egyptians and Israelis bore witness to what had happened. No government is interested.

I have often found myself while watching al-Jazeera, translating the interviews into English in my head, wishing I could transmit them, wishing that people who could not speak Arabic could somehow have access to what was being said: to all our humanly varied points of view.

The Language of the Veil[1]

1923: Stepping down from the train in Cairo Central Station, Hoda Hanim Sha'rawi lifts her hand to the side of her face, undoes a golden clasp, and her fine white crêpe de Chine yashmak flutters to the ground. At that moment, the Turkish-style veil ceased to be *de rigueur* for Egyptian women of the upper class. Sha'rawi was handsome, wealthy, widowed and securely aristocratic, with powerful political connections through both her father and her husband. She had been in Rome on behalf of the Egyptian Women's Union, a trip that was one more chapter in Egypt's modernisation project. The gesture, at its final moment, resolved a debate that had occupied Egyptian society for almost thirty years.

Or, at least, everyone thought it had. How strange and how telling that now, some eighty years later, here we are talking once more about 'the veil'. How odd, also, that we don't have one word in Arabic equivalent to 'the veil'. But perhaps not odd at all, for doesn't English have bowler hats and top hats and trilbys and cloth caps and boaters and Stetsons, while Arabic only has *qubba'ah*, 'hat'? And when the West – always so inordinately interested in what Arab (or 'Eastern') women wear – talks about 'the veil', doesn't it mysteriously elide the 'seductive' veil as worn by, say, Colette in her Egyptian Tableaux, and the 'forbidding' veil as 'forced' on to contemporary Eastern women? To the West, 'the veil', like Islam itself, is both sensual and puritanical, is contradictory, is to be feared. It is also concrete, and is to do with women, and since cultural battles are so

[1] The *Guardian*, 8 December 2001.

often fought through the bodies of women, it is seized upon by politicians, columnists, feminists . . .

And so it is that, having refused many times to write about 'the veil', I am now trying to put together some thoughts about the 'dress code' of Arab or Muslim women. But I immediately run into problems. Muslim women are not all Arab. The conditions of Irani women are different from those of the women of Pakistan, Turkey, Indonesia and now, famously, Afghanistan. And they are all different from the Arabs. And not all Arab women are Muslim. Thirty years ago, you could not have told whether an Egyptian woman was Christian or Muslim by her dress. In Palestinian villages, you still can't tell. So whose dress code shall I talk about? Where? The clusters of women you see around the shops in Knightsbridge, tented in black, their faces muzzled with leather-and-brass-beaked masks, are from the Gulf states and would (and do) look equally out of place in the shopping malls of Cairo and Beirut. Similarly, the women with layers of black chiffon over their faces and Jimmy Choo slingbacks tripping out from under their black abayas are Saudi, and their face coverings send out a different signal from those of an Egyptian or an Algerian. So let us say, for the moment, that we're looking at the dress codes of Egyptian women. Let us further say that the women we will look at will be urban.

In every country, social, cultural and political changes manifest themselves in dress. In Europe, we see this in the loose 'empire' cuts favoured by French ladies after the Revolution, or in the flapper styles that swept England after the First World War, or indeed in the miniskirts that came along the late 1960s with the sexual revolution and the crystallisation of women's lib. None of this is news. And the principle holds for us in the Arab world as well. Except that, in the Arab world, there has been – since the end of the nineteenth century – an additional factor: the powerful presence of the West in our lives and its influence on our social, cultural and political changes. It is interesting, for example, that the Bedouin societies of the Arabian peninsula who came into contact with the West only in the past fifty years or so, and whose contact was essentially political and economic, rather than cultural, and who were also in a position of strength due to their oil, have seen no need for the wholesale adoption of Western fashion by their men any more than by their women.

That image of Hoda Sha'rawi unveiling in public was present in the school books of Nasser's Egypt, and to us – the school children of the time – the contradiction in it was not immediately apparent. Sha'rawi was part of the struggle to break free from the grip of a European power, yet she publicly adopted the 'revealed face' code of that same power. My parents' and grandparents' generations were able to live with this contradiction, because they thought (at least, the ones that thought about it did) that politics and culture existed in two separate realms – that even though we needed to shake off the West's political yoke, the Western was the more advanced culture and it was, therefore, progressive to adopt it. As overwrought Arabic narrative forms already in decline gave way to the adopted novel, and the folkloric 'shadow-play' transmuted into the three-act drama; as Egyptian sculptors started to exhibit their works and musicians to incorporate waltzes into the traditional Arab quarter-tones, so men doffed their jibbahs and qaftans and climbed into suits, and women uncovered their faces and hair and donned tailored skirts and jackets and flowered frocks.

A picture I'm looking at now shows a leading Egyptian journalist interviewing Indira Gandhi in 1955. The journalist, Amina al-Sa'id, is wearing a sleeveless, almost off-the-shoulder flowered dress. No one thought anything of it. Yet I'd lay odds that no Egyptian journalist working today would allow herself to be photographed so uncovered. Why? What happened?

Four Women of Egypt is a brilliant documentary exploring the lives, arguments and friendship of four very different women. At one point, we see stills from the 1960s and 1970s showing Safinaz Kazem, a well-known writer and columnist, svelte and alluring in an assortment of slinky suits and Audrey Hepburn-type shift dresses. Then Kazem, in 1998, in loose clothing and a scarf covering her hair, says, 'For years, we ran around in short skirts and bare arms saying to them, "Look, see, we're just like you." Enough. It got us nowhere. We're not like them, and they shouldn't matter. We have to find a way to be ourselves.'

It seems it has taken our defeat in the war with Israel in 1967, Nasser's death and Sadat's coming to power in 1970 to bring us back to the position of one of the pioneering feminists, Malak Hifni Nasif, who wrote in 1906 that the veil was, so to speak, a red herring. Her view was that the question of the veil was central in the debate about women's place in society only because the West (personified in Egypt then by Lord Cromer) had made it so. She urged that reformers should concentrate on questions of education, health and economic independence – i.e., the opportunity to work outside the home – and let the veil take care of itself. In the Cairo of the time, women covered their hair with a tarha, a thin material in either black or white. For their faces, they had a choice of the white yashmak, which was drawn across the face under the eyes and connoted the aristocracy and their imitators; the bisha, which could be casually thrown over the whole face and was neutral in class terms; and the burqu', a rectangle of the same fabric as fishnet stockings that was hung from under the eyes with a small decorative gold or brass cylinder at its centre over the nose. This last was very much the accessory of the bint al-balad, the 'native woman' of the working or lower middle class, who had no desire to imitate the yashmak or bisha-wearing ladies. It is, of course, different from the Afghani 'burka', and would not have afforded much of a disguise in the Simpson and Ridley antics.[2]

---

[2] John Simpson and Yvonne Ridley who entered Afghanistan during the bombing disguised in Burkas.

When I was growing up in the 1960s, the tarha was generally worn by women of the working class and by traditional women over, say, fifty of all classes. The burqu' could still be glimpsed as a piece of exotica in some popular districts of Cairo, but the bisha and the yashmak were to be found only in sepia photographs.

1971: Until the early 1970s, if you sat in the Café Riche on Qasr el-Nil Street watching the world go by, you could tell fairly accurately what a person was by their clothes. And, generally, the more affluent a person was, the more Westernised they looked. That woman there, the slim one in the well-cut suit with the skirt just above the knee, in sunglasses; she might be an engineer/doctor/lawyer/academic/ranking civil servant, or married to one; or she may own one of the new boutiques that have started appearing as Sadat yanks the reins sharply right towards a capitalist, open-door economy. That child hurrying across the street in slippers and an ill-fitting dress with a white kerchief binding her hair is a servant-girl, sent out to fetch something in a hurry. And here come two women deep in conversation – one has her hair covered in a kind of filigree bonnet, the other wears hers in a bun; they walk slowly in their sensible shoes, and they wear what most Cairene women wear: a straight, dark gabardine skirt ending just below the knee and over it a shirt in a floral or geometric pattern with an open collar and sleeves just above the elbow. They are (or are married to) minor civil servants, school teachers or legal workers, but they might also be the wives of men in trade, or workers in the large public-sector factories: textiles, pharmaceuticals, food, steel and so on. In other words, they are either the petty bourgeoisie or the upwardly mobile working class. As for that comely, plump woman hurrying along, her long, black overdress similar to that of the peasant-woman, her head covered in a loose black transparent tarha over the flowered scarf that binds her hair, she might be married to a butcher's or grocer's assistant, she might work as a cleaner in a school or a hospital or a government office.

Men pass, too, but we ignore them as we watch a bevy of young women saunter by in skirts above the knee and jeans, in tight jumpers and silver bracelets, their hair flowing on their shoulders or cut short *comme les garçons*. These are students from one of Cairo's various universities, arts academies and colleges.

If we're watching closely, the silver bracelets should tell us something, for since the mid-1960s there has been a revival of interest in traditional culture. Folkloric dance troupes have been formed, the Arabic Music Ensemble plays to packed houses, motifs from Egyptian epics find their way into three-act dramas, the comfortably-off are ordering bits of mashrabiyya and appliqué tapestries for their homes (to the relief of the craftsmen, who were dying out fast) and the fashionable silver jewellery blends Pharaonic design with inscriptions of classical Arabic poetry. Some women artists, such as the documentary film-maker Atiyyat al-Abnudi, in the absence of a national costume, adopt a modified version of the peasant-woman's smocked and colourful galabiyyas, getting them made up in pure cottons or rich velvets.

2001: Thirty years have passed as we take our seats today at the Café Riche, which – thank goodness – is still there: Qasr el-Nil Street throngs with three times more people than it did on that October afternoon long ago, and the daughters of those women we watched then are having a harder time getting through the crowds. Most of the women struggling to keep a foothold on the pavement are in a variant of the old uniform: the straight gabardine skirt is now just above the ankles, the patterned shirt is longer, and now has long sleeves. The head is covered with a scarf folded into a large, concealing triangle.

This has become the 'default' dress. In the 1970s, the regime of President Anwar Sadat did three things: it switched the Egyptian economy from socialist to capitalist and opened the door to foreign investment, it signed a peace treaty with Israel and, to weaken the opposition critical of both these policies, it nurtured and funded the political Islamist groups. The sky-high inflation resulting from the economic policy and the corruption that came along with it led whoever could to head for the oil-rich Arab states, thus opening the way for their brand of puritanical Islam to enter Egypt. The ones who did not leave – the majority of the population – became increasingly disenfranchised, hard-up and angry; except, that is, for the very, very few who were making money rapidly.

The treaty with Israel, when it was not followed by a just settlement for the Palestinians, and even though it won back the Sinai for Egypt, generated more anger still; except, that is, for the very, very few who developed vested interests with Israel. Both these policies – involving, as they did a turning-away from the Soviet Union – were perceived as Western-backed. So people questioned whether following the West was good for Egypt. Perhaps, they thought, we should look back at ourselves, at our own history and traditions, and find the way forward there. Sadat's third policy ensured that the anger and questioning had no outlet, no platform or expression except the Islamist one. Covering her hair then started as a woman's act of political protest and a symbol of a search for an Egyptian, non-Westernised identity. In two decades, it became simply what you did – unless you took a conscious decision not to.

Many young women in the street today are in hijab: a long, loose garment topped with a large plain scarf securely fastened so no hair, ears or neck show through. Some wear it because they believe this is what a good Muslim woman should wear, and, they add, why should men who are not entitled look at my hair or my figure? It neutralises, they say, men's tendency to look at women as sex objects. Some wear it because it deals with the economic problem posed by the need to wear different outfits for different occasions, and makes you a good Muslim into the bargain. Some wear it because their friends are wearing it and they don't want to stand out, and if their friends think it makes you a good Muslim, well, why not?

Today, I see only one woman in the full niqab, a black hijab outfit with a thick, black cloth over the face and a narrow slit to see through. She hurries along, her every movement as deliberate as her garb, which says loud and clear: 'I am a political Islamist. I believe our only solution lies in creating an Islamic state. I am in opposition to this government.' It takes guts to do this in these days of arbitrary detentions and torture. Guts, or desperation.

Tyres shriek. A woman has started to cross the street and is almost run over by a speeding Cherokee. The driver leans out of the window. Her hair is expensively streaked and her lip-lined mouth screams at the pedestrian: 'Open your eyes, you backward one.' She wears an imitation tiger-skin top, and if she were to step out of the car we would see that she is in boots and leather trousers. In the back seat, there is a small Filipina nanny, which means that her daughter, in Gap jeans in the passenger seat, probably does not speak Arabic. This is the family of one of the businessmen who have made it big in the new economic climate.

The woman who was almost run over adjusts her head-scarf and dusts down her brown, gabardine skirt. She mutters something about 'the pashas of these sooty times' and passers-by shake their heads in sympathy. She is a teacher married to an architect. Unable to make ends meet in the inflation-ridden 1970s, they had migrated to Kuwait, but were asked to leave after the Gulf War. They lost their savings in the collapse of the big Islamist investment companies, and are now more or less back where they started. There are many, many like her. Where do they go from here?

For at least 4,000 years, Egyptian women have understood the power of the image and have, when they could, manipulated it to their advantage. Nefertiti, reigning with her husband Akhenatun as the first co-monarch, had herself depicted as the goddess Isis, a PR coup to be followed by Cleopatra some fourteen centuries later when she made her triumphal entry into Rome as Caesar's honoured guest. In more modern times, Shahindah Miqlid, who presented herself as a traditional beauty in her portrait of 1953, transformed herself in 1966 into a modern 'woman of the people' as she demanded that the murder of her husband (allegedly) by a feudal family be investigated. And Rawiyah Atiyyah, running for elections after Suez (or, as we know it, the Port Said war) created an icon by celebrating her victory in battle fatigues.

So what do we do now? The image we need to project should embody our Egyptian notion of ourselves at this moment. It should also appeal to the audience. But we are multiple and varied, and who's sitting in the dress circle? Many think there's no longer any point in playing to the West. And there is no Second Power. And – until the bombing of Afghanistan – political Islam had lost credibility in the Egyptian street. If only we had a national costume, such as a sari or a sirwal qamis, a lot of us would probably be wearing it right now.

Cabool Cotillion[1]

Philip Hensher, *The Mulberry Empire*

Penning (or keying in) the final sentences of his novel on Good Friday 2001, Philip Hensher could not have known that by the time *The Mulberry Empire* was published the name of the city he wrote of, the 'jewelled city of Kabul', would once again be on everyone's tongue. And if post-colonial awareness means that London isn't quite dancing the 'Cabool Cotillion' as it did some 160 years ago, the progress of history also means that today's power-reshuffle has cost thousands more Afghani lives than the ill-starred British adventure of 1839.

The novel, starting some few years before 1839, moves between Afghanistan on the one hand, and Britain and Russia, the two powers vying to possess it, on the other. Alexander Burnes, on a 'geographical' expedition, is waiting in a Kabuli house, for an audience with the Amir Dost Muhammad Khan, Prince of the Afghans. When Burnes, back in London, publishes *Travels into Bokhara and Cabool* he is received by royalty, fêted by society, loved by Bella Garraway and crystallised into an apologist for 'benevolent' and expanding imperialism. He returns to the East as an agent of empire.

The counterpoint to the triumphal, public, outward-bound – and ultimately disastrous – movement of imperial expansion is the disgrace and retreat into the countryside of Bella Garraway. But in her banishment, with her life pared down to essentials (among which, tellingly, are 500 books and a sofa on which to read them) Bella finds true love and happiness.

[1] The *Guardian*, 23 March 2002.

The story of Bella, in her ruined, moated castle, its unused rooms still with false memories, is echoed and varied by the story of an Afghani woman, Jamila (also 'the beautiful one'). And the story of Jamila, whose lover loses her by going out to seek wealth before returning (too late) to claim her is in turn a contrast to the story of Akbar who acts – and quickly – to claim what is his.

The novel is full of such deft patterned echoes, such hints at similarity and contrast. The princes of the Amir Dost Muhammad's court are humiliated by his weekly audience with the common people because 'what honour could possibly reside in being the noble designed by ancient custom to hand the Amir his rice, if any Kabul ironmonger could just as easily whisper in the Amir's ear, simply by turning up on a Friday morning?' Reading this we are reminded of London society's thoughts – having dressed for a grand salon some fifty pages earlier – that you drew 'what satisfaction you may from the fact that when you have to go home, outside there may be poor people who may be prepared to gawp, who, you hope, are eaten up with envy of you; because if no-one in London envies you in your party-going plight, it is hard to see why you should continue the exercise'.

In one throwaway moment Hensher offers us an image: a river and in it 'a table, upturned, floating down. And in the table stood a man with a long pole . . . the table drifted along, pushed by the current. The man in his makeshift boat stirred confidently, ineffectively at the river . . . and the river drove him onwards.' If this is a metaphor for life then the image of 'the Amir's empire, so carefully subdued and brought together, like a basket weaved of Jew's-hair thread' will serve as a metaphor for what art does to life. And *The Mulberry Empire* does this with delicacy and gusto. There is pleasure there in passion and in absurdity, in landscape and in conversation, in costume and in food. There is pleasure, I think, above all, in writing. The novel pays elegant homage to Shakespeare, Austen, Tolstoy, Balzac and many others. It puts forward brilliantly realised minor characters then allows them to sink back, out of sight, into their own, unobserved lives. It offers odd little apperçus and improvisations: Masson breaks off from the Persian he has mastered to count in English, '. . . nine, ten, eleven – that was the thing you never got rid of, the counting in your first language'.

The action of the novel is framed by two narratives: Burnes' account of his first journey to Kabul and a circus performance of the reunion of General Sale and his wife Florentia at the end of the campaign. The first, as we know, had dire consequences. The second, as we also know, was a sentimental falsification – but the audience loved it. Are there tricky questions here about writers, representation, responsibility?

It's been said – I forget by whom – that artists are the antennae of society. So perhaps Philip Hensher did sense, early last year and the year before that, that Afghanistan was floating, once again, into bull's-eye in the sights of the powerful.

In an afterword to *The Mulberry Empire* he acknowledges indebtedness to Antonia Byatt for telling him 'bluntly' that he had to write a long novel. We too are in Byatt's debt, for Hensher has given us a delightful entertainment, a timely social and political commentary and a highly literary and ambitious novel.

It Matters[1]

Gilles Kepel, *Bad Moon Rising*

Is the United States' (and Britain's) invasion of Iraq the first move in a far larger game targeting the entire region? Many commentators think so. The tens of millions of the world's citizens who marched last spring were, I believe, opposing not just this war but everything they sensed would follow in its wake.

Would the treatment meted out to Iraq over the last decade – the sanctions, the betrayals, the invasion (with its attendant lies and spin) and now the attempt to exploit and remould the country – would all this have been so easily undertaken had it not been underpinned by a deep prejudice against Arabs and Muslims and a profound ignorance of their histories and cultures?

The American historian, William E. Leuchtenburg, remarked that 'the most striking aspect of the relationship between Arab and American cultures is that to the Americans, the Arabs are a people who have lived outside history'. As for the prejudice, the briefest exposure to mainstream American media confirms it. And since September 11 the language of the more unguarded members and friends of the US administration – their repeated references to 'uncivilised' and 'backward' parts of the world, to 'snakes in swamps' and other images – has been unashamedly racist. Can this state of things be reversed? Can it even be halted?

I now find myself looking at every sentence, every image, that purports to tell the West about the Arabs and the Muslims with this question in mind: to what extent does it feed into existing stereotypes and established prejudice?

[1] July 2003.

What, therefore, do I make of Gilles Kepel's odd little book? While Kepel's previous works have been lengthy results of a fair amount of research, this one comes in at 136 small pages. It is a diary of his stay in what the blurb describes as 'history's most contentious region': twenty-two days in Arab cities and three days in Israel. In the English edition we get a further twelve days in New York, Cambridge and LA. Starting in October 2001, the entries are in the manner of dispatches from the front (vide the book's French title, *Chronique d'une guerre d'Orient*), impressionistic snapshots, short records of conversations, and so on.

In his previous books Kepel has set out the story of the rise of political Islam, charting the post-1967 failure of national governments in the newly decolonised Arab and Muslim countries, their lack of democracy and alternative ideologies; a narrative that most Arab historians agree on. He distinguishes – as all do – between two Islamist tendencies: the young urban poor, made ambitious by education then radicalised into militancy by their disenfranchisement and their lack of any viable economic future, and the 'pious middle classes', influenced by the petro-dollars of Wahhabist Saudi Arabia and sympathetic to the idea of an Islamic state. He freely admits that he was first alerted to this division by Isam al-Iryan, a veteran of the Muslim Brothers.

Kepel's current thesis, articulated in his last book, *Jihad: the Trail of Political Islam* is that political Islam has failed. The violent methods of the young militants have alienated both their popular base and the pious middle classes who fear for their own economic interests. The attacks of 9/11 (and the later ones in Bali and Saudi Arabia and any more that may yet take place), he argues, are nothing more than the death throes of militant Islamism.

Bad Moon Rising demonstrates some uncomfortable traits – as well as giving the Creedence Clearwater Revival song a new twist. The moon here presumably refers to the crescent symbol of Islam. Is the 'bad moon', then, meant to be militant Islam? And if so, why is it 'rising' when Kepel's thesis is that it is on the wane? A book that deals with a specific topic can focus on its research and forego the larger picture. But such a focus becomes a false limit in a book of impressions of people and places. Kepel presents everything through the prism of religion. The graffiti that in Gaza 'covers every available surface with scrupulous calligraphy, no matter what the political tendency' surprises him. 'So much political iconography is unusual in a Sunni land,' he muses 'and is rather reminiscent of Tehran or the southern suburbs of Beirut.' But what other 'Sunni land' is living the conditions of Gaza?

A similar shoe-horn effect is apparent when he describes the portraits of the late President Hafez al-Asad of Syria flanked by his two sons as projecting the 'subliminal image of the Alawite holy trinity'. A Syrian friend of mine commented that Tony Blair and his Cabinet could, by the same reasoning, represent Christ and the Apostles. More serious, though, is his throwing away of an interview with Sayyid Hussein Fadlallah, the leader of Lebanese Hezbollah, a formidable and highly articulate man. He entertains us with the information that Fadlallah's family name translates as 'God's favour' (it would have been more interesting to point out that it is one of the Arab names common to Christians, Jews and Muslims) and ascribes his dismissal of Osama bin Laden as a true thinker and leader to sectarian rather than political or intellectual differences: bin Laden is Sunni, Fadlallah is Shiite. He leaves the interview and goes on to wonder whether Fadlallah was 'implying that the time of the Islamic revolution, and the chimeras it engendered, is past?' To which the obvious response is, why didn't you ask him?

Kepel speculates that 'perhaps religion is only the crystallization of far larger conflicts: the language in which to express, for lack of a better alternative, the vast disquiet in the civilization of Muslim societies, the relationship – both intimate and conflicted – in which they are intertwined with the Western world'. Well, OK, but why 'perhaps'? The conflicts are not in themselves, after all, religious; they are to do with land, human rights, resources, trade agreements and so on. But the real problem here is that picking out the Islamist discourse as the only language being addressed by the Arab and Muslim world to the West is false. It's true that this is the discourse picked up and highlighted by much of the media and many of the scholars of the West. Newspàpers carry daily bulletins on this mullah and that sheikh and the other ayatollah, but does the Western reader see any mention of the joint appeal of the students of Palestine and Israel to the international community? What about the recent communiqué from the Faculty Club of Cairo University to academia worldwide? Or the sorrowing bulletins from the Christian authorities in Jerusalem, Bethlehem and Nazareth? Or the various statements by Tunisian NGOs, position papers by the Egyptian trade unions or the reports of Arab Press Freedom Watch? The ether is teeming with 'alternative languages' in which the East is addressing the West. Kepel the scholar, Arabist, and expert so very much at home in the region, gives them no mention.

Another disturbing trait is to do with representation. Not in the main foregrounded statements of the book, but in the seemingly gratuitous, throwaway lines. Let me detail one example: the book begins with Kepel's arrival in Cairo on 14 October 2001. By paragraph two he is telling us about the 'grey fog' in the air: 'this is the heavy oppressive smoke from the burning of rice straw. Agriculture was liberalized three years ago in the Nile Delta, and the *fellahs* fell upon the profitable planting of rice. Then they burn the straw to plant in its stead fava beans, clover, wheat. Government prohibitions, the straw-compacting machines they were offered – they care nothing for these. And every autumn they calmly asphyxiate the city's inhabitants.'

Now it's true that what Cairenes call 'the black cloud' hangs over Cairo from mid-October for about a month. And it's true that the burning of rice straw is partly responsible. But that's not the whole story. The pollution levels in Cairo are very high. The city accommodates two million cars, then there's the Shubra Electricity Plant which accounts for about 25 per cent of the pollution, the rubbish dumps located just outside the city now deal not only with massively more refuse than they were meant for but also with new kinds of garbage such as plastic bags, containers, etc. Add to that the erosion of practically all the green spaces in the city and the random building that has swallowed up the fields that used to encircle it and the pollution is tipped over into visibility when the Sharqiyya farmers burn their rice straw.

Now for the burning: after the rice harvest the farmers are left with the stalk and the husk. The ashes of the stalk provide an essential fertiliser for the land – in fact Ministry of Agriculture regulations specify that it *has* to be burned and mixed back into the soil. The husks were used as insulating material for crop storage but are no longer needed because villages now have agricultural refrigerators. The farmers are obliged by law to get rid of the husks within a short space of time because if left lying around in quantities they generate particular pests. The problem became apparent in 1998 when liberalisation meant that more farmers grew rice. In 1999 the Ministry of Agriculture told the farmers to pile up the husks at the end of their fields and they would be collected. The collection never happened and the farmers burned the husks when they became a liability. The Ministry of the Environment then fined them 1,000 pounds each for pollution. The farmers lobbied the government and were told that they would be supplied with straw-compacting machines. But neither the Ministries of Agriculture nor of the Environment had the budget for these machines. Eventually the Ministry of Petroleum and some cement manufacturers provided funds and machines were bought in 2000. But the machines' capacity could deal with only ten per cent of the husks that needed to be compacted in the allocated time. What the farmers then did was get together in informal collectives to process ten per cent of their husks, burn the rest and divide the thousand-pound fine amongst themselves so each one paid a more manageable sum.

The farmers are constantly negotiating with government inefficiency, bureaucracy and lack of funds and coming up with creative solutions to try to keep their work viable. They are also liaising with local NGOs – such as the Hapi Centre for Environmental Rights – which have made the information available to anyone interested. A different picture, I think, from Kepel's *fellahs* (as he calls them in standard colonial parlance) going 'calmly' about their business 'caring nothing' for the law or the environment: ripe, possibly, for a Paul Bremer to come and modernise them.

One could say that this is a small point, but when a book is made up of impressions then small points add up.

Here's another, this time in the first paragraph of the book. Of the Egyptian festival of Shamm-en-neseem we learn that 'Only radical Islamists boycott it: it would distract believers from the exclusive adoration of God. But even their curses cannot stop the month when the fragrance of crushed sugar cane fills the air . . .' But 'exclusive adoration of God' is not a Muslim concept, evidence the famous Hadith where the Prophet, seeing a man praying in a mosque every day at all hours, asks him how he can afford to devote so much time to prayer? The man answers that his brother supports him; 'then your brother is more beloved of God than you,' says the Prophet. If the most radical of the Islamists boycott Shamm-en-neseem it would be simply because it's a pagan festival.

And then again, there's the point of view that the reader is invited to share. Meeting some young journalists in the offices of Cairo's *Akhbar al-Adab* (Literary News), Kepel finds them condemning the sanctions on Iraq and 'especially vehement in condemning the US's failure to intervene in the Israeli–Palestinian conflict since . . . Autumn 2000. In the name of anti-imperialism, these same nationalists – or their parents – once railed against America's superpower interference; today, it is accused of benign neglect, and of allowing the stronger party, Israel, to dominate its Palestinian adversary.' This rather amused 'look at the paradox' attitude will not do. America's intervention (objected to in the past) had the effect of strengthening Israel. It has led to a situation where only America's intervention (demanded today) can ensure a decent solution to the conflict. Where is the paradox?

Similarly in a paragraph which captures very well the conflicted relationship existing today between the Arabs/Muslims and the West: 'A curious relationship with America and the West in general has developed in our globalised universe: declarations of distrust are combined with a very powerful attraction; rejection of the paradigm with admiration for a democratic system of which most of the Muslim world's societies are still deprived; and claims of cultural specificity with a desire for recognition and the irrepressible wish to participate equally in universal culture. And, failing America, I am asked why Europe does not . . . play a mediating role to avoid breaches that would have potentially catastrophic consequences for Arabs and Muslims, first and foremost, if Bin Laden or the Taliban managed to capture the popular imagination in any lasting way.'

What, exactly, is 'curious' about this relationship? What attitude would not be 'curious'? Complete trust in America's intentions and policies despite the evidence? Absence of admiration for democratic systems? Renunciation of cultural specificity? Refusal to participate in universal culture? Isn't a nuanced position much more of a valid response to the power structures of the world today? And isn't it the response of many nations other than the Arabs and the Muslims – nations who just don't happen to be in the eye of the storm right now?

Then there are the linguistic tricks that have become so drearily familiar. 'A missile has fallen on the building al-Jazeera was broadcasting from in Kabul' (I checked the

French: '*Un missile est tombé* . . .') not 'the Americans have bombed al-Jazeera's office in Kabul'. Or, in Ramallah, Kepel goes to see 'the site of the attack that destroyed a house the previous night, killing a Fatah cadre and two children from another family. The building has collapsed inward without damaging the surrounding structures.' The agent of the killing here is not Israeli soldiers in aircraft but an impersonal 'attack'. The killed person is equally impersonal – and a Fatah 'cadre', which provides justification for the killing. Unfortunately two children were killed as well but damage to buildings was kept to the necessary minimum. On the other hand, we are told that 'the previous evening, in the Arab city of Umm al-Fahm, in Israel, two people speaking Arabic opened fire on a young Jew killing him immediately'. Here we know exactly who the killers are, we see them open fire and we hear them speak Arabic. The killed person is defined by Jewishness (not, for example, by nationality or political allegiance) and further personalised by his youth. Since all we know about him is that he's Jewish and young, his killing is unjustified and possibly random.

This short book boasts scores of such examples of sleight of hand, misrepresentation, imbalance and blinkered vision. The skewed texture belies the objective, mostly true, status of its upfront statements. So while it tells you, openly, that Arabs and Muslims, for example, want to share in universal culture not destroy it, it suggests at the same time that they are backward, inconsistent, vaguely schizoid and given to random murder. It's not unique in this; just one more example of much of the discourse that is used in the West to define the Arab and the Muslim worlds.

Does it matter? In a recent review of books on Islam (Kepel's *Jihad* among them) in the *NYRB* (3 July) Clifford Geertz concludes that 'the conception of Islam being so desperately built up before our eyes by professors, politicians, journalists, polemicists, and others professionally concerned with making up our minds will be of great importance in determining what we do. Here, for once, the line between writing and the world is direct, explicit, substantial and observable. And, we shall doubtless soon see, consequential.'

It matters.

Rebel with a Cause[1]

Jean Genet, *Prisoner of Love*

When *Prisoner of Love* was first published in France in 1986, *Le Matin* declared that 'Genet was assuredly one of the greatest French prose poets of this century, reaching the same heights as Proust and Céline. *Un captif amoureux* has all the sacred fire and poetry of his earlier works.' Yet today several bibliographies do not list the book and even readers familiar with Genet are sometimes unaware of its existence. I was amused to see that when the French theatrical Compagnie Lara adapted *Captif* into a play and performed it in April 2002 as part of the Prague Writers' Festival (dedicated to Genet) the performance was mentioned in the British press as 'a new production of Genet's last play'.

In fact Genet's last play, *The Screens*, about the Algerian revolution, was written on the eve of Algerian independence from France in 1961. Three years later, following the death of his companion of some nine years, the high-wire artist Abdalla Bentaja, Genet (having, it is said, destroyed his manuscripts) left France. His relationship with his homeland had never been simple. Born in 1910 and abandoned as an infant to the '*assistance publique*' he had, by the age of sixteen been jailed for petty theft. At eighteen he was sent to Syria as a volunteer for the Foreign Legion which he deserted eight years later, setting off on a '*vagabondage*' across Europe towards France and jail once more. Genet's extraordinary 1940s saw him in and out of prison while producing the great narratives that won him the admiration and solidarity of

---

[1] Introduction to Genet's *Prisoner of Love* for the *New York Review of Books* edition, 2003; *The Nation*, 24 February 2003; the *Guardian*, 12 July 2003.

Cocteau, Sartre and André Breton: *A Thief's Journal*, *Miracle of the Rose*, *Our Lady of the Flowers*, *Funeral Rites* and *Querelle*. In the 1950s he created the plays which are his great bequest to European post-war theatre: *The Balcony*, *The Maids* and *The Blacks*, followed in 1961 by *The Screens*.

'Obviously,' Genet said in an interview in the early 1980s, 'I am drawn to peoples in revolt – because I myself have the need to call the whole of society into question.' But if all Genet's preceding work subverted the values and arrangements of society, *The Screens* was the first to engage with a specific revolt. Perhaps it was this that then drew other 'transgressors' to appeal to him. Genet, as he said in the same interview, responded. He wrote an '*hommage*' for the young revolutionary Daniel Cohn-Bendit in '68, smuggled himself across the Canadian border into the US to speak on behalf of the Panthers at Stony Brook in March 1970 and, in the autumn of that year, fetched up in the Palestinian bases in Jordan. He was to stay till May '71 and then – intermittently – till the end of 1972. His involvement with the Palestinians is the story of *Prisoner of Love*.

But Genet did not, as it were, go home and start writing. Another ten years were to pass before he started work on the new book. During this time he was to say in an interview for Australian radio: 'I no longer have the need to write . . . I have nothing further to say.' Then, in September 1982, Genet (at the request of his Palestinian friend, Leila Shahid) visited Beirut and found himself in the middle of the Israeli invasion of the city. He was, it seems, one of the first foreigners to enter the Palestinian refugee camp of Chatila after the Christian Lebanese Phalange, with the compliance of the Israeli command, tortured and murdered hundreds of its inhabitants. There, pushing open doors wedged shut by dead bodies, Genet memorised the features, the position, the clothing, the wounds of each corpse till three soldiers from the Lebanese army drove him at gun point to their officer: ' "Have you just been there?" [the officer] pointed to Chatila. "Yes." – "And did you see?" – "Yes." – "Are you going to write about it?" – "Yes." '

The essay 'Four Hours in Chatila' was published in 1983 and in October of that year Genet began writing *Prisoner of Love*. It is as if, through the long years of virtual silence, everything was being saved up for this last book which he finished just before his death of throat cancer in 1986. Serious and playful, romantic and unflinching, literary and factual, *Prisoner of Love* is a coming together of everything that was Genet: his art, his politics and his humanity.

But Genet is at pains to point out that 'I'm not an archivist or historian or anything like that.' *Prisoner of Love* accumulates its power though a staggering display of leaps between times, places, styles and modes of consciousness. Taking in events from the beginning of the twentieth century to the time of writing, shifting from polemic to lyrical, from exposition to prophecy, fusing disparate bits of the world into living images, it refuses to be confined by definitions or summaries. 'This', said Genet, 'is my Palestinian revolution, told in my chosen order.'

His revolution is – at the beginning, amidst the hills of Ajloun – 'a party that lasted nine months. To get an idea of what it was like, anyone who tasted the freedom that reigned in Paris in May 1968 has only to add physical elegance and universal courtesy.' And at the heart of the party were the young guerrillas, the 'fidayeen'.

The party, however, was being held in grim circumstances. Expelled from their lands in 1948 and again in 1967 these Palestinians were refugees in King Hussein's Jordan. Radicalised by the Arab states' defeats in both wars they had started to take matters into their own hands by forming guerrilla organisations. In 1970 there were at least five such organisations operating in Jordan and the King had started to fear them. Their raids on Israel brought Israeli attacks on Jordanian villages and there were several skirmishes between the fidayeen and Hussein's Bedouin troops. Although Arab governments tried to contain the conflict it escalated till, on 6 September, the Popular Front for the Liberation of Palestine (PFLP), led by George Habash, hijacked three aeroplanes. They demanded the release of some 100 Palestinians from Jordanian jails and blew up one of the planes – after releasing the passengers and crew. On 16 September the King launched a full-scale attack on the Palestinians. In the civil war that raged for ten days some 3,000 Jordanian and 2,000 Palestinian fighters were killed. It was at the end of this 'Black September' that Genet arrived at Ajloun: 'War was all around us. Israel was on the watch, also in arms. The Jordanian army threatened. But every fedayee was just doing what he was fated to do.' What they did was train, discuss revolution – and make music. One of Genet's recurring images is his memory of two young fighters 'drumming on wood, inventing more and more cheerful rhythms' on a pair of deal coffins; coffins that were clearly destined to be either their comrades' or their own, for 'nearly all of them were killed. Or taken prisoner and tortured.'

The root *fda* in Arabic signifies something relinquished in the certainty of gaining something more precious: a ransom, perhaps, or a sacrifice. 'What made the fidayeen supermen', Genet wrote, 'was that they put the predicament of all before their own individual wishes. They would set out for victory or death, even though each still remained a man alone with his own sensibilities and desires.' In them he rediscovered one of the central themes that had occupied his earlier work. In *The Miracle of the Rose* Genet had written 'Only children who want to be bandits in order to resemble the bandit they love . . . dare have the audacity to play that character to the very end.' In the Palestinian fidayeen in 1970 he finds young men – boys almost – with the audacity to play the revolutionary to the very end. And with them, this 'pink and white' sixty-year-old French eminence, although he never thought of himself as Palestinian, felt 'at home'.

One of the unique qualities of this book is that Genet never exhibits any of the characteristics we have learned to expect from white men or women writing about Arabs. He has no inclination to 'go native' but he never goes in for generalisations on 'Arab customs' or the 'Arab mind' in either his descriptions of the Palestinians or his reflections on them and on his feelings for them. More than that, his opening scene, where he finds himself sipping tea among the women in the camp at Baqa – women who laugh and joke when he asks if their husbands would mind his presence among them – is set up as a swipe at 'orientalist' references and as a joke at his own expense: 'Something told me my situation was not what I'd have expected from my previous knowledge of the East: Here was I, a man, alone with a group of Arab women. And everything seemed to reinforce this topsy-turvy vision of the Orient.' From then on, in image after image he fuses together his own French, Catholic world and this new one he is experiencing: the Bedouins dance, 'twelve or fourteen soldiers holding arms like Breton bridegrooms', an annexe of the Fatah office makes him think of 'the 1913 Russian Ballet: with five Parisian stage-hands standing by, several Nijinskys in striped costumes flecked with moss and dead leaves waiting to leap on-stage in *Le Prélude à l'apres-midi d'un faune*', a Circassian village on the Golan Heights, after six years of Israeli occupation, like a village 'in Normandy after the landing at Avranches. Looted by the Yanks.' And then, in what becomes a motif of the revolution throughout the book, the image of the young fidayee, Hamza, and his mother 'linked to that of the Pieta and Christ'.

But if Genet was '*bouleversé*' by the fidayeen – as his friend Leila Shahid put it – he retained a clear eye for the circumstances surrounding them: '[the fidayee's] brightness protected him, but worried the Arab regimes . . . What was it the Arab world so urgently needed, that the Palestinian resistance should come into being?' In training, not just his eye, but his heart and his genius on the Palestinian revolution, Genet also sees the world surrounding it: the Palestinian leaders who 'serve two masters', the Arab rulers 'faithful to America', America: 'Does she support Israel . . . or just make use of her?' And Israel: 'If you're against Israel you're not an enemy or an opponent – you're a terrorist. Terrorism is supposed to deal death indiscriminately, and must be destroyed wherever it appears. Very smart of Israel to carry the war right into the heart of vocabulary . . .' And the revolution itself? 'There's a small shop in Chatellerault where I once saw a knife as small as a penknife with blades that opened slowly one after the other and then gently shut again, after having threatened the town in all directions . . . open, this small provincial masterpiece swelled up until its forty-seven blades resembled a porcupine at bay or the Palestinian revolution. That too was a miniature threatening in all directions: Israel, America and the Arab kingdoms. Like the penknife in the window it turned on its own axis and no-one wanted to buy it.'

Time and time again as I read *Prisoner* I found myself wishing that Genet were alive today. As Edward Said wrote in 1990, he 'fully intuited the scope and drama' of what the Palestinians were living through, recording 'a seismographic reading, drawing and exposing the fault lines that a largely normal surface had hidden'. And in doing this he was also reading the future. It could be said that for Genet the enemy was always the rigid form: a movement that became a government, a revolution that turned into an authority. The Palestinians were the antithesis of rigidity; he was captivated by the flexibility of their identity. It could embrace, it seemed, anyone who wanted to be part of it: German and Cuban doctors, a French priest, a nun, two young Frenchmen called Guy, a young Israeli who had renounced Zionism: everyone was welcome at the party. And – as is testified to by Genet's failure to realise that the fedayee leader he knew as 'Abu Omar' was in fact a Christian – 'Palestinian' always came before 'Christian' or 'Muslim'.

Yet this openness itself, Genet saw, could in the prolonged absence of victory prove a weakness. In a passage just after the middle of the book he examines the French expression *'entre chien et loup'* – 'dusk': a time when one creature might metamorphose into another. For a moment Genet pulls back from his image: 'In order to record the next phase of the story,' he suggests, 'perhaps I ought to draw back at first and take a run at it.' What he's taking a run at is his fear of the fedayeen metamorphosing into Islamic militants; the 'logical conclusion', of his feeling that 'the expression *entre chien et loup*, instead of connoting twilight, describes any, perhaps all, of the moments of a fedayee's life'. The proposition brings 'howls of protest . . . from the PLO officials'. But Genet's premonition is so strong that – uncharacteristically – he records the exact date of its occurrence: 'But as one of their leaders told me today, 8 September 1984, that such a thing was impossible, let's pretend this digression was never either written or read.'

This remarkable passage is very much Genet at work. Like a miraculous street artist he beckons us over to watch as he paints prophetic lines and shadows on the pavement. The image complete, he walks away with a shrug.

But what he has to say is of tremendous importance and he knows it. There is no doubting that once again he has nailed his colours to the mast of the oppressed, to the 'metaphysical revolution of the native'. In this instance the Palestinian, as before it had been the Black Panthers and before that the Algerian revolution. Said reports that in Beirut in the fall of 1972, speaking of Sartre's strong pro-Israeli stance, Genet had said, 'He's a bit of a coward for fear that his friends in Paris might accuse him of anti-Semitism if he ever said anything in support of Palestinian rights.' Genet would probably not have been surprised to see otherwise admiring critics, like Edmund White, fearful that such an accusation might be levelled against him, seeking to separate the genius of the book, somehow, from its politics. Similarly Clifford Geertz (*NYRB* 19 November 1992) has written that 'Genet is, for all his sympathy for the Palestinians' predicament not so much a partisan . . . as a connoisseur of pure rebellion.'

Genet himself would have rejected such expedient distinctions. 'It's not the justice of their [the Palestinians'] cause that moves me,' he writes, 'it's the rightness.'

And yet, if the Palestinians found in Genet a passionate friend and a thoughtful interpreter, Genet, writing in the early Eighties, found in them the subject that would draw from him a powerful and layered articulation of the themes that had informed his work of the Forties and Fifties: the heroism of the outlaw, the beauty of the constant, wilful overturning of the established order, the transfiguration of eroticism into chastity, the power of a non-religious spiritual life, the weightlessness of death, the continuation of a feeling beyond the life of the individual who felt it, and the tensile and creative relationship between the image and its reality.

This is a book about the Palestinian revolution (with some pages about the Black Panther movement) but it is also about art and about representation. In *The Balcony*, *The Maids* and *The Blacks* the central theme is the relationship of appearance to reality. For Genet the image is central both to art and to life. It can make reality more bearable and keep memory alive: 'Every district in the camp tried to reproduce a village left behind in Palestine . . . Nazareth was in one district, and a few narrow streets away Nablus and Haifa. Then the brass tap, and to the right Hebron, to the left a quarter of old Jerusalem. Especially around the tap, waiting for their buckets to fill, the women exchanged greetings in their own dialects and accents, like so many banners proclaiming where each patois came from.' But its mask can also be used to manipulate reality to sinister ends. Genet cites the murder of three Palestinian leaders in Beirut by three pairs of Israeli commandos camping it up as ringletted queens who 'kissed one another on the lips to shock the bodyguards into thinking they were just shameless, giggling Arab pansies . . . Newspapers all over the world described the assassination, but none of them called it terrorism on another country's sovereign territory. No, it was considered as one of the Fine Arts, deserving the relevant Order and receiving it.'

Then, and most importantly, there is the image which needs to be created in order to convey reality, to make it, so to speak, real. 'It's not enough just to write down a few anecdotes. What one has to do is create and develop an image or a profusion of images.' And this is the task that Genet has set himself in *Prisoner of Love*. For an image, he suggests 'is the only message from the past that's managed to get itself projected into the present'. It is a measure of Genet's pinpoint accuracy, the hard-headed realism that accompanies his poetics of the image, that today – two decades on – the Palestinians are more than ever embroiled in an 'image' battle, while Genet's friend, the one-time Black Panther leader, David Hilliard, is embarking on a fight to rescue the image of his group from a new and different group calling itself by the same name. 'This is about more than the ownership of a trademark,' Hilliard is quoted as saying, 'it's about who controls and defines history.' (*Guardian*, 12 October 2002)

In his 1982 interview for Australian radio Genet insisted that the work he had done of his own accord, the novels written in prison, had been done in the certainty – because of the certainty – that it would never be read. His plays he dismissed as having been written to commission, except for *The Screens* which – because of its cast of 107 characters – he had thought would never be performed. In *Prisoner* the possible absence of a reader is at once reassuring and troubling: 'This book will never be translated into Arabic,[2] nor will it ever be read by the French or any other Europeans. But since I'm writing it anyway . . . who is it for?'

Sartre had written – in praise of Genet's work – that 'he reduces the episode to being merely the manifest illustration of a higher truth . . . He reconstructs the real on every page . . . in such a way as to produce for himself proof of the existence of God. That is, of his own existence.' It is not surprising that, in 1982, Genet brushes this aside with

---

[2] *Un captif amoureux* was translated into Arabic and published in Cairo in 2001.

'[Sartre's] book called "Saint Genet" was really about himself.' For in the work that he was about to embark upon, unconstrained and uncommissioned, Genet was engaged upon a project at once more artful and more truthful. The Palestinians, he saw, were no good at making images: 'The . . . journalists, describing the Palestinians as they were not, made use of slogans instead. I lived with the Palestinians, and my amused astonishment arose from the clash between the two visions. They were so opposite to what they were said to be that their radiance, their very existence, derived from that negation. Every negative detail in the newspaper, from the slightest to the boldest, had a positive counterpart in reality.' It is this reality that Genet devoted his final years to recording. He feared the revolution's defeat and 'the evidence, rarely accurate but always stirring, vouchsafed to the future by the victors'. Age and illness were against him. Pain was there too. In the last months he refused painkilling drugs to retain the lucidity that he needed to create, for the future, his image of the reality of the Palestinian revolution: 'Would Homer have written or recited the *Iliad* without Achilles' wrath? But what would we know about Achilles' wrath without Homer?' Genet, the great subversive image-maker knew that he had found his subject and his subject had found him.

Genoa: City of Light and Shadow[1]

Let me start in a room flooded with light. The yellow
carnations, crowded, erupting out of the polished black
bowl delight in the sunshine. Rejoicing, they fling some
gold of their own back at the room, at the patterned parquet
of the floor, at the heavy blue silk curtains and beyond, into
the glassed-in terrace which draws me out to stand, my
elbows on the warm stone parapet, leaning out into the life of
the street below. All quiet. Quiet, now, for the siesta. But
soon the shops will roll back their shutters and the gracious
colonnades will brim with young people in jeans and in a
hurry, with elderly couples strolling hand in hand, the men
in suits, the women in sensible shoes and good, formal dresses
and jackets. The tables on the sidewalk will fill with early
diners. And all these people will be going about their
business at a junction, a hinge, between ancient and modern
times.

Or I can start somewhere else; at a place where a dense
grove is all you can see from the road. If you were a stranger
– as I was a stranger – you would assume, reasonably, that
the trees clustered uninterrupted all the way down to the sea.
But the car turns into a massive iron gateway and drives
along a shingled path lined with citrus trees. It rounds a
generous curve and stops in front of what looks to me like a
house in a fairy tale. A small palace, its walls made of cream
and pink stone. Enchanted, from the broad marble steps
which lead to the glass front doors up to the belvedere
nesting in the pines. The signora who greets me feels like
someone I have known for a long time; a friend of my aunt's

[1] Published by the Bogliasco Foundation, Genoa, 2003.

perhaps from the times when your friends in Cairo were as likely to be Italian or Greek as Egyptian. The tea, the china, the embroidered cloth on the tray all remind me intensely of home as it used to be when I was small. It is as though I have stepped both into my grandfather's house and into the past.

Later, upstairs in the room I have been given, I find a shelf-full of books left by other people over the years. I pick out a book and open it and a sheet of typed paper falls to the floor. It is a letter, dated some twenty-five years ago, and it ends '*Be, Carissimo Papi, se non ti scrivo piu prima di partire per l'Egitto, riceverai tante cartoline firmate da noi tutti.*'

Again and again during my stay in Genoa a sense of affinity washes over me. Much has been made of Khedive Ismail, Egypt's great modernising ruler in the late nineteenth century, modelling his new grand Cairo on Paris. But when he wanted to issue the first Egyptian stamps in 1866 it was to Genoa that he turned to have them designed and printed. All the sphinxes and pyramids and mosques and kings on every Egyptian stamp for the next ninety-five years were printed in Genoa. The Genoese apartment blocks with their ornate façades, the patterned mosaic floors in the houses, the curve of the armchairs all speak to me of the great debt that Cairo and Alexandria owe to Italian style. It is with a shock of recognition that I come upon the names of 'Pontremolli' and 'Buccelati' on shopfronts here in Genoa. For in Cairo Pontremolli was the most succesful manufacturer of furniture and all artists (and school children) bought their art supplies from Buccelati in Mustafa Kamel Square. At an earlier time the architectural debt is reversed: the austere, simple columns of Sant'Agostino hark back to the Mosque of Ahmad ibn Tulun, the striped façades of churches and palazzi to many of the Mameluk mosques of Cairo. But it is in the small manifestations of daily life that the resonances are strongest: in the washing hanging out to dry from the windows, the ice-cream shops and patisseries on every street, the large families eating companionably in a pizzeria, the elderly couples out shopping together, the odd person nipping into a house of God in the late afternoon for a quick pray, the silence in the middle of the day for the siesta, the presence, everywhere, of children.

Children are being taken, in a line, to see an exhibition at the Palazzo Ducale. I am heading downstairs, to an exhibition of front pages of *La Repubblica*. Accounts of strikes, stories of the 'red' Doria, photographs from the events of 2001 are blown up and ranged on the walls. Genoa's name has meant different things at different times: a maritime trading power, a crusading city, a financial centre. After the anti-globalisation protests of July 2001 'Genoa' came to mean a time/place where peaceful protest was hijacked by 'disruptive elements' and radicalised by 'state brutality'. A friend writing to me from Cairo in April 2003, while Egyptian police were beating up and arresting students protesting against the war on Iraq, wrote that 'if Thursday was our Seattle, Friday was our Genoa'. Yet this is a civic building and on the floor above there is a peaceable bookshop and, above that, an exhibition of Genoese painters and up at the highest level a music school where the notes from the piano chime melodiously through the long whitewashed vaulted corridors. Genoa lives with her contrasts.

In fact, I've come to think that Genoa relishes her contrasts, enjoys her own paradoxes. Uses them to surprise, to subvert expectations, to reinvent herself whenever she feels like it. Look at her name: 'Genoa', we are told, derives from the Latin 'janua' (door), a clear reference to the city's position as a port, a doorway to the sea. One of her principal deities was Janus, the two-faced god of doorways, one of his faces gazing steadily at the past, the other turned firmly towards the future. But the name, we are told, could also be from 'genoux' (knee) because of the shoreline's local shape. And is it to be ignored that the city's old name 'Zena' is in Arabic 'the beautiful one'? And where did her people come from? Who were they, those men and women, who some 2,500 years ago arrived at this narrow strip of rock, sheltered by craggy but green hills, and decided to stay? Well, they are clearly Etruscan, clearly Greek, clearly Phoenician or clearly Celtic – depending on the source you read. But, whoever they were, they quickly became Genoese and settled into the dialectic that was to inform their entire history.

It is tempting to read the story of Genoa as you read her façades, the play of light and shadow in her streets and on her buildings, as a constant balancing of opposites, a narrative of contrasts, to see her as a city achieving her very character from the tension between feuding principles: commerce and war, the nobility and the *popolo*, individual and communal interests, secrecy and openness, privacy and hospitality, capital and craft, the need of art and patronage for each other and the function of art as a subversive force 'speaking truth to power'. The creative genius, my psychologist father once told me, if it is to be productive, has to rest on four abilities: perseverance is one, maintaining direction is another, flexibility is the third, and the fourth and crucial one is tolerance of ambiguity. He was speaking of the creative individual. But I like to think that the theory can be extended. Any city that has survived for a length of time can be said to possess the first two abilities: its goal is to survive, it has maintained its direction towards that goal and persevered in its pursuit. In a city's reinvention of herself we can read flexibility. But it may be that it is in the fourth, in the tolerance and even embrace of ambiguity that Genoa excels.

I see the Palazzo Ducale for the first time under somewhat extraordinary circumstances. The ambassador of the United States of America is coming to Genoa and he is holding an audience. Some of my American friends have been invited and I go with them because, it is said, the Sala del Minor Consiglio will be opened – and that is a rare event. The sala is, by all accounts, splendid. We enter the wonderful atrium of the palazzo and proceed up the broad, shallow marble steps – shallow, it is said, so that horses could canter down them in procession. I can just see it: the Doge's procession, the thunder of hooves on marble as the horses, magnificently caparisoned, perhaps with feathers on their tossing heads, gallop down and burst like a wave on the crowds gathered in the piazza outside. No such sight this evening shatters the tranquillity of the vast porticoes and we file into the sala and take our seats to wait. The ambassador is late. Very late. So I have ample time to admire the huge mirrors, the marble floors, the chandeliers, the decorations. But what captures my imagination most is the painting of *The Arrival in Genoa of the Ashes of St John the Baptist*.

I have read that the ashes are housed in the San Lorenzo Cathedral next door and that every year on 23 June they are carried ceremonially down to the harbour for a ritual appeasement of the sea. And that, of course, has set me thinking about the ceremony that has taken place in Egypt every August for the last 4,000 or so years when, at the peak of the flood, the ruler of Egypt goes in a magnificent procession of boats on to the Nile and lowers a life-size doll into the water. In possession of his 'bride' the river will subside and recede from the fields leaving them enriched once more with the black soil that will ensure the people's survival for another year. I was trying to remember whether I'd ever seen a pictorial representation of that ceremony and I was looking at the painting in the Sala del Minor Consiglio.

In the central position above the podium, *The Arrival of the Ashes* is clearly an 'official' painting full of pomp and circumstance: the Doge's party, under a canopy on the left, receives the ashes, which arrive in a procession of ambassadors and churchmen from the right. The sea, the mountains, the Lanterna are all visible in the background. The angels are looking down from heaven and everything is in its proper place. In their proper place also are the helmeted soldiers holding back the people. But they're doing it with a certain amount of violence. And the people, on the whole, are women and children and – because of the perspective of Carlo Giuseppe Ratti, the artist – they are in the foreground and so are larger and more detailed than the grandees beyond them. One man is fully turned towards us, the viewers, as he looks up at a soldier. His bare chest and upturned face are iconic and the lighting on him ensures that he provides an alternative focal point for the picture. It is not surprising, then, that artists (together with nobles and politicians) were regarded as the most serious threat to the established order and that the prison tower in the Palazzo Ducale was kept exclusively for their use.

Outside, on a sunny Saturday, young people sit on the steps. Two trumpets play a duet and the fountains wash the air of Piazza de Ferrari. In March 2003 the city is festooned with the rainbow-coloured banners of peace and young women are collecting signatures outside Feltrinelli. I am back on Via XX Settembre which is fast becoming one of my favourite streets in the world. I continue to be amazed at its pavements, at their mozaic patterns of flowers and birds and intricate geometric designs. I cannot comprehend how people seem to be walking on them so casually, with such ease. A burly, stocky man with a white beard and the legs-apart, rolling walk of the sailor or the cowboy is looking at this floor with intent concentration. As I watch he bends to pick up the spent stub of a cigarette, examines it carefully and places it in his pocket.

I wander into the Mercato Orientale and there it comes again, that whoosh of nostalgia. This time for the market on Shari' al-Murgan where my grandfather had his furniture shop. Fruit and vegetables and meat and flowers. Women shopping and men carrying sacks of produce. Abundance. What a pleasure it would be to come down and choose a perfect artichoke, a polished aubergine, some shiny satsumas and go back and cook a wholesome meal for your loved ones.

It occurs to me that this austere, reserved city will sense the instant when you surrender to her, when you let her guide your thoughts and your footsteps, and at that instant she may, sometimes, vouchsafe you a moment almost of epiphany.

Badly bombed during the Second World War, Genoa was nevertheless the only city that managed to liberate itself. When the Allies arrived the city was already liberated.

I retrace my steps and stop under the arches of the Ponte Monumentale to read the tablets on the wall. Genoa has always celebrated the foreigners who came and contributed – has always invited foreigners to come and contribute. And she has been rewarded. Painters, architects and poets have given her of their best. Gallant men have come to her aid and here, on this wall, are the names of some who laid down their lives for her. ASUR AMENARKOV (AMERKANOFF), USSR; RUDLE ALDBOURS, SOUTH AFRICA; ERNEST ALEXANDER, GREAT BRITAIN; GEORGES SOMMERHALTER (PARIGI), FRANCE; PETER JOSEF (LUPO), POLAND; DIMITRIYK DIMITRNEVIC (MITTA), YUGOSLAVIA; the list goes on, fifteen young men from Britain and fifteen from the USSR, six from France and four from Poland, two from Austria and one each from Holland, South Africa, San Marino and Yugoslavia. PARTIGIANI STRANIERI CADUTI PER LA LIBERTA. CITTADINI HONORARI DI GENOVA. 25 APRILE 1945.

In front of them, on the ground, tall, dark, slim young men have laid out their pirated CDs and computer games on the patterned pavement. They stand and call out to the passers-by in an Italian flattened and opened out, an Italian without shadows, like an African landscape in this hilly Ligurian city.

A city caught up in a headlong rushing life, impelled, from time to time, to pause and nail down the moment, to hammer out in stone the record of a person or an event: CONSACRE QUESTE CARCERI IL SANGUE DI JACOPO RUFFINI MORTOVI PER LA PEDE ITALIANA 1833 or GENOVA CELEBRA OGGI 24 APRILE 1980 O COMPANION DE PAXO RIPRISTINATO NELL'ANTICA SEDE AUSPICE A COMPAGNA GENEROSAMENTE PARTECIPI IL COMMUNE EI CITTADINE. And the city records the bad as well as the good: IOANNI PAULO BALLI HOMINUM PESSIMO, FLAGITYS OMNIBUS IMBUTO, IMPURO, SICARIO, MONETAE PROBATAE, ADULTERINAE, TONSORI, CONFLATORI . . . AD AETERNAM IGNOMINIAN NEFANDAE SUI MEMORIAE LAPIS HIC ERECTUS ANNO MDCL.

And often, these formal mural proclamations are counter-pointed by urgent messages handwritten large upon the walls: PALESTINA LIBERA is a favourite. Another is DISOBBEDIENZA. A more argued text is LO STATO OPPRIME E REPRIME. NESSUNA DISOBBEDIENZA MA RIVOLTA APERTA E RADICALE.

Perhaps it is only natural that with so dramatic a setting Genoa should think of itself in theatrical terms. From the beginning it has presented itself to the traveller coming in from the sea as a welcoming but well-defended place, bristling with the towers of its noble families: the Embriachi, the Doria, the Fieschi, the Spinola . . . A theatrical city. A drama queen. Affording you a tantalising glimpse of a corner of balustraded terrace half concealed behind pines and fig trees. Leading you down dark and narrow alleys to surprise you with a sumptuously in-your-face striped marble façade, beckoning you through barred windows into a lavishly hospitable courtyard, teasing you with the shadows of half-open blinds.

In 1352 Petrarch, having visited the city, described it as 'a celestial abode . . . the buildings of marble at the foot of the hills second to no one in royalty and enviable to any city'. The art and architecture of Genoa constantly and con-sciously strove to create an image of the idealised, classical city harmonising the concerns of family, commerce and religion. The project of the Strada Nuova (now the Via Garibaldi), planned in 1550 and completed in 1591 is the great example of this. Opening out from the Piazza delle Fontane Marose it allowed for ten family palaces ranged on both sides of a wide street closed in at the far end by the gardens of the palace of Luca Grimaldi; not a 'strada' at all but rather an *albergho*, a neighbourhood, it echoed the alberghi down in the medieval part of the city but with major differences: whereas each of the old alberghi had belonged to one noble family, the Strada Nuova was a patrician ensemble representing the unity of these families, symbolising their common interests and power. It was set high up in the city and was open, wide and light in contrast to the dark, narrow streets below. It was a display case for the power and wealth of the nobility aimed at both the local Genoese and visiting personalities. It was the location of hospitality for important visitors and a larger-than-life stage set for local occasions and ceremonies when the terraces of the piani nobili would transform naturally into viewing galleries. This was the civic power of the city at its most visible. Today the palazzi are banks and museums.

I walk the street, admiring but not touched, until I notice, on the cobbled paving stones, a scattering of tiny discs of coloured paper. Confetti. I follow the trail and find myself in the Palazzo Tursi, the Town Hall. And at the top of the first flight of the magnificent staircase is a statue. The figure stands in thoughtful, almost humble, pose: his head lowered, his hands folded in front of him. Giuseppe Mazzini. Surely one of the most attractive figures to be found in the history of the world. I am so glad to have found him. The most rational of Romantics, many Italian cities have named streets and piazzas after him. But it was in Genoa, in Via Lomellini and the university nearby that Mazzini developed his own mix of Romanticism, idealism and hard-headed political activism – and paid for it by spending his life exiled from his native city. A young Genoese student who read Homer, Ossian, Vico, Lamartine and the Qur'ān. A patriot who believed that patriotism should always serve the wider interests of humanity. An activist for a unified Italy who believed power should be devolved to elected local authorities as a check on central government and who hoped for a 'league or society' of independent European nations. A thinker whose advice to a friend was to use his newspaper (*Roma del Popolo*) to fight against the 'official economists' who championed the selfishness of free enterprise based on individual rights and not social obligation. His was a voice that struck a deep chord in the hearts of his compatriots. In 1849, on board a ship that docked briefly in the port of Genoa, he could not disembark for fear of being imprisoned. But Gladstone (the sometime British Prime Minister) reported that passing through the city he saw pictures of Mazzini and Garibaldi proudly displayed in the shop windows.

Out there the Lanterna, throwing its light fifty-five kilometres out to sea, drawing in the ships. In they came, and in, as far as the houses now looking over Piazza Caricamento where, right now, two preachers in black suits are entertaining a small crowd. The sailors, I imagine, would saunter down the gangplanks, the traders would unload their merchandise under these colonnades, the oldest in the city. Currency would be exchanged and, later, customs tax would be paid here, at the Palazzo San Giorgio where you can still see the post boxes set out to receive complaints or the odd bit of anonymous information. Above the post boxes the stone tablet listing the goods on which customs duty is payable conjures up the feel, the smell, the bustle of this quayside: from golden wheat to red wine, timber from Lebanon, spices, linens, silks and oils – and slaves. The whole world on the quayside.

During the course of her history Genoa acquired – and lost – colonies. She took part in the Crusades. But her image is far more the city going out to trade than the city going out to conquer. And the cultural exchanges that are the off-shoots of trade are to be seen in the architecture of the colonnades on Sottoripa – the architecture of North Africa looking so much at home on the northern coast of the Mediterranean.

We sit at a small table, eating farinata and watching the emissaries of the world go by. A cluster of men surround a trader emptying his wares from a large plastic sack on to the pavement. But long after the jeans and trainers are arranged to catch the eye of the buyer the men are still there, lounging, smoking, waiting. It is, apparently, from this corner that ships' captains used to recruit their crew. What are these men waiting to enlist for? A group of German tourists passes them by. Just off a cruise liner, cameras banging against their chests, they make way for a small man with Chinese features and a yellow parka who staggers by, bottle in one hand, the other tight on a leash at the end of which a scruffy black and white terrier scampers along, his head cocked, his questioning eyes fixed on his master's face. Three dark-haired little girls skip along counting their skips in French: *vingt-et-un, vingt-deux* . . . the clatter of plates from the farinata counter mixes with the sustained excitement of the commentator's voice on the radio – funny, I think, how the rhythm of the voice tells me it's football even if I can't make out the words. The last time I was here, back in 1982, you just had to say 'Paolo Rossi' to a stranger and you were instantly best friends. A woman, huge diamanté earrings swinging out from under her grey hair carries a knapsack and a cage with two green budgies. A tough-looking man in a leather jacket licks at a double ice-cream. A child in a red hood plays with a yo-yo. A group of three: the young man in the middle has his baseball cap on backwards. The girl on his left holds his hand and drapes her other arm round his chest. She nibbles at his neck while over the bouquet of blue ribbons twined in her hair he chats with the friend walking at his other side. The pigeons, heads bobbing back and forth, scuttle and hop among the passing feet as they've done for hundreds of years.

And sometimes the city takes matters into her own hands, guiding you to where you need to be. So it was that a poster on a wall showing a turbaned man on a mule – a medieval Arab merchant, I guessed – led me to the Museo Diocesiano. The museum was closed, but next door to it, the State Archives were open. I climbed and climbed till I arrived at the top of the staircase and a kindly woman who listened to my somewhat incoherent request and asked me to wait. Then a man came to see me, thin, intense, serious. I already felt I was wasting his time asking simply to look at 'old documents'. He shrugged. The gesture of his arms took in the whole building: from top to bottom it was crammed with old documents. 'I'm from Egypt,' I offered, 'I'm looking, perhaps, for some links . . .' He set off and I followed him down some corridors, cupboards on either side bulging with paper. He turned into a side room where he reached down for some files and put them on the table in front of me.

A big volume. The first, he tells me, Notary Register, it records contracts between Genoa and Alexandria written on Arabic paper. A dozen years of contracts: 1154 to 1166, Iounni Scriba records in his neat hand in ink which has faded now to a pale brown. *Ego Ugo Sfreldo accepte . . . Ego Simon . . . Bonefacio . . . Ego Soliman . . .*

In a white folder, separate treaties, unbound. Again the small formal writing in pale brown ink: 'Ego—' The 'E' a lyre, a harp, a bow, 'Ego andrea capo peccore . . .' and in a scimitar slash from bottom to top of the page, written against a pale five-line grid like a musical score, comes the Arabic large and dark and ornate '. . . and the people of the Levant and all the races of the Franks . . .' I find one sheet, separate, covered in neat numerals: 'iii x viii . . .' someone was counting something? Doing accounts? And then there is a pattern and I know straight away it is a doodle. A doodle from the thirteenth century. He (he?) got so bored with his figures he let his mind wander and drew these stylised flowers – or butterflies. Complex, curvy shapes, a respite from the straight lines and angles of the Roman numerals; circles and tipped ovals, the shaded areas carefully alternating, each shape connecting up with another as his mind wandered further and further away from his business. The figures. And the odd thing was that the shapes I saw before me were exactly the kind of shapes I fall into drawing when my mind is absent and a pen is in my hand. I looked up, to bring myself back to today, and caught the eye of the library assistant detailed to keep watch over this room. Something in my face makes him come over, asking 'What is it?' I point at the paper – at the contained floral shapes in the middle of the rows of 'iii's and 'xxx's and 'ccc's and watch the recognition light up his face:

'It is like what you do when you're speaking on the telephone,' he says. Then he tells me he has been to Alexandria and Port Said many times. He tells me of a Genoese sailor, long ago, who settled in Morocco and became a Sufi. His shrine is still there, in Fez: Sidi Abd-Allah al-Jinawi, San'Abd-Allah the Genoese. He tells me he used to work on the boats and he tells me he thinks this whole 'clash of civilisations' talk is ignorant nonsense. Then he leaves me with the archives and steps outside for a cigarette.

Something about him makes me think of my uncle, dead now these ten years yet still much beloved. I can imagine them playing chess together in the Café Commerciale in Alexandria. My uncle adored Italy, spoke some Italian and visited Genoa several times. When I was four years old he taught me a song: 'Lo sai che . . .' I learned it by heart but it was only a few days ago that I found out what it meant. He taught it to me because, with my father, I was about to set sail for Genoa. We were passing through, my father and I, on our way to join my mother who was studying in London. Practically everyone who went to Europe from Egypt (or the Levant) went through Genoa. And returned home through Genoa too as we did much later, another time, when we left our belongings in the port and explored the Ligurian coast in a train full of singing soldiers.

Back in the city we stayed briefly in a hotel near the Stazione Principe. I go back now to try to find it and find myself face to face with the statue of Christopher Columbus in Piazza Aquaverde. A deeply politically incorrect statue; Columbus's outstretched hand presents to the beholder a squaw with a feathered head-dress who sits in docility at his feet. Her breasts are bare and pert, her eyes are averted modestly. Genoa had declined to finance Columbus's expedition but the success of the native son demanded commemoration. The controversy surrounding this issue is brilliantly captured in an episode of (the American television series) *The Sopranos* where a group of Italian-Americans setting out on their traditional Columbus Day parade are amazed and indignant to find themselves fending off the jeers and insults of activists for the rights of the Native Americans.

Tony Soprano's men would have a great time in this area. I have been warned not to go into the port district near the Stazione Principe. Not a good area, I've been told. But I see a young woman with a baby in a sling headed down and I decide if it's safe enough for her it's safe enough for me. I swing down behind her and there are the familiar lanes of the poorer districts of Cairo or twenty other Mediterranean cities: the houses practically nose to nose across the alley, the doors of sheet metal standing slightly ajar to give you a glimpse of the dingy hall inside, the stairway with bites taken out of its uneven cement balustrade. And there are the smells of cooking and the sound of the televisions loud behind closed doors and the occasional raised voice of a woman. A turn down an alley and suddenly I'm in a different place, still poor but here the women are standing around in groups of two and three. They're almost all quite healthily plump and wedged into tight blue jeans. They are North African or black or mixed. Black guys hang about. Separately, but keeping an eye. The few white men around look old and furtive. I quicken my pace. Every other shop here offers the facility of telephone calls abroad or of sending money – also abroad. One more turn and happily I find myself in the noise and bustle of Via Soziglia and within seconds I'm part of a crowd clapping and stamping to the sound of a four-man band making music on an accordion, a tabla, a cello and a qanun. They play 'O Sole Mio', 'La Vie en rose', 'Kalinka' and 'Debka Libnani'. A bearded man hesitantly offers me a copy of the street paper *Terre di Mezzo*. For half an hour the Piazza Soziglia feels like the hub of the world.

The University of Genoa was founded in 1243 and now occupies a whole neighbourhood around Piazza della Nunziata down to the port. Turning into the Via del Campo from the Porta dei Vacca (built in fear of an attack by Frederick Barbarossa) you can see a modern classroom practically embedded in the medieval city walls. But it is the main buildings, the palazzi along the Via Balbi that hold the real treasure. In the Palazzo dell'Universita I peeped into the lecture theatre on the ground floor and found benches and students and above them the most magnificent decorated ceiling centred with a vast chandelier. And in another, hidden away on an upper level, Jupiter, Neptune, Demeter and a variety of gods, goddesses, muses and rivers surveyed the library catalogue from on high. A smallish room, filled with students working at their desks, gave me the overpowering sense of being inside a jewellery casket, so perfect was its ceiling of egg-shell blue curving down, not a sharp angle anywhere, to meet the walls in joyous bursts of gilded flowers and foliage. But most entrancing was a large square study room with a frieze of vivid erotic scenes running round the walls just below the ceiling. An elderly professoressa sat reading at a table while above her a fair, voluptuous woman, tendrils of hair escaping from the auburn pile on top of her head was being tied up by a swarthy, muscular man. Near them two women turned towards each other while a mischievous child put his mouth to an exposed nipple. All around the tops of the walls women were being carried away, tied up and chastised amid laughing cherubs and an abundance of flowers and fruit while down below the life of the mind ran its course unheeding. Leaning against a computer were the *Confessions of Saint Augustine* and Origene's Commentary on the Gospel According to Matthew.

And here is another of Genoa's paradoxes: the cemetery at Staglieno, a city towering high above the living city. A city for the dead yet somehow boisterous with life. Here the chiaroscuro of Genoa is dispensed with, the city sheds her gloom and Staglieno lies open to the sunlight. Evelyn

Waugh called it a 'terraced hillside beginning with the strong echo of Canova and ending in a whisper of Mestrovic and Epstein'. It teems with angels in sexy drapery, with animated family groups, with ladies in starched lace and gentlemen in ruffled cuffs. It feels as though the artists, the architects and sculptors working on it had a good time. Gardens and galleries and halls, catacombs that bring to mind a library catalogue, each drawer holding a life-full of information. Mark Twain, who visited it in 1869 – while it was still being built – believed that his party would 'continue to remember it after we shall have forgotten the palaces'. Its sheer audacity is amazing.

'*La morte non esiste, non può nemmeno concepirsi; la vita è vita, è immortalità,*' said Mazzini.

In March 1872, when his body was brought home for burial, shops in the city were shut and ships in the bay lowered their flags. Thousands of people accompanied the funeral procession to Staglieno. In the half-hour I spend in front of his tomb three different sets of young people come to visit it. I take this as a sign of hope for it seems to me that the world needs his voice more than ever today. It was, I believe, through my uncle that I first heard of Mazzini. And thinking of them both, and others dear to me whom I shall never see again, the song I used to sing when I was small sings itself in my head. A song I carried with me all my life till I could put it in front of the signora in the enchanted house and she could tell me what it meant:

> Lo sai che papaveri son' alti alti alti
> Lo sai che papaveri son' alti alti alti
> E tu sei picolina
> E tu sei piccolina
> Che cosa c'e vai fa?

I picked up a couple of pine cones from the ground and slipped them into my pocket, then, taking a winding route down uneven steps almost overgrown with grass, I came upon a simple grey tomb. Its cover was at the height of my hip, a large flat grey stone with no ornament, the names engraved on it could have been anybody's; they were worn so smooth. It sat in its grassy nook for all the world like a picnic table, or a bench where a pair of lovers might whisper for an hour, or a space where a weary traveller might wrap herself up in her cloak and sleep.

We have not finished with Genoa. We can never finish with Genoa. But let us return now to one of my beginnings. Leave the enchanted house and walk along the Via Aurelia till you come to Cinema Paradiso. Run across the train tracks, bend to the left and a few paces down a piazza opens to your right. A wide, serene, communal space with a scattering of wooden benches shaded by spreading trees, it is spacious and homely at the same time. Mothers chat next to empty push-chairs while their *bambini*, released, play in the dappled sunlight. An elderly man reads a newspaper bought from the *giornaliero* on the corner.

I stand at the edge of the piazza watching the mothers and children, the tranquil everyday life of the square. Every day, weather permitting, it will be more or less the same, unchanging scene. Time will pass. Children will grow up, others will take their place. Mothers who used to be young and loaded with nappies, toys and bottles will come into the square more slowly, more quietly, with wraps and newspapers. Black, white and grey pebbles make a swirling pattern on the piazza floor, and I am a child again and entranced by these same patterns on the winding paths of Cairo Zoo. A movement to my right. The priest has come out of the dark doorway of the church and is standing to one side, waiting. A small knot of elderly men has gathered. Before I've worked it out, without my seeing it approach, the black hearse is there, its rear door already wide open, the widow's hands in the hands of the priest – I turn away quickly from this private moment. Out at sea, in the bay to the east a flock of young men in black diving suits are surfing the waves. Eleven I count. Above them, in the lighter blue of the sky, a formation of gulls swoops and soars. And almost at my feet, interrupted in its erractic bouncing rush downhill, caught in the shrubbery is a shining red football.

I am indebted to George L. Gorse's article on the Strada Nuova, published in the *Art Bulletin*, 6 January 1997. Also to Dennis Mack Smith's *Mazzini*, Yale University Press, 1994.

Edward Said, My Friend[1]

It was twelve years ago that Edward called me, early on a summer evening, to tell me he had just been diagnosed with leukaemia. There was no hushed tone, no sadness, no fear in his voice. There was surprise and anger. It was 'Guess what? I've got fucking leukaemia. Apparently I'm dying.' I said you can't be dying. It was an impossibility as far as I was concerned, and continued to be an impossibility – until today.

Our loss cannot be measured.

For twenty-two years Edward has been my friend. And the friendship started in a way typical of him. He heard I was in New York. He'd read my first published story. He phoned up and invited me and my husband to dinner at his house. We met Mariam, his wife, Wadie and Najla, his kids, and a few other people. At the end of the evening he walked Ian and me out. At the door of the lift we all shook hands then he opened his arms and gave me a huge hug. We had become old friends.

Now I say to myself he was sixty-eight, he had a wonderful family, he saw his children grown up and had huge happiness and pride in them, he leaves us his work, he has touched and influenced millions of people across the world and, in the end, death comes for each and every one of us. But it brings no comfort.

The loss to his family I cannot speak of. For us, his friends, we are orphaned. What shall we do without him? He brought love and concern and loyalty and charm to his friendships, and he kept them in good repair. He was ready

[1] The *Guardian*, 26 September 2003. Edward Said died on Thursday 25 September 2003.

with help before you even knew you needed it. Many times, alone in a strange city, my hotel phone would ring and it would be a friend of Edward's: 'He said I had to look after you so I'm coming round to take you out.'

When I told him last Christmas I was going to Rome he gave me a phone number: 'Get in touch with her. She's a wonderful woman. You'll love her.' It was his music teacher, from Cairo, from half a century ago. She still adored him. She said he had never lost touch and that she and her husband prayed for him every night. 'Edward and his three thousand close friends' is how one of us puts it.

Yet, when with him you always felt unique. He noticed if you wore your hair differently, he commented on your clothes, on what you chose to eat. In my car, recently: 'Would you mind switching off this dreadful racket,' of a currently popular Egyptian singer. And then, turning to me, 'But if you like this stuff how can you bear not to live in Cairo?'

It is a measure of his no-holds-barred friendship, that alone one night some two years ago, with the diagnosis of my husband's lung cancer just off the fax, it was to Edward in New York that I turned. He talked me through that first hour and gave me phone numbers of doctors, medical centres, and friends who had been through it. When I made contact I found he had already called them and told them, again, to 'look after' me.

The last two of his public events I attended with him – one in Brighton, the other in Hay-on-Wye – people were coming up afterwards just to touch him. It was as though he was a talisman. He laughed it off: 'You know me, I'm just an old demagogue,' he said.

But he wasn't. He was a guide and an example. In the most private conversation, as well as in public, he was always human, always fair, always inclusive. 'What is the matter with these people?' he asked after a recent debate. 'Why does no one mention truth, or justice any more?' He believed that ordinary people, all over the world, still cared about truth and justice. My life and many others' are desolate without him.

Address in Memorial Event for Edward Said[1]

Ladies and gentlemen, my friends,

I am very moved to be the first of Edward Said's friends to speak here tonight.

I am also grateful that Mariam, Edward's wife, is with us tonight, so that what we say is said in the presence of the person closest to him, the person he loved the most, and I thank Mariam for this generous gift which her presence has given us.

We are here to do honour to Edward Said.

We are also here to prolong, if I can put it that way, our contact with him.

For a sizeable part of the lives of many of us, an Edward Said event has been a high point in our calendar: we have rushed to read what he's written, to listen to what he has to say, to watch him in action on screen and in person. To-night, how much happier we would have been, if we were here to listen to Edward speak. But we can no longer do that, and so we have come here to speak of Edward, and in doing so, to hold on to him for a little longer.

Our loss is great indeed. His family, his few thousand 'close' friends, his colleagues and students and protégés and disciples and comrades. And all those who never met him, but felt that in some way he was theirs. And it is of that greater circle of people, and of our common loss that I want to speak.

How many times in the last six weeks have each of us thought – how many times have we said to each other: Who is out there for us now? And we don't just mean for us Palestinians, us Arabs, us Muslims, us Third Worldeans – us the people he spoke *up* for – we also mean that wider 'us' which was happy to align itself with the positions and with the attitudes he articulated. The us he spoke *for*.

Who will speak for us with his clarity, his passion and his wit? Who will put our case? Who will rally us with his incision, his unfailing humanity, his humour?

The question is stark and frightening. I have been trying to understand why Edward's death has hit so many of us with a feeling of fear, of foreboding. After all, it was not the case that he could prevent bad things happening. Bad things happened throughout his life. Lies and deceit, killings, expulsions, torture, you name it. Why then does it feel as though the world is more likely to go up in flames because he has gone?

I think the answer I arrived at was that as long as Edward was there I had felt that injustice could not finally triumph. Because for injustice to triumph all resistance to it must stop. And that could never happen as long as he was around. So whatever defeats we suffered, whatever setbacks, whatever betrayals – they could never be final because he would not allow them to be final but would articulate a powerful and reasoned response to them. And we, each one of us, could stake our lives on the certainty that he would never give up.

But now he is no longer here.

I think we have also come here tonight because we need to draw strength from each other; to feel that we are not alone – each one of us – with their loss and their forebodings. It is, after all, still Edward who brings us together here.

In Bethlehem, in Jerusalem and Nablus last week, I saw that Edward's picture had taken its place on the walls of the houses, alongside those of other Palestinians, whose lives now are in the hearts and memories of their people. A photograph in a local paper even showed an Israeli soldier aiming his gun with Edward observing him from the wall.

A friend said to me, 'You saw the picture? Edward is with

the masses.' And that was doubly true because across the towns and villages of occupied Palestine you can see that same Edward Said combination: resistance twinned with grace. For Edward – and this is important – made resistance attractive. Much has been made of his charm, his civility, his love of life, his interest in clothes and cuisine. But who says that intellectual rigour and moral clarity have to come with sloppy cooking or a badly cut suit?

The lettering on Edward's poster said: 'We will continue on your road – Your thought shall be immortal.' Yes, we can see this as a cliché. But clichés are often true and wise.

I do believe that we are not alone, that we have each other, we who choose to occupy the space that Edward created for us. I believe that the way out of the fear sparked by his loss is for each of us to resolve, like him, never to allow injustice a final victory. And I believe that the most honour we can do Edward, and the way we can hold on to him and not lose him twice over is to work, like him, for the causes he believed in. Like him to hold on to our humanity, our tolerance, our inclusiveness, always. To denounce cruelty, hypocrisy and phoniness wherever we find them. To keep our friendships in good repair. And to get back soon our humour and our joy in life without which he would not have tolerated five minutes in our company.

Palestinian Writers[1]

When I finally get Liana Badr on the mobile she is in her car in the centre of Ramallah, unable to reach her office or to turn and go back home. She sounds distraught: 'They're invading the town. Going into the banks. The kids are throwing stones and there's word that one person has been killed—'

My questions seem a bit theoretical, but we agree that I will fax them through anyway: 'Does the occupation affect you as a writer?'

'Yes it affects my writing. I can't work for very long. It's as though concentration becomes claustrophobic. The situation controls you. It affects you like a fever; it's always there. It's very hard to concentrate on one thing. I find myself trying to work on several projects at once.'

When I first met Badr, ten years ago, I was impressed by her energy, her output, her looks, her will to optimism. When I saw her last year there were dark circles under her eyes, her words seemed speeded up, her energy more brittle. Badr was born in Jerusalem and brought up in Ariha (Jericho). In 1967 she fled with her parents to Amman, but Black September drove them out to Beirut in 1970. Then the Israeli invasion drove them out of Beirut in 1982. She lived in Damascus and Tunis and returned to Palestine after Oslo in 1994. 'The writer', she has said, 'feels a need to create the world from the beginning every time – and that need is even stronger as you see your world vanishing in front of your eyes.' Moving from city to city she produced four

[1] Written March 2004. Short version published by the *Guardian* in September 2004.

novels, *Balcony over the Fakahani* (1983) establishing her as a major Arab writer. But, today, writing is particularly challenging: 'The given are very ugly. I'm obsessed now with the emotions that a person has as she tries to remain human under circumstances like these. To try to create aesthetic form under such ugly circumstances is a big challenge.'

This is the challenge that every Palestinian writer faces. Adania Shibli tells me she retreats into 'a kind of autism'. Shibli is the current most talked-about young writer on the West Bank. Slight and tomboyish in jeans and cropped hair she whizzed me around the streets of Ramallah in a small white car. She is from a Palestinian village inside the Israeli border but says she can no longer bear to live in it because 'Israeli control transforms every place into a completely consumer society'. She works with young artists in a Palestinian cultural foundation. It was Friday when we visited. I wandered around the light rooms looking at posters, computers, magazines; the instruments of cultural activity. On a table were some books sent over by an organisation that works with children from the camps. They were 'My Story' books where the children set down in words and pictures their history and their wishes. Every one I picked up said it was very difficult to see the future. Many of them wrote that they dream of becoming doctors, many asked, 'Am I going to end up performing a martyrdom operation?'

Shibli describes sitting in front of a man 'who's talking about how a missile hit his car and killed his wife and his three children and I am taking in the details of how much grey he's got in his hair. That's fiction. Reality now is too frightening, impossible to grasp. Yet you could say that fiction becomes a kind of perversion.' Her short story 'Performing with Many Particles of Dust' (2002) is a study of a young woman's day: she goes to the post office in Jerusalem to send a parcel, visits a friend in Ramallah and considers whether to buy meat. That's all. But it takes the concentration of a tight-rope artist to maintain enough neutrality (or cool) to get through the day without mishap – and it leaves you exhausted as you share the minutiae of the character's thoughts and counterthoughts and metathoughts.

One of Shibli's novellas, *Masas* (Touching), has now come out in French. But she was first published in *al-Karmel*, the literary magazine that has shared the Palestinian liberation movement's fortunes since it was started by the poet Mahmoud Darwich in Beirut in 1981. It is run by the writer and translator Hassan Khader and, since 1996, has been coming out of Ramallah. Khader has always been part of the Palestinian movement and has lived through its wars of the last three decades. *Al-Karmel* is an example of how Palestinian culture sees itself: strongly rooted in Arabic with an internationalist outlook. In the last six months it has published pieces by Herbert Baker, Russell Banks, Coetzee, Dwight Reynolds, José Saramago, Efrat Ben-Ze'ev as well as many Arab authors.

Darwich, still the magazine's mentor, has said that the highest aim of the writer is to give his work an aesthetic that enables it to live in a different time and in a different consciousness. Khader feels that the current chaos instigates a fictional response: 'It's seductive, but it's treacherous too.' It poses the danger that the writing it produces will be too raw, too premature to survive the transplant into another consciousness. His strategy is to create a distance between himself and what's happening, 'trying to let events "cool down" a little, sometimes allowing a space of time (not just an emotional or psychological space) – to assert itself – these are all formulae to lessen the risk'.

Once, when I was living in Riyadh, a child I knew was hit by a car and died. I did not see her die. I only heard about it. And I saw the altered road – and her mother. I was unable to turn my hand to anything until I had written Melody's death. I put this to Hassan Khader down a crackly and threatened phone line and he tells me that earlier that same day he had been walking back from his office and was about a hundred metres from the ruins of the Muqata'a when he heard shots. On the six o'clock news he learned that a man had been killed in Ramallah when he tried to throw explosives at Israeli soldiers. 'I felt ashamed as I listened to the news, because at three-thirty I had thought that the shots I'd heard might have been been aimed at someone. That silent thought had taken perhaps a second to pass. And at six it turned out that the shots had indeed been aimed at someone, someone who had died at that moment. I was ashamed of what had happened at three-thirty, but that didn't stop me having my dinner, and there's another source of shame. Every day on my way to and from my office I will pass the spot where he fell. How many times will I feel that someone died here? And how many times shall I walk by and not remember?' The situation, he says, robs death of its eloquence, of its awe.

But Khader is an editor as well as a writer – under curfew, he once sent his final proofs to the printer's in an ambulance – and *al-Karmel* is still managing to come out twice a year. 'When the [Israeli] soldiers trashed the Sakakini [Cultural Centre],' he says, 'my office got off lightly. Yet the papers were all over the floor and I still keep the draft of a poem with the print of a muddy boot on it. Maybe the soldier who trod on it didn't even notice, but he left his signature on that poem.'

Last October I read at the centre, a beautiful nineteenth-century Ottoman villa donated by the Khalil Sakakini family and standing in the heart of Ramallah. The hall was full; people had braved the closures and come in from Jerusalem, the eighteen-kilometre journey taking up to three hours. 'We so rarely see anyone from the outside,' they said. 'We need to breathe the fresh air.' Nobody wanted to talk about the 'situation' or about the Israeli incursion into the town earlier that day which netted a fighter believed responsible for killing two soldiers; they just wanted to talk about fiction. In the middle of the reading there was an explosion. I stopped. Someone went outside and came back saying it was just a container of cooking gas. It's nothing, everyone said, carry on, and we did. I slept in a friend's house that night and at three in the morning I woke up to a terrible banging. The Israelis have come, I joked to myself and pulled the quilt over my head. But the banging went on and a nearby mosque started to sing out Qur'ānic verses. It wasn't a joke. I found my hostess standing in the shadows of her roof terrace watching as, across the narrow street, a group of six soldiers deployed at the door of a house. Two would attack it with a kind of battering-ram while the other four would train their guns on the street and the houses. Then they'd crouch and run and swap places and start again. Their postures, their flares, our darkness; it was like watching a film, and the rest of the audience was out there too, in their darknesses, watching, while the soundtrack of mellow chanting circled round us exploded by the thunderous bangs. 'Go to bed,' my friend said. 'That house is empty, and they'll only leave at dawn.' Next day I learned that a young lawyer, a cousin of the captured fighter, knowing he had explosives, thought to remove them before the soldiers came back. But he knew nothing about explosives so he had been blown up – while we discussed fiction at the Sakakini.

Can a novelist or a poet ignore the situation? Is there room to write outside the situation? Darwich has famously asserted his right to write about things that are not Palestine, his right to play, to be absurd. Yet in his obituary of (Palestinian poet) Fadwa Touqan who died last November he asks what the poet should do at a time of crisis? A time when he has to shift his focus from his inner self to the world outside, when poetry has to bear witness. The poet Mourid Barghouti, after thirty years, finally succeeded in obtaining a permit to visit Ramallah, his home town, for two weeks in 1997. That journey became *I Saw Ramallah* (2000). 'The problem with writing what is outside yourself,' he says, 'writing as part of a collective, is that this will not produce literature unless it has truly become part of yourself – it is no longer "outside". It becomes part of your inner structure. There is no point in setting down events, anecdotes. But do events pass over us like mercury on paper? The moment of contact between the event and your soul, that's where literature is born.'

Every Palestinian writer I spoke to insisted on their right to make a professional or aesthetic decision not to write about the situation – but it's a theoretical right. The events that make contact with the soul are all shaped by the occupation. 'There is no bit of my life that is not under their control,' Liana Badr says. 'They control our health, they control our friendships. I wasn't able to go see Fadwa Touqan before she died – in Nablus, her friends kept away from her till she died.'

Perhaps that's why so many are turning to the essay, or to what they call 'fragments': literary responses to events that, as writers, they need to speak of immediately without waiting for the desired transfiguration into fiction or poetry. Hassan Khader's 'Splinters of Reality and Glass' (Autumn 2002) examines what it's like to experience the occupation simultaneously on the streets and on television. It is a wonderfully articulated account of the dynamic relationship between, on the one hand, violence on or by Palestinians and, on the other, the media – whether Palestinian, Arab or international: how the image has subsumed and then shaped the reality. Perhaps predictably, everyone I spoke to saw the militarisation of the Intifada and the suicide attacks in negative terms. And yet, what space is the media giving to the civil resistance to the barrier in Palestinian villages today?

Jean Genet, writing in 1985, describes the Palestinian fidayeen in Jordan in 1970 obligingly posing with their guns for a Western media they were never able to understand – let alone use. He states the misrepresentation the media went in for: 'The journalists, describing the Palestinians as they were not, made use of slogans instead. I lived with the Palestinians . . . they were so opposite to what they were said to be that . . . every negative detail in the newspaper, from the slightest to the boldest, had a positive counterpart in reality.'

We still live with the problem. If the suicide bombers or

the gunmen or the members of the PA can be said to have colluded with their own misrepresentation, it's hard to see how the same can be said of other Palestinians – writers, say. Yet I found the attitudes ascribed to Palestinian writers – by, for example, Israeli writer, David Grossman in a recent article by Linda Grant[2] – hard to square with what I knew. Grant wrote that friends in Britain had suggested to her that 'Israeli writers . . . create an alliance with their counterparts on the Palestinian side, to find some solidarity with each other . . .' Grossman describes how in the early 1990s he organised a group which met for three years 'secretly under the umbrella of some foreign embassies'. But, he says 'there's almost no contact now between Israeli and Palestinian writers' because of 'hints from Arafat' to the Palestinian writers 'not to contribute to the normalisation of Israel'. He also believes that Palestinian writers thought Israeli writers 'could change the politics here and when they saw that we couldn't deliver . . . they despaired of the possibility of doing something with us'.

This makes Palestinian writers into Arafat's tools. It also makes them politically naïve, first to meet with Israeli writers in 'foreign embassies' then to expect them to change the policies of their state. So I asked the Palestinian writers I spoke to how they viewed Israeli writers. Their immediate response was literary: Liana Badr says she's read them all and thinks some of them are brilliant. She adds that she doesn't think they present a national phenomenon like, say, Latin American writers; the terms of reference of each writer connect up to different cultures. Hassan Khader praises David Grossman and Applefeld. Mourid Barghouti says he was always moved by the poems of Yehuda Amichai. I ask if a writer's political allegiance colours their perception of her/him. Adania Shibli tells me the writer she admires most among the Israelis is Shai Agnon, and 'he wasn't particularly nice to the Palestinians'.

[2] See Linda Grant in the *Guardian*, 31 January 2004.

I asked whether they saw any possible relationship between themselves and Israeli writers. Hassan Khader told me that he had translated Grossman's *The Smile of the Lamb* when Grossman contacted him (in 1993 in Tunis where Khader was living at the time) to thank him and to offer his help with any linguistic problems. When Khader returned to Palestine after Oslo the two met at distant intervals. Their talk was of politics. In March 2000 Khader ran a long interview with Grossman in *al-Karmel*. The interview, he wrote, had taken two years to set up, but he understood Grossman's reluctance: 'When an Israeli (most often from the left) meets Palestinians and writes about them it is his version that will be published, and his sympathy for the Palestinians endorses his view of himself as a defender of certain values . . . Also the craft of writing persuades you that rendering someone in an imaginative linguistic discourse doesn't just give them a voice but "captures" them as well.'

A few days after Camp David failed (October 2000), Grossman contacted Khader to organise a meeting between Palestinian and Israeli writers in Jerusalem: 'He said Yehoshua, Oz and even Yitzhar Simlanski wanted to come. I agreed but said if we were to have a formal meeting we had to agree on some points. I wrote down: Israeli withdrawal to the 1967 lines, dismantling the settlements, Jerusalem one unified capital for two states, Israeli recognition of its moral responsibility for the problem of the Palestinian refugees, and I put in some explanatory notes and faxed it. A few days later he responded saying my note read as though it had been written by a lawyer. So the meeting never happened.'

Khader has written a book about the crisis of identity in Israeli literature: 'Their works tell you more about them than the statements they give to the press. Oz, for example, is a declared lover of peace – maybe he really does love peace. But his works show a racist attitude to Arabs and Palestinians. Yehoshua transforms Jewish existential crises into narrative forms and looks for fictive solutions which are at odds with his declared political stands. He is supposed to be politically a hardliner, but he expresses a true sense of crisis and vulnerability in his work. Grossman went against the current and wrote a novel that was critical of the occupation and suffered the inevitable attacks. He showed considerable sensitivity in his fictional treatment of the Palestinians. I admire his honesty and I admire *Look under: "Love"*, the wonderful book he wrote about the Holocaust.'

Mourid Barghouti puts it more trenchantly: 'They all carry a whiff of the establishment. Look at South Africa: the white writers who allied themselves with the liberation movement rejected apartheid, clearly and publicly. Some of them joined the ANC. As long as the Israeli artist subscribes to the official Israeli narrative, there is a great big hole in the heart of his "alliance" with the Palestinians. You cannot hold on to your ideological position and then join the Society for the Prevention of Cruelty to Palestinians. The ones with the kindly hearts – there are many of those, we meet them, we talk to them. Politically, it leads nowhere. It does them a lot of good – the Israelis – it eases their consiences, it pays dividends, it plays well on the world stage. It does nothing for the Palestinians.'

Badr is more diplomatic: 'It seems that the price of loyalty – of belonging – to Israel is very high. So you have writers who by any criterion are secular – and yet they posit that this land is theirs through a two-thousand-year-old covenant! Or take Yehoshua: on the whole he doesn't harbour bad felings towards Arabs but he still thinks in a racist way, and believes in the politicisation of religion – to allow for a Jewish state of Israel. Or take Amos Oz, or Grossman; they believe themselves progressive but they are entranced by their collective mythology and lament the future of Zionism. Their literature is more developed than their ideology. We have to give them that they are genuinely seekers of peace, and democratic, and artists. At the same time they cannot let go of their Zionism. It's a great contradiction in their lives. So they write about the narrowly personal. Yehoshua in *The Lover* has an Arab character, Naim, a character that's really vivid. In an interview he said the character had run away from him. Brilliant writers imprisoned by ideological justifications. But in the end we have to say that they are for peace – of a kind.'

New York academic Ella Habiba Shohat has written about the rationale of the Israeli government's funding of New Wave films that attempted a 'relatively critical' representation of the conflict. What she says could equally apply to 'sympathetic' writings of Israeli novelists: 'Although the films offer progressive images within the history of Israeli representation of the conflict, they operate within the . . . framework of Zionism. Rather than expressing any clear ideological perspective, they reflect the Sabra bewilderment at the realisation of the existence of the Other, the Palestinian, as victim. This dynamic . . . softens the threatening edge of the films and allows for official support.' The Israeli establishment, she says, 'draws its Western support on the basis of its reputation as "the only democracy in the Middle East" ' and the films ultimately help in projecting 'the liberal image of a country with free speech'. This is not to say that either film-makers or writers wish to be used in this way, but it does mean that Palestinian intellectuals have a point when they refuse to cooperate with what they regard as essentially fig-leaf activities.

Shohat's analysis of Sabra films shows that they 'betray acute discomfort at the very idea of a Jewish victimiser. The Jewish people, after all, are historically unaccustomed to the role of the oppressor . . . Nothing in the historical culture of Judaism prepares its artists for such a tale.' The film-makers' solution is to project the Israeli peace activist as 'the real martyr caught between two violent worlds'. Shohat lists among these films Shimon Dotan's *The Smile of the Lamb* – based on Grossman's novel about the Palestinians. What comes across in many of the statements given by Israeli writers is that they are against the occupation for their own sakes; for the harm it is doing to Israeli society, to the Israeli image and to the Israeli psyche. While this is legitimate it does somewhat overshadow their concern for the overall human injustice of the situation. It's hard to imagine, say, Nadine Gordimer, being more concerned for the image and psyche of South Africa's whites than for the injustice of apartheid and the damage done to all the people of her country – white and black.

As Israeli documentaries have far outstripped features in recognising the truth of Palestinian dispossession, and its implications, so have Israeli journalists outstripped imaginative writers. Israeli writers, Khader says, are facing more and more a situation similar to that of French writers at the time of the Algerian war of independence and American writers at the time of Vietnam: 'Should they take a stand against colonialism or should they agree to be a cosmetic instrument for it? They have not yet made up their minds.'

The problem is that the occupation – which Israeli writers are against and which they think is so bad for the Israeli soul – has now been shown (by Israeli historians among others) to be the natural continuation of the Zionist project in Palestine. If hundreds of Palestinian homes are being demolished today, entire villages were erased in 1948. Is it possible to be against the occupation and hold on to the idea of Israel's noble origins? Well, yes, if the Palestinians will agree to subscribe to the liberal Israeli view that all was well until 2000, until 1993, until 1967 – any date, really, apart from 1948. But the Palestinians cannot agree to that because it is a denial of their history and a betrayal of half their nation. Right-wing Israelis accept the truth of what happened in '48 – but they don't have a moral problem with the occupation. The Palestinians have already accepted Israel's de facto right to exist – on 78 per cent of historic Palestine. That is a humbler right than a promise made by God – but it would, in the end, save more souls.

Is it possible to disentangle your Jewishness from your Zionism? Only Israelis can answer that. Palestinians, on the whole, agree that they are in a less difficult position than Israelis. As Khader puts it, he may have problems with his passport but he has none with his identity. And he knows that what he's fighting for is his freedom.

Over the difficult phone lines, by fax and e-mail, I asked the Palestinians about the future? 'My poems now', said Mourid Barghouti, 'seem to be all about death. But then half the numbers in my phone book no longer answer.' 'Terror and destruction', Liana Badr replied, 'and killing on both sides until Israel stops thinking in military terms. Until they become really democratic – not just among themselves but with everybody.' Hassan Khader was not optimistic: 'Probably a more overt apartheid system which continues for years. But it shall eat away at the soul of the Israeli state.'

Palestinian writers respond to quotes from Israeli writers

DAVID GROSSMAN: 'Maybe we were different because we never had the opportunity until now to inflict cruelty and suffering. That is such a nightmare for me.'

LIANA BADR: The difference between us is that we look for what is human in general. We are in a ghetto so we try to belong to a general human community. The Israelis believe they are different and are in love with their specific identity. They each carry a mirror and look admiringly at themselves. If we gazed at ourselves like that we would go mad.

HASSAN KHADER: This type of psychological interpretation is very current in Israeli discourse. I dislike them. I asked Grossman once what the Israeli problem was, he said they wanted to be loved by the other side.

AHARON APPLEFELD: 'What is happening here in Israel has to wait fifty years before becoming literature.'

KHADER: Applefeld is a specific phenomenen among Israeli writers. He always writes about the Holocaust but he never tries to use it for political or ideological purposes as others do.

MOURID BARGHOUTI: The Holocaust has been written as novel, as poetry, as music, as theatre – as everything – in the Fifties and Sixties. It didn't have to wait fifty years to be written. Israel has been established for fifty-six years and the West Bank has been occupied for thirty-seven years. They have been occupiers for thirty-seven years and that's not long enough to look at themselves and see what they have become? Where exactly is their human gaze directed? How did Breytenbach, Coetzee, Gordimer manage to do what they did?

A. B. YEHOSHUA: 'After the Six Day War the abolition of the border poisoned the two peoples.'

KHADER: So the relationship was a positive one before the Six Day War? And how was the border 'demolished'? Yehoshua loves figures of speech but is it not more honest in this case to speak of 'occupation'? In any case, many Israelis hold the occupation responsible for the rise of extremism and fundamentalism in their society and hanker after 'the good times' before 1967. Of course from this position they don't even see the Palestinians. Their 'good times' were completely imaginary.

BADR: Is he blind? He ignores that the Israelis occupied Palestine in '48? He was friends with Khalil Sakakini. He mentions Sakakini in his writings. So why does he not admit what happened in '48? They are very selective in their view of the world.

YEHOSHUA: 'Understanding the Arabs is the key to understanding ourselves.'

KHADER: He said to me once, 'You accept your limits, we'll accept ours.' The problem is that what we see as our limits doesn't please them, and their way of teaching us our limits doesn't please us. They talk of security; on the surface that means borders, water, arms, etc. But perhaps they feel that our sense of national identity as Palestinians is in itself a security threat. There's a deep wish to engineer Palestinian identity itself in a way that serves Israel's need for emotional security.

GROSSMAN: 'Since the Intifada and the anti-Semitism in the Islamic world, the average Israeli feels swept into the Jewish world of tragic aspect, of being the eternal outsider, and all the old feelings surface.'

BARGHOUTI: If the original Zionist project had worked and they had colonised part of Uganda, you would not today have heard anything about anti-Semitism in the Islamic world. If there had been a conflict it would have been characterised as white vs. black and we would have watched it on TV along with the rest of the world.

ADANIA SHIBLI: The religious dimension has been forced on the Palestinian question. What I see is the colonialist dimension dressed in different terminology. It used to be East/West, Black/White, now it's Muslim/Jew. The terminology changes according to the time and how well it allows the victimisation of a certain group. Recently the Israeli Deputy Defense Minister posed the question whether 'the Palestinian terror is caused by a genetic defect'. So, should we talk, perhaps, of a biological dimension to the conflict?

On the Geneva accords

David Grossman calls the introduction he wrote for the Geneva accords his 'bestseller'.

KHADER: The main flaw is that it does not include an Israeli admission of what happened in 1948: the destruction of the Palestinian entity and the transformation of most Palestinians into refugees. Personally, I believe in negotiation and I support the two-state solution. But I do not believe a real solution is viable which does not include an admission of responsibility by the Israelis.

BADR: It's not the solution of our dreams but it would get the area out of its crisis. Israel's agreement to compensate the refugees implies a recognition of what happened in '48. But it lacks a formal apology from the Israelis to the Palestinians.

SHIBLI: I don't understand why we have to keep running around different cities: Madrid, Oslo, Taba, Sharm . . . when it is completely clear what should be done. It's just delay. Maybe they don't feel it so in Geneva but here, in Palestine, we feel its consequences very well and every minute. If Switzerland wants to contribute to the peace I suggest that they invite – with all the money Europe is investing – Israeli soldiers from the checkpoints to have a ski vacation in the Alps – a vacation from occupying us.

Acknowledgements

I would like to thank Karl Millar who first published me in the *London Review of Books*, Miriam Gross who first commissioned me for the *Observer* and Ian Katz who gave me my first space in the *Guardian*.

Conversations with my family and friends have been essential in forming the articles in this book. I am particularly indebted to Susan Glynn for rescuing me in the small hours and helping to clarify my ideas across the kitchen table.

We would like to thank the newspapers and news websites who allowed us to use a short extract to front the political essays, as follows. Every effort has been made to contact copyright holders. The publishers would be glad to hear from any who may have been unintentionally omitted and would be pleased to insert the appropriate acknowledgement in any subsequent edition.

'Mystery surrounds rules of engagement', Julian Borger, *Guardian*, 3 October 2000 © *Guardian*; 'Intifada 2000 dwarfs the original', Brian Whitaker, *Guardian*, 27 October 2000 © *Guardian*; 'Hijackers ram two jetliners', by Serge Schmemann, *New York Times*, 12 September 2001, © *New York Times*, all rights reserved; 'In this together', *Al-Ahram Weekly*, 13–19 September 2001; 'Wanted: Dead or Alive', *The Times*, 18 September 2001; 'Secret plans for 10-year war', *The Times*, 20 September 2001; 'We are at war with terrorism', *The Times*, 17 September 2001; 'Bush: the hour is coming', *The Times*, 21 September 2001; 'The battle is joined', *The Times*, 8 October 2001; 'Battle of Kabul', *The Times*, 12

October 2001; 'A federal judge's decision', *The Nation*, 22 May 2004; 'The Bush regime', Les Blough, www.axisoflogic.com, 13 August 2003; 'Seisint Inc', Oj, www.alternet.org, 21 May 2004; 'Hundreds of protesters', *Al-Ahram Weekly*, 30 March 2002; 'Defiant Israel', Ed Vulliamy and Graham Usher, *Observer*, 31 March 2002 © *Observer*; 'America turns sights on Iraq', *The Times*, 9 October 2001; 'Iraq War Was about Israel' from 'Turning into Israel?' by Juan Cole published by Salon.com, 16 April 2004 at this url: http://www.salon.com/news/feature/2004/04/16/israel/index.html; 'Much to the displeasure', *Al-Ahram Weekly*, 5–11 June 2003; 'US forces in Iraq', Julian Borger, *Guardian*, 9 December 2003 © *Guardian*; 'Before the war' from 'America's Blankness' by Stephen Holmes published by Salon.com, 17 April 2004 at this url: http://www.salon.com/opinion/feature/2004/06/17/anti_americanism/index.html; 'International Women's Day', *Al-Ahram Weekly*, 13–19 March 2003; 'For well over a century', *Al-Ahram Weekly*, 21–27 March 2002; 'Bitter harvest in West Bank', Chris McGreal, *Guardian*, 14 November 2003 © *Guardian*; 'The IDF's Military', *Haaretz*, 23 June 2004; 'Shock new details', P. Beaumont, C. Stephens and Jason Burke, *Observer*, 2 May 2004 © *Observer*.